Pro Excel 2007 VBA

Jim DeMarco

Apress®

Pro Excel 2007 VBA

Copyright © 2008 by Jim DeMarco

ISBN-13 (pbk): 978-1-59059-957-0

ISBN-10 (pbk): 1-59059-957-8

ISBN-13 (electronic): 978-1-4302-0580-7

ISBN-10 (electronic): 1-4302-0580-6

Printed and bound in the United States of America 9 8 7 6 5 4 3 2 1

Lead Editor: Tony Campbell
Technical Reviewer: Mark Etwaru
Editorial Board: Clay Andres, Steve Anglin, Ewan Buckingham, Tony Campbell, Gary Cornell,
    Jonathan Gennick, Kevin Goff, Matthew Moodie, Joseph Ottinger, Jeffrey Pepper, Frank Pohlmann,
    Ben Renow-Clarke, Dominic Shakeshaft, Matt Wade, Tom Welsh
Project Manager: Kylie Johnston
Copy Editor: Damon Larson
Associate Production Director: Kari Brooks-Copony
Production Editor: Liz Berry
Compositor: Linda Weidemann, Wolf Creek Press
Proofreaders: Linda Seifert, April Eddy
Indexer: Carol Burbo
Artist: April Milne
Cover Designer: Kurt Krames
Manufacturing Director: Tom Debolski

Distributed to the book trade worldwide by Springer-Verlag New York, Inc., 233 Spring Street, 6th Floor, New York, NY 10013. Phone 1-800-SPRINGER, fax 201-348-4505, e-mail orders-ny@springer-sbm.com, or visit http://www.springeronline.com.

For information on translations, please contact Apress directly at 2855 Telegraph Avenue, Suite 600, Berkeley, CA 94705. Phone 510-549-5930, fax 510-549-5939, e-mail info@apress.com, or visit http://www.apress.com.

Apress and friends of ED books may be purchased in bulk for academic, corporate, or promotional use. eBook versions and licenses are also available for most titles. For more information, reference our Special Bulk Sales–eBook Licensing web page at http://www.apress.com/info/bulksales.

The source code for this book is available to readers at http://www.apress.com.

This book is dedicated to my beautiful wife, Marlene, who continually challenges me to excel (no pun intended). I would also like to dedicate it to my two very talented teens, Jimmy and Melanie, who never fail to impress us with their creative powers.

Contents at a Glance

Contents

About the Author

JIM DEMARCO is Director of Application Development at the Hudson Center for Health Equity and Quality (HCHEQ), in Tarrytown, NY. HCHEQ is a not-for-profit organization whose mission includes advocacy for equitable healthcare policy in government and the development of information technologies to improve healthcare quality, safety, and efficiency. Previously, Jim was a product manager at Sharp Electronics, where his responsibilities included the development of their handheld organizer product line.

Jim has been building Microsoft Office applications ever since he first received a copy of Microsoft Access 1 in the early 1990s. He discovered object-oriented programming when taking a Visual Basic 5 course, and has been a strong proponent of that paradigm ever since. Jim has published numerous articles on this subject and has also published articles on Microsoft Access programming. He has worked as a software trainer for local adult education facilities, a position that has helped tremendously when designing user interfaces.

Jim is currently leading a team of developers using cutting-edge .NET technologies to streamline the processing of Medicaid applications in New York state. He is the software architect for a system that streamlines that process, providing huge cost savings to all users of the system, as well as providing data efficiencies.

Jim is also a working musician and music producer; music from his projects is available locally and nationally.

About the Technical Reviewer

 **MARK ETWARU** is an information technology strategy consultant in New York, NY. Mark originates from Guyana, South America, and currently resides in New York with his immediate and extended family whose roots in New York date back to the 1960s.

Mark holds a BS in information technology and business management from York College, New York, earned in 2002. He is currently pursuing an MBA with a concentration in technology management from the University of Phoenix Online. Mark is a seasoned technology professional, expanding his knowledge through academic and work-related activities. In addition, Mark is a member of PMI, as well as many other acclaimed organizations.

Beyond Mark's passion for technology, he also enjoys reading, traveling, and spending time with his loved ones. His future aspirations include expanding his consulting services into the financial services marketplace, assembling a technology training institution for the underprivileged, and expanding his travels of the world.

Acknowledgments

I would like to first thank my family for being so understanding and supportive during this endeavor. Over the last three or four months, in addition to my normal (and large) amount of side projects (computer- and music-related), I spent whatever "free" time I had putting together this volume. Their patience is truly appreciated and made a busy period of my life pass with ease.

I would like to acknowledge my technical reviewer Mark Etwaru. Mark is a very talented developer and project manager in his own right, and his input was invaluable in putting this book together. Thanks again Mark for a job well done!

I would like to thank Dilshan Jesook for getting me started with the .NET examples in this book. I have yet to find a technology that he is not able to implement in short order.

I would also like to thank Mor Hezi and Chris Bryant at Microsoft for taking the time to talk to me about Excel 2007 and helping me understand Microsoft's vision for the Office product.

Thanks to all at Apress for giving me this opportunity and for guiding me through a process that is very complex. As a first-time author, I did not know what to expect, and the folks at Apress were so very understanding and helpful at all times.

And finally, I would like to acknowledge the readers of this book. Thank you for purchasing it and I hope this book helps you understand the power of VBA in Microsoft Excel 2007.

Introduction

Did you ever wonder whether there is more to Excel than data displayed in rows and columns or pretty charts? If you want to learn how to bring data into your Excel 2007 projects, or learn to work with XML, or see how object-oriented programming can be used in Excel 2007, this book will provide you with that information.

I wrote this book because I've always enjoyed writing applications in Excel when it is the required solution. Excel is often overlooked in coding situations, but as you'll see in the pages of this book, it has many, many possibilities, and it is relatively easy to learn. Excel 2007 has expanded XML support. XML data is easily brought into and out of an Excel project so your client spreadsheet data can be shared. Excel UserForms give you the ability to create simple user interfaces for your clients and allow you to create easy-to-use data collection tools. Excel charting and PivotTables have always been a strong suit for data summary, and in Excel 2007, PivotTables are greatly enhanced.

This book also addresses object-oriented programming to a great degree. Just because you're not writing a .NET or even a classic Visual Basic application, there's no reason you can't use object-oriented coding techniques in your projects. It provides you with the same advantages in Excel that you get in the full-fledged programming languages: ease of reuse, easier code maintenance, encapsulation, and more.

You will find sample files and code solutions in the Source Code/Download section of the Apress web site, at `www.apress.com`.

Who This Book Is For

This book is intended for developers who would like to learn to use Visual Basic for Applications (VBA) to extend the power of Microsoft Excel 2007. You should have some knowledge of or experience using the VBA or classic Visual Basic programming languages and their related development environment.

Anyone with VBA, Visual Basic, Microsoft Access, or .NET experience will readily understand the concepts in this book, but anyone with any coding experience should have no problem with the material.

How This Book Is Structured

This book gives a view into the many features available to today's Excel developer, from a tour of the Visual Basic Editor, where coding is done, to its debugging features. It also provides modern coding techniques, including object-oriented programming. You'll learn about data access, XML, charting, and PivotTables, UserForms, and more.

Chapter 1 is a basic tour of Excel 2007 coding features, from the development environment to other tools you'll use. It begins with an examination of the Visual Basic Editor and shows some of its features. It then looks at the Excel Macro Recorder and the code it generates for you, talks about the different types of code modules available to you, and discusses the types of code you can write.

Chapter 2 details methods of bringing data into and out of Excel projects. It covers importing from Microsoft Access data, text files, and SQL Server data. It also discusses the many data access options available, including DAO, ADO, and ODBC.

Chapter 3 discusses using the XML features in Excel 2007. Examples include importing and exporting data to an XML file and appending data from an XML file. It shows how to build a custom object in a class module to work with XML files. It also shows how to build a custom user interface component using XML.

Chapter 4 looks at Excel 2007 UserForms and the tools they provide. Its examples show how to build simple and complex data entry forms, and how to use classes to add functionality to the UserForms.

Chapter 5 explores charting in Excel 2007. After examining the code created by the Macro Recorder, it shows how to use the Chart object in code.

Chapter 6 takes a look at Excel PivotTable reports. PivotTables are powerful data analysis tools, and they're easy to create and modify. The code samples show how to create and modify PivotTable reports.

Chapter 7 is an overview of VBA debugging tools and techniques. The Immediate, Locals, and Watch windows are shown in detail. The section on error handling shows how to effectively trap for errors and how to provide positive feedback to the user.

Chapter 8 is all about integrating your Excel solution with other Microsoft Office applications. Its examples include building a chart report in Word 2007 and building a PowerPoint presentation that includes text and charts from an Excel workbook.

Chapter 9 shows how to use components built in Visual Basic 6 and Visual Studio 2005 in your Excel 2007 projects. Examples from earlier chapters are re-created using ActiveX technologies in Visual Basic 6 and .NET assemblies using Visual Studio 2005 and Visual Studio Tools for Office 2005.

Prerequisites

Microsoft Excel 2007 is required for the examples in this book. For Chapter 8, "Office Integration," you'll need Microsoft Word 2007 and PowerPoint 2007.

SQL Server 2005 Management Studio Express is used in our SQL data examples. This is available for download from the Apress web site (www.apress.com), in the Source Code/Download section.

To create the code for Chapter 9, "ActiveX and .NET," you'll need Visual Basic 5 or 6 (for the ActiveX section) and Visual Studio 2005 and Visual Studio Tools for Office 2005 SE (for the .NET section). If you do not have one or both of the above, the compiled components for each example are provided on the Apress web site. The .NET Framework 2.0 should be installed on your PC for the .NET examples to run. If you do not have Visual Studio 2005, you'll be able to run the samples, but you won't have direct access to the code.

Downloading the Code

The source code for this book is available to readers at www.apress.com, in the Source Code/
Download section. Please feel free to visit the Apress web site and download all the code there.
You can also check for errata and find related titles from Apress.

Contacting the Author

Contact Jim DeMarco at jim.demarco@hcheq.org. For more information on HCHEQ and
its mission, go to www.hcheq.org. For information on Jim's musical endeavors, go to www.
fiftyhabit.com or contact him at info@fiftyhabit.com.

CHAPTER 1

The Macro Recorder and Code Modules

This book is written for experienced coders. You may have experience in many languages, but not in the Excel (or Office) VBA IDE. We will be writing quite a bit of code as we move along, but before we do that, let's take a quick look at Excel's Macro Recorder and the Visual Basic Development Environment. The Macro Recorder has been a part of Excel for quite a long time, and it's still the best way to get a look at some of the objects that make up the Excel Document Object Model (DOM), and a great way to get the core of your code written for you as you start your development projects.

Macro Security Settings

Excel's default security settings do not allow any macro activity. Before you begin exploring macros in Excel and the Macro Recorder, you will need to tell Excel which security settings to use to control what happens when you open a workbook that contains macros (or one that will contain macros). If you use antivirus software that works with Microsoft Office 2007 and you open a workbook that contains macros, the virus scanner will check the workbook for viruses before opening it.

You can make changes to the macro security settings in the Trust Center:

1. Click the Microsoft Office button, which looks like the following:

2. Click the Excel Options button, select Trust Center, click the Trust Center Settings button, and finally click the Macro Settings item.

Alternatively, on the Developer ribbon, click the Macro Security button in the Code Group section. (Depending on the network security level at your organization, you may or may not have rights to change these settings).

■**Note** Macro setting changes made in Excel's Macro Settings section apply to Excel only; they do not affect any other Microsoft Office applications.

Table 1-1 lists the Excel macro security settings and explains each setting.

Table 1-1. *Macro Security Settings*

Setting	Purpose
Disable all macros without notification	Use this setting if you don't trust the source of a workbook containing macros.
Disable all macros with notification	This is the default setting. Use it when you want macros to be disabled, but you want to get security alerts if there are macros present. You can decide when to enable those macros.
Disable all macros except digitally signed macros	This is the same as the "Disable all macros with notification" option, except that when the macro is digitally signed by a trusted publisher, the macro can run if you have trusted the publisher.
Enable all macros (not recommended, potentially dangerous code can run)	Use this setting to allow all macros to run.
Trust access to the VBA project object model	This setting is for developers only.

■**Caution** The "Enable all macros" setting makes your computer vulnerable to potentially malicious code. It is not recommended that you use this setting permanently. For the examples in this book, we use this setting, but it is highly recommended that you choose another option in your production code.

Trusted Publishers

This section lists the currently trusted certificates that can be used by developers to sign documents and add-ins. When you open a digitally signed document, the digital signature appears on your computer as a certificate. The certificate names the VBA project's source, plus additional information about the identity and integrity of that source. A digital signature does not necessarily guarantee the safety of a project, and you must decide whether you trust a project that has been digitally signed. If you know you can always trust macros from a particular source, you can add that macro developer to the list of trusted sources when you open the project.

Trusted Locations

This is where you can define trusted locations. These are folders on your PC or network where files with macros can be stored. Excel will trust any document in a folder designated as trusted and will run any macros in those files.

Caution Be careful when defining trusted locations! Documents in trusted locations can run without being checked by the Trust Center security system. If you add or change a location, make sure the new location is secure.

The Remove Button

If you added a certificate to your list of trusted publishers when you first opened a VBA project signed with that certificate, and later choose not to trust that publisher, you can use the Remove button to remove the certificate from your list of trusted publishers. The next time a project signed with that certificate is opened, the virus protection behavior corresponding to the setting on the Security Level tab will occur.

The Remove button in the Trusted Locations section lets you remove locations from the list in the same manner.

Lowering the Security Level

Before you can begin recording and playing back macros, you must lower the macro security level. By default, all macro activity is disabled.

To temporarily set the security level to enable all macros, do the following:

1. On the Developer ribbon, in the Code group, click Macro Security, as shown in Figure 1-1.

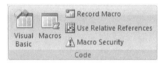

Figure 1-1. *Code options on the Developer ribbon*

2. If the Developer tab is not available, do the following to display it:

    a. Click the Microsoft Office button (shown in the following image).

    b. Click Excel Options.

    c. In the Popular category, under "Top options for working with Excel," select the "Show Developer tab in the Ribbon" check box, and then click OK.

3. Under Macro Settings, click "Enable all macros (not recommended, potentially dangerous code can run)," and then click OK, as shown in Figure 1-2.

> **■Warning** To help prevent potentially dangerous code from running, it is recommended that you return to any of the settings that disable all macros after you finish working with macros.

Once this is done, you can record your macro.

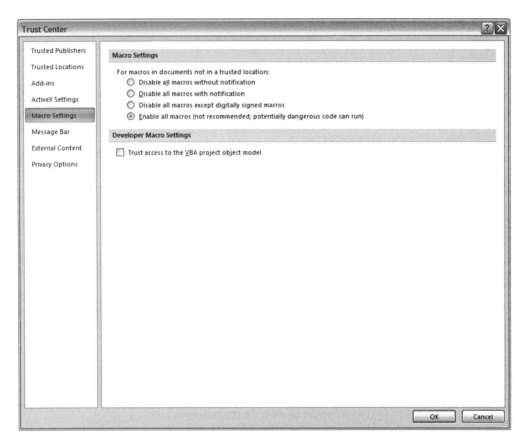

Figure 1-2. *Excel Trust Center Macro Settings options*

The Visual Basic Development Environment

Open the Developer ribbon and choose Visual Basic to display the Visual Basic Editor (VBE). Figure 1-3 shows the VBE.

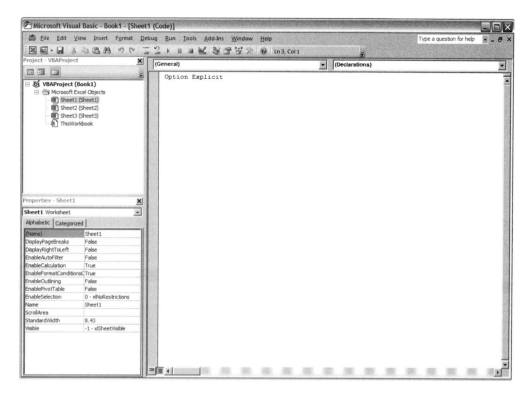

Figure 1-3. *Excel's Visual Basic Editor*

The default view is divided into three panes: the Project Explorer, the Property Sheet, and the code window.

The Project Explorer (Figure 1-4) lists open projects (workbooks) and the objects they contain. These can include worksheets, the workbook itself, standard code modules, class modules, and any UserForms in the project.

Objects are stored in folders representing their function. In Figure 1-4, you can see the worksheet objects in the Microsoft Excel Objects folder. Code is placed in its own folder, as are UserForms.

At the top of the Project Explorer pane is a toolbar that provides access to view code, view the selected object (choosing this command with Sheet1 selected will bring you to the Excel window with Sheet1 active), and toggle the folder view on or off. Toggling the folders off lists all of the objects together in one list regardless of type of object, as in Figure 1-5.

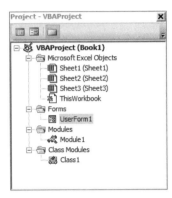

Figure 1-4. *Excel objects grouped by object (with Toggle Folders on)*

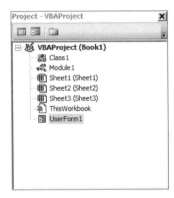

Figure 1-5. *Excel objects with Toggle Folders off*

The Property Sheet lists properties for the currently selected object in the Project Explorer, and will look very familiar to those VB 6.0 coders among us. Figure 1-6 shows an example of the Property Sheet for an Excel worksheet.

Use the code window to write, display, and edit Visual Basic code. You can open as many code windows as you have modules, so you can easily view the code in different forms or modules, and copy and paste between them.

You can open a code window from

- The Project window, by selecting a form or module and choosing the View Code button

- A UserForm window, by double-clicking a control or form, choosing Code from the View menu, or pressing F7

You can drag selected text to

- A different location in the current code window

- Another code window

- The Immediate and Watch windows

- The Recycle Bin

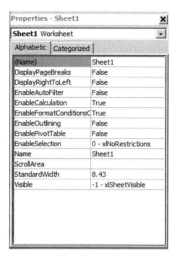

Figure 1-6. *VBA Property Sheet*

The code window shown in Figure 1-7 will look very familiar to those with VB 6.0 experience.

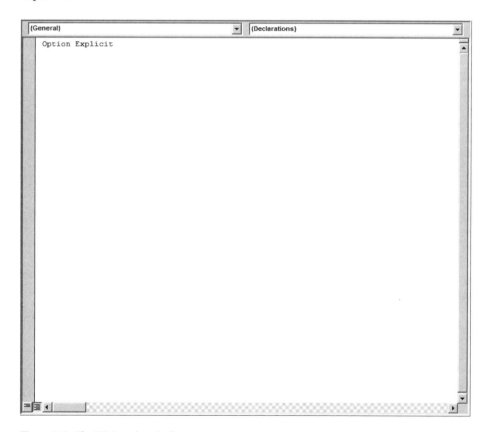

Figure 1-7. *The VBA code window*

At the top of the code window are two drop-down lists. On the left is the Object box, where any objects associated with the current selection are listed. On the right is the Procedure/Events box, where all methods and events for the currently selected object are displayed.

With Sheet1 selected in the Project Explorer, choose Worksheet from the Object box in the code pane. The default method for the worksheet object, Worksheet_SelectionChange, is inserted into the code window. Open the Procedure/Events box to see other methods and events available to you, as shown in Figure 1-8.

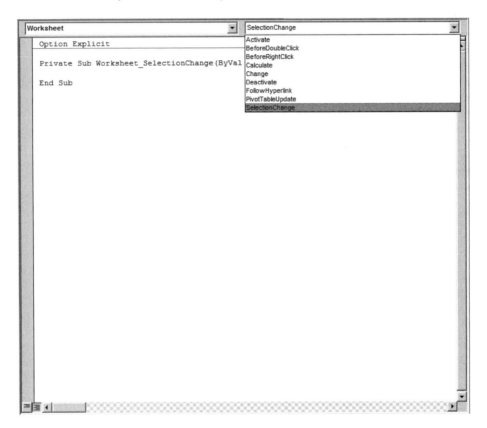

Figure 1-8. *The code pane with the procedure list open*

In the bottom-left corner of the code pane are two command buttons that determine how your procedures are displayed: Full Module View and Procedure View (shown in Figure 1-9).

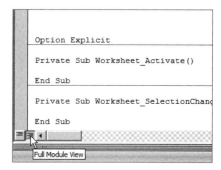

Figure 1-9. *Full Module view*

By default, Excel shows all procedures in a module (Full Module View). Clicking the Procedure View button (Figure 1-10) filters out all code except the procedure in which the cursor is located.

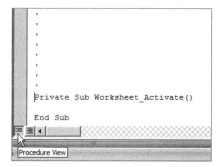

Figure 1-10. *Procedure view*

Immediately above the vertical scroll bar is the split bar, shown in Figure 1-11. Dragging this bar down splits the code window into two horizontal panes. Each pane can be scrolled separately, allowing viewing of two sections of a module at once. The information that appears in the Object box and Procedure/Events box applies to the code in the pane that has the focus. Dragging the bar to the top or the bottom of the window or double-clicking the bar restores the pane to its original single-pane view.

```
Sub TotalSales()
'Author: Jim DeMarco
'Date: 6/24/07
'Purpose: Adds total sales for all regions
Dim sFormula As String

sFormula = "=SUM(R[-5]C:R[-1]C)"
range("B8").Select
ActiveCell.FormulaR1C1 = sFormula
range("C8").Select
ActiveCell.FormulaR1C1 = sFormula
range("D8").Select
ActiveCell.FormulaR1C1 = sFormula
range("E8").Select
ActiveCell.FormulaR1C1 = sFormula



End Sub
```

```
Dim sFormula As String

sFormula = "=SUM(R[-5]C:R[-1]C)"
range("B8").Select
ActiveCell.FormulaR1C1 = sFormula
range("C8").Select
ActiveCell.FormulaR1C1 = sFormula
range("D8").Select
ActiveCell.FormulaR1C1 = sFormula
range("E8").Select
ActiveCell.FormulaR1C1 = sFormula



End Sub
```

Figure 1-11. *Code window with split panes*

In addition to these items, there are a few other windows to help you write and test your code: the Immediate window, the Locals window, and the Watch window.

The Immediate Window

The Immediate window (Figure 1-12) allows you to do the following:

- Type or paste a line of code and press Enter to run it

- Copy and paste the code from the Immediate window into the code window, but not save code in the Immediate window

Figure 1-12. *The Immediate window*

The Immediate window can be dragged and positioned anywhere on your screen unless you have made it a dockable window from the Docking tab of the Options dialog box.

You can close the window by clicking the Close box. If the Close box is not visible, double-click the Title bar to make the Close box visible, and then click it.

Note In break mode, a statement in the Immediate window is executed in the context that is displayed in the Procedure box. For example, if you type **Print variablename**, your output will be the value of variablename. This is the same as if the Print method had occurred in the procedure you were executing.

The Locals Window

The Locals window (Figure 1-13) automatically displays all of the declared variables in the current procedure and their values.

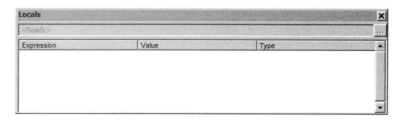

Figure 1-13. *The Locals window*

When the Locals window is visible, it is automatically updated every time there is a change from run to break mode, and when you navigate in the stack display, as shown in Figure 1-14.

Expression	Value	Type
⊞ Module1		Module1/Module1
Region	"North"	String
GetRegionalTotals	0	Long
lngReturn	1000	Long

Figure 1-14. *The Locals window shows function values.*

You can use the Locals window to do the following:

• Resize the column headers by dragging the border right or left.

• Close the window by clicking the Close box. If the Close box is not visible, double-click the Title bar to make the Close box visible, and then click it.

Locals Window Elements

The Locals window is made up of the following components. These window elements allow you to open the call stack and see the actual values of your variable as they are processed.

Call Stack button: Opens the Call Stack dialog box, which lists the procedures in the call stack. The call stack lists all the functions that are currently being executed. Figure 1-15 shows that the GetRegionalTotals function is being run from within the GetTotals function. The function on top is called by the function below it.

Figure 1-15. *The call stack*

The Locals window shows the following items in its columns:

Expression: Lists the name of the variables. The first variable in the list is a special module variable that can be expanded to display all module-level variables in the current module. This data is read-only.

Value: Lists the value of the variable. When you click a value in the Value column, the cursor changes to an I-beam. You can edit a value here to alter your code execution.

■**Note** All numeric variables must have a value. String variables can have an empty value.

Type: Lists the variable type (read-only).

The Watch Window

The Watch window (Figure 1-16) appears automatically when watch expressions are defined in the project (Figure 1-17).

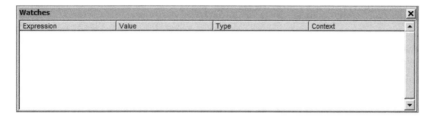

Figure 1-16. *The Watch window*

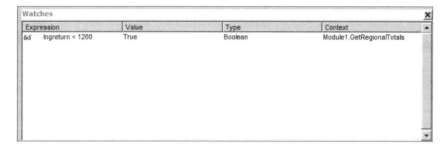

Figure 1-17. *The Watch window takes action when values meet certain criteria.*

You can use the Watch window to do the following:

- Change the size of a column header, by dragging its border to the right to make it larger or to the left to make it smaller

- Drag a selected variable to the Immediate window or the Watch window

Close the window by clicking the Close box. If the Close box is not visible, double-click the Title bar to make the Close box visible, and then click it.

Watch Window Elements

The Watch window list box columns display information about your watched expressions.

Expression: Stores a conditional phrase defined by the developer to evaluate the value of the watched variable. For example, if you wanted to know when a string variable named sCity was equal to New York, you would enter an expression of sCity = "New York".

Value: Lists the value of the expression at the time of entering break mode. You can edit a value here to alter code execution.

Type: Lists the expression type.

Context: Lists the context of the watch expression.

You can close the window by clicking the Close box. If the Close box is not visible, double-click the Title bar to make the Close box visible, and then click it.

Recording a Macro

In an Excel workbook, open the Developer ribbon and choose the Record Macro command to display the Record Macro dialog box, shown in Figure 1-18. The Record Macro dialog will display. The dialog box shows the default macro name, allows you to assign a shortcut key, lets you choose where to store the macro, and provides a text field where you can enter text describing the macro's function.

By default, Excel 2007 stores macros in the current workbook. If you want your macros to be available to any workbook, you can choose Personal Macro Workbook from the "Store macro in" drop-down list.

Figure 1-18. *The Record Macro dialog box*

1. In the Macro name text box, enter a name for your macro: MyMacro.

2. Add a shortcut key if you like.

3. From the "Store macro in" drop-down, choose This Workbook.

4. Add descriptive text if you like.

5. Click OK.

6. Enter the data shown in Figure 1-19.

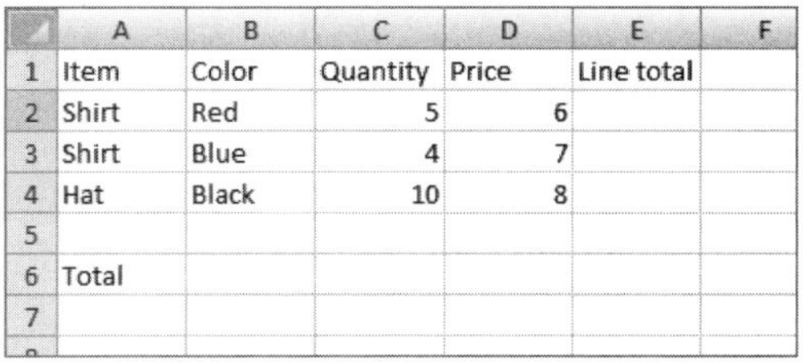

	A	B	C	D	E	F
1	Item	Color	Quantity	Price	Line total	
2	Shirt	Red	5	6		
3	Shirt	Blue	4	7		
4	Hat	Black	10	8		
5						
6	Total					
7						

Figure 1-19. *Recording data entry*

7. Choose the Stop Recording command from the Developer ribbon.

Let's take a look at the code Excel 2007 created for us. To open the Visual Basic Editor (VBE), choose the Visual Basic command from the Developer ribbon or use the Alt+F11 short-cut key combination.

A new standard code module named Module1 has been inserted in your project. Open Module1 by double-clicking the Modules folder, and then click Module1 to view the Macro Recorder–generated code. Listing 1-1 shows the code the Macro Recorder generated for us.

Listing 1-1. *Macro Recorder–Generated Code*

```
Sub MyMacro()
'
' MyMacro Macro
' Enter test data
'

'
    Range("A1").Select
    ActiveCell.FormulaR1C1 = "Item"
    Range("B1").Select
    ActiveCell.FormulaR1C1 = "Color"
    Range("C1").Select
    ActiveCell.FormulaR1C1 = "Quantity"
    Range("D1").Select
    ActiveCell.FormulaR1C1 = "Price"
    Range("E1").Select
    ActiveCell.FormulaR1C1 = "Line total"
    Range("A2").Select
    ActiveCell.FormulaR1C1 = "Shirt"
    Range("B2").Select
    ActiveCell.FormulaR1C1 = "Red"
    Range("C2").Select
    ActiveCell.FormulaR1C1 = "5"
    Range("D2").Select
    ActiveCell.FormulaR1C1 = "6"
```

```
    Range("A3").Select
    ActiveCell.FormulaR1C1 = "Shirt"
    Range("B3").Select
    ActiveCell.FormulaR1C1 = "Blue"
    Range("C3").Select
    ActiveCell.FormulaR1C1 = "4"
    Range("D3").Select
    ActiveCell.FormulaR1C1 = "7"
    Range("A4").Select
    ActiveCell.FormulaR1C1 = "Hat"
    Range("B4").Select
    ActiveCell.FormulaR1C1 = "Black"
    Range("C4").Select
    ActiveCell.FormulaR1C1 = "10"
    Range("D4").Select
    ActiveCell.FormulaR1C1 = "8"
    Range("A6").Select
    ActiveCell.FormulaR1C1 = "Total"
    Range("A7").Select
End Sub
```

Excel 2007 has created a subroutine for us, and we can see each cell we selected and the data we entered into each. One interesting thing to notice is Excel's choice of the `FormulaR1C1` property to assign the data to the `Range` object (cell A1 in the second line of code generated), `ActiveCell.FormulaR1C1 = "Item"`. We did not enter any formulas, and yet Excel uses a property used to reference a formula. As you're coding, you'll most likely assign a value to a cell or range by using the `Range` object's `Value` property, and use the `FormulaR1C1` property to insert formulas.

1. Change the line `ActiveCell.FormulaR1C1 = "Item"` to `ActiveCell.Value = "Item"`, and then delete all of the data from the worksheet. Run the MyMacro macro.

2. Click the Macros command from the Developer ribbon.

3. Choose MyMacro from the Macro dialog box.

4. Click Run.

Cell A1 contains the word `Item` as its value as it did in the previous example. The `Value` property is a bit more intuitive to use when typing code.

Let's create two more quick macros, one to format our data table and one to add formulas, to get a look at the code Excel creates.

Formatting the Table

1. Select the Record Macro command.

2. Name the macro FormatTable and click OK. (You cannot use spaces or special characters in your macro names.)

3. Select cells A1:E1 using the mouse, and apply bold formatting to them.

4. Select cell A6 and apply bold formatting.

5. Choose the Stop Recording command from the Developer ribbon.

The code Excel generates is very straightforward:

```
Sub FormatTable()
'
' FormatTable Macro
' Formats the table
'


    Range("A1:E1").Select
    Selection.Font.Bold = True
    Range("A6").Select
    Selection.Font.Bold = True
End Sub
```

We select the range containing our data. Each Selection object's Font property has a Bold property that is set to True.

Adding Totals

1. Select the Record Macro command.

2. Name the macro AddTotals and click OK.

3. Select cell C6, choose the AutoSum command, and then press Enter (AutoSum can be found on the Home ribbon or the Formulas ribbon, as shown in Figure 1-20).

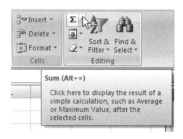

Figure 1-20. *The AutoSum button on the Home ribbon*

4. Select cell E2 and choose the AutoSum command. Press Enter.

5. Copy the contents of cell E2 to cells E3:E4. Press Enter.

6. Select cell E6 and choose the AutoSum command. Press Enter.

7. Choose the Stop Recording command from the Developer ribbon.

Taking a look at the code, notice that Excel uses the FormulaR1C1 property of the ActiveCell object, and this time it makes sense because we are entering formulas. One thing to note is that, depending on how you copy the formula from cell E2 to the rest of the column in step 5, Excel will create different lines of code.

Same Task, Different Code

If you use the fill handle and Ctrl-drag the contents into the range E3:E4, the code Excel generates might look like this:

```
Range("C6").Select
ActiveCell.FormulaR1C1 = "=SUM(R[-4]C:R[-1]C)"
Range("E2").Select
ActiveCell.FormulaR1C1 = "=SUM(RC[-2]:RC[-1])"
Range("E2").Select

'Used fill handle to copy formula to E3:E4
Selection.AutoFill Destination:=Range("E2:E4"), Type:=xlFillDefault
Range("E2:E4").Select
Range("E6").Select
ActiveCell.FormulaR1C1 = "=SUM(R[-4]C:R[-1]C)"
Range("E7").Select
```

If you select cell E2 and choose the Copy command, select the range E3:E4, and then choose the Paste command, Excel will generate this code:

```
Range("C6").Select
ActiveCell.FormulaR1C1 = "=SUM(R[-4]C:R[-1]C)"
Range("E2").Select
ActiveCell.FormulaR1C1 = "=SUM(RC[-2]:RC[-1])"
Range("E2").Select

'Used Copy command to copy formula to E3:E4
Selection.Copy
Range("E3:E4").Select
ActiveSheet.Paste
Application.CutCopyMode = False
Range("E6").Select
ActiveCell.FormulaR1C1 = "=SUM(R[-4]C:R[-1]C)"
Range("E7").Select
```

The code is identical up until the second Range("E2").Select command. In the first example, the fill method of copying was used, and we see Excel's AutoFill method invoked.

The AutoFill method takes two arguments, the range to fill (including the source range) and the type of fill to apply. The Type argument takes a value whose data type is xlAutoFillType enumeration. These correspond to the Series dialog and can contain the values listed in Table 1-2. These values can be combined by using the And operator (as in xlFillSeries And xlFillFormats).

		es and formats from the source range to the target
		mes of the days of the week in the source range into ge
		ermine the values and formats used to fill the target
		the formats from the source range to the target range.
		names of the months in the source range into the target
xlFi...		e values in the source range into the target range as a ., "1, 2" will be extended as "3, 4, 5")
xlFillValues	4	Copies only the values from the source range to the target range
xlFillWeekdays	6	Extends the names of the days of the workweek in the source range into the target range
xlFillYears	8	Extends the years in the source range into the target range
xlGrowthTrend	10	Extends the numeric values from the source range into the target range; assumes that each number is a result of multiplying the previous number by some value (e.g., "1, 2" will be extended as "4, 8, 16")
xlLinearTrend	9	Extends the numeric values from the source range into the target range, assuming that each number is a result of adding some value to the previous number (e.g., "1, 2" will be extended as "3, 4, 5")

The copy-and-paste method is very straightforward:

1. Select the range to be copied: Range("E2").Select.

2. Choose the copy command: Selection.Copy.

3. Select the destination range: Range("E3:E4").Select.

4. Choose the Paste command: ActiveSheet.Paste.

Another interesting line of code is: ActiveCell.FormulaR1C1 = "=SUM(R[-4]C:R[-1]C)". The default cell or range reference behavior in the Macro Recorder is to use R1C1 notation. This provides you with row and column offsets from the active cell. It can be useful in situations where you must calculate cell addresses to be used in your formulas.

R1C1 notation uses the R value to show the row offset from the active cell and the C value to show the column offset from the active cell. The offset value is enclosed in brackets; it can be a negative number to show rows or columns with a lesser value than the active cell row or column, or a positive number to show rows or columns with a greater value than the active cell. If the reference is to the same row or column as the active cell, there is no value entered—only the letter R or C.

In the preceding example, the first call to the SUM function refers to the range R[–4]C:R[–1]C. This is interpreted as a range starting four rows above the active cell (C6) in the same column and ending in the cell one row above the active cell in the same column.

You may be used to seeing the SUM function used with direct cell references like =SUM(A1:A4), especially if you're entering formulas directly on a worksheet. If you are adding a total to cell A5, this is a direct way to get the total of that range. But what if you need to add a total value for a number of columns across a row under your data range through VBA code? Using R1C1 notation, the formula =SUM(R[-4]C:R[-1]C) will always refer to rows 1 through 4 in the same column as the active cell (where the active cell is located in row 5).

As you've seen, the VBE is where Excel's Macro Recorder stores the code it creates, and it's where you will create and save the code you use in your daily tasks as well as in this book's examples.

Writing a Macro in the VBE

In this example, you'll create a macro by typing code directly in the VBE.

Open the file 1-MacroExample01.xlsx (shown in Figure 1-21), and open the VBE.

■**Note** You will find all the example files and source code for this book at www.apress.com in the Downloads section of this book's home page.

	A	B	C	D	E	F
1	QTR 1 Sales					
2		North	South	East	West	
3	CDs	24	23	82	28	
4	DVDs	58	82	44	43	
5	Hats	36	67	28	74	
6	Shirts	47	35	74	41	
7						
8	Total	165	207	228	186	
9						
10	Grand Total	$786.00				
11						

Figure 1-21. *Sales data for the first quarter of the year*

We see tour sales for the fictitious band "VBA," which are received quarterly by their management office and need to be totaled. Using R1C1 notation, we'll create one subroutine that will total these numbers, and since it is a relative reference to the cells, we'll see that we only need to create one formula.

First, we'll add a standard code module to the project. In the VBE (Alt+F11 from an Excel workbook), in the Project Explorer section (top-left pane), choose the top-level item, named VBAProject (1-MacroExample01.xlsx), right-click it, and choose Insert ➤ Module, as shown in Figure 1-22.

Figure 1-22. *Inserting a standard code module (shortcut menu)*

The Project Explorer shows our new module, named Module1 by default, as shown in Figure 1-23.

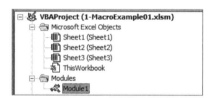

Figure 1-23. *New standard code module added*

More Macro Security

In the code pane, create a new empty subroutine called `TotalSales`, as shown in Listing 1-2, and save the file.

Listing 1-2. *Empty TotalSales Subroutine*

```
Sub TotalSales()

End Sub
```

The prompt shown in Figure 1-24 will appear.

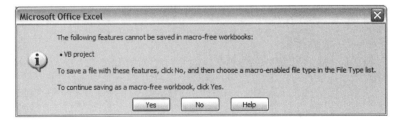

Figure 1-24. *Macro-free workbook warning*

The file you opened has an extension of .xlsx, which is the default file format for any new Excel workbook. This format is not macro-enabled and cannot be macro-enabled. To use macros in Excel 2007, you must choose a macro-enabled format from the list of file types in the Save As dialog box.

Choose No from this dialog to display the Save As dialog box. In the "Save as type" drop-down list, choose Excel Macro-Enabled Workbook (*.xlsm), as shown in Figure 1-25, and click OK.

Figure 1-25. *Selecting a macro-enabled file type (*.xlsm)*

Other macro-enabled file types available are listed in Table 1-3.

Table 1-3. *Macro-Enabled File Types*

File Type	Extension
Macro-enabled template	*.xltm
Macro-enabled add-in	*.xlam
Non-XML Excel binary workbook	*.xlsb

Our TotalSales method will create a formula to insert in the first cell in the Totals section (B8). That formula will be reused in the rest of the cells in the Totals row on the worksheet.

Let's determine the R1C1 coordinates of our formula. Once that's done, we'll assign that to a variable so we don't have to type it multiple times or copy and paste it.

The first cell in the Totals row is cell B8. On the worksheet, put the cursor in cell B8. For illustrative purposes, arrow key up until the cursor is in B3 (the first cell in the data range for that column), counting rows as you move. Of course, it's much simpler to just subtract the row numbers (8 – 3 = 5 in this case). Now we have our starting row, R[–5], five rows above our formula's cell location. Since we're working in the same column as our formula, the column reference will be C. This gives us the starting cell in our formula range of R[–5]C. Use the same technique to determine the last cell location (I've used the cell above the formula even though it does not contain any data; this is how Excel's AutoSum command works). Our finished range reference is R[–5]C:R[–1]C.

Add a string variable to hold the formula:

```
Dim sFormula As String
```

Once we've done this, we can assign the variable to each cell in the Totals data row individually.

The finished TotalSales code should look like Listing 1-3.

Listing 1-3. *Completed TotalSales Macro*

```
Sub TotalSales()
'Author: Jim DeMarco
'Date: 6/24/07
'Purpose: Adds total sales for all regions
Dim sFormula As String

sFormula = "=SUM(R[-5]C:R[-1]C)"
Range("B8").Select
ActiveCell.FormulaR1C1 = sFormula
Range("C8").Select
ActiveCell.FormulaR1C1 = sFormula
Range("D8").Select
ActiveCell.FormulaR1C1 = sFormula
Range("E8").Select
ActiveCell.FormulaR1C1 = sFormula

End Sub
```

As you can see, we created the formula once, assigned it to the sFormula variable, and then selected each target cell and inserted the formula. Of course, this is not the most efficient method we can use to achieve this.

Using Excel's Range object, we can walk through the cells in a given range and set the formula. Add a second subroutine to Module1 as follows:

```
Sub TotalSales2()
'Author: Jim DeMarco
'Date: 6/24/07
'Purpose: Adds total sales for all regions by looping through cells in a range
Dim sFormula As String
Dim cell As Range

sFormula = "=SUM(R[-5]C:R[-1]C)"
For Each cell In Range("B8:E8")
    cell.FormulaR1C1 = sFormula
Next cell

End Sub
```

We've added a variable called cell which is of type Range. You'll recall that a range in Excel can be anything from one to multiple cells. We then walk through the range B8:E8 using a For...Each statement, visiting each cell in the referenced range. This is much more concise, easier to read, and easier to maintain. Of course, like in the first example it also assumes you know the addresses of the cells in the range to receive the formula.

Let's look at one last example that, while not completely dynamic, will show you a method whereby you could easily adapt it to determine the locations for your formula.

Add one more subroutine to Module1:

```
Sub TotalSales3()
'Author: Jim DeMarco
'Date: 6/24/07
'Purpose: Adds total sales for all regions by moving across columms
Dim sFormula As String
Dim i As Integer

sFormula = "=SUM(R[-5]C:R[-1]C)"
For i = 2 To 5
    Cells(8, i).Select
    ActiveCell.FormulaR1C1 = sFormula
Next i

End Sub
```

This time we're using a counter variable, i, to loop through columns 2 through 5. We select each cell in turn and apply the formula to it. Using this method, it becomes apparent that if we can use code to determine our start and end points for the For loop, we can very easily create a dynamic method of adding our formula to a variable number of columns or rows.

The Object Browser

The Object Browser, shown in Figure 1-26, is displayed by choosing View ➤ Object Browser or by pressing the F2 function key. It displays the classes, properties, methods, events, and constants available from any object libraries, and it also shows the procedures in your project. You can also use it to find and use custom objects you create.

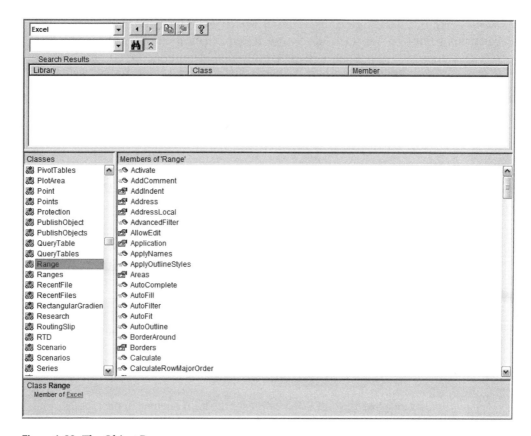

Figure 1-26. *The Object Browser*

Object Browser Window Elements

The Object Browser window contains window elements that enable you to search for a method or property within an object library and to get information about the selected method or property.

> *Project/Library Box*: The Project/Library box displays the currently referenced libraries for the active project (Figure 1-27). Libraries can be added in the Tools ➤ References dialog box. The <All Libraries> selection allows all of the libraries to be displayed at one time.

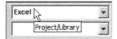

Figure 1-27. *The Library drop-down list box*

Search Text box: This text box contains the string that you want to use in your search. You can type a string or choose the string you want from the drop-down list. The Search Text box contains the last four search strings that you entered until you close the project. You can also use the standard Visual Basic wildcards when typing a string. You can search for a whole word by using the Find Whole Word Only command from the shortcut menu.

Go Back button: This allows you to go back to the previous selection in the Classes and "Members of" lists. Each time you click it, you move back one selection.

Go Forward button: This allows you to repeat your original selections in the Classes and "Members of" lists each time you click it.

Copy to Clipboard button: This copies the current selection in the "Members of" list or the Details pane text to the clipboard.

View Definition button: This moves the cursor to the place in the code window where the selection in the "Members of" list or the Classes list is defined.

Help button: This displays the online help topic for the item selected in the Classes or "Members of" list. You can also press F1 to access this.

Search button: This searches the libraries for the class, property, method, event, or constant that matches the string you typed in the Search Text box. The result of the search is shown in the Search Results pane.

Show/Hide Search Results button: This opens or hides the Search Results pane.

Search Results list: This list displays the library, class, and member that matches the items that contain your search string.

Classes list: This list displays all of the available classes in the library or project selected in the Project/Library box.

"Members of" list: This list displays the elements of the class selected in the Classes pane by group and then alphabetically within each group.

Details pane: This pane shows the definition of the class member. The Details pane (Figure 1-28) contains a hypertext link to the class or library to which the element belongs. Some members have hypertext links to their parent class. For example, if the text in the Details pane states that TextBox1 is declared as a text box type, clicking text box takes you to the TextBox class. You can copy or drag text from the Details pane to the code window.

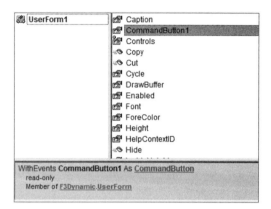

Figure 1-28. *The Details pane*

Split bar: This splits the panes so that you can adjust their size. There are split bars between the following:

- The Classes box and the "Members of" box

- The Search Results list and the Classes and "Members of" boxes

- The Classes and "Members of" boxes and the Details pane

Standard Code Modules

A standard module is a code module containing only procedure (Sub or Function), type, and data declarations and definitions. Module-level declarations and definitions in a standard module are public by default. In earlier versions of Visual Basic, a standard module was referred to as a code module.

Whenever a new macro is created in an Excel session, a standard module is inserted into the workbook to hold the macro. Any additional macros created in that session will also be inserted into this standard module. Once the workbook is closed and reopened, Excel will create a new standard module if the Macro Recorder is invoked.

■**Note** You will have to copy and paste your code if you want to keep it in one place or provide a specific location for your code.

Standard modules are inserted into your project by choosing Insert ➤ Module or by right-clicking an object in the Project Explorer and choosing Insert ➤ Module from the pop-up menu.

Subprocedures

A *subprocedure* (also called *subroutine*) is a procedure that performs a task within a program, but does not return a value. A subroutine begins with a Sub statement and ends with an End Sub statement. Any version of the TotalSales code you wrote previously is an example of a subroutine.

```
Sub TotalSales3()
'Author: Jim DeMarco
'Date: 6/24/07
'Purpose: Adds total sales for all regions by moving across columms
Dim sFormula As String
Dim i As Integer

sFormula = "=SUM(R[-5]C:R[-1]C)"
For i = 2 To 5
    Cells(8, i).Select
    ActiveCell.FormulaR1C1 = sFormula
Next i

End Sub
```

Functions

A *function* is a procedure that performs a task within a program and returns a value. A function begins with a Function statement and ends with an End Function statement. Functions (and subroutines) can receive arguments passed in from calling procedures or passed in directly.

The following is a function that returns the total for a range passed in to the function as an argument. We pass in the range reference to make the code flexible enough to reuse on any range that needs to be totaled.

```
Function GetSalesTotal(RangeToTotal As Range) As Currency
'Author: Jim DeMarco
'Date: 6/24/07
'Purpose: Returns value of sales total
Dim currReturn As Currency
Dim cell As Range
Dim temp As Currency

    For Each cell In RangeToTotal
        temp = temp + cell.Value
    Next cell
```

```
    currReturn = temp
    GetSalesTotal = currReturn

End Function
```

To use the function, we can create a subroutine or function to call it. The following adds a label and inserts the total next to it on the worksheet:

```
Sub AddSalesTotal()
'Author: Jim DeMarco
'Date: 6/24/07
'Purpose: Places value of sales total on worksheet

    With Range("A10")
        .Value = "Grand Total"
        .Font.Bold = True
    End With

    Range("C10").Value = GetSalesTotal(range("B8:E8"))

End Sub
```

Type Statements

Type statements are used at module level to define a user-defined data type containing one or more elements. In the following example, we define Employee as a data type and then use it in a subroutine, setting values and displaying them.

```
Type Employee
    ID As Long
    Name As String
    Title As String
    Phone As String
End Type

Sub SetEmployee()
Dim empMyEmployee As Employee
    empMyEmployee.ID = 123456
    empMyEmployee.Name = "John Doe"
    MsgBox empMyEmployee.ID & " " & empMyEmployee.Name
End Sub
```

Class Modules

If you've done any amount of VBA or VB coding, you have more than likely used objects in your code. Any time you've gone out to a database and retrieved records using ADO, you may have declared and instantiated a variable like this:

```
Dim rs As ADODB.Recordset
Set rs = New ADODB.Recordset
```

Some of the examples you've seen thus far have also used some of Excel's built-in objects, like the Selection object, which has a Font property, or the Range object, which has many properties and methods you can use in your code.

Using Excel's VBE, you can create your own objects that contain custom properties and methods that you define. You do this by creating classes in class modules. Here's the definition of an object (from Microsoft's ASP.NET forums at http://forums.asp.net/p/1117506/1933142.aspx):

Class: The formal definition of an object. The class acts as the template from which an instance of an object is created at run time. The class defines the properties of the object and the methods used to control the object's behaviour.

In a standard code module, public functions and subroutines you create can be called from anywhere in your code simply by referencing the procedure. Code in a class module must be explicitly instantiated, as in the preceding ADO Recordset example. Until an object is instantiated in this manner, its methods and properties are not available to your code.

Another difference is that standard code modules can contain any number of related or unrelated procedures (although best practices dictate that code in a given module should be related to specific functionality, reality tells us that this is not always the case, and there is no enforcement of this practice within a standard code module). Code in a class module by definition defines the methods, properties, and events for objects that you create from a class. These methods, properties, and events are all directly related to the object, and their inner workings do not need to be known to implement or use the object. The term used to define this relationship to the object is *encapsulation*.

Encapsulation can be defined as *the capability of an object to conceal its inner workings from client code or other objects*. It is one of the fundamental principles of object-oriented programming (OOP). If an object has clearly defined properties and methods, it will be easily reusable and will require limited (if any) documentation. When we look at the ADO recordset object, we can easily understand what its Open or AddNew methods do for us with no concern for how they provide their services. Your objects will be as well defined as any of the Visual Basic objects, and therefore easy for you or anyone else to implement in their applications.

Class modules contain only code—there is no visual interface. Classes you create in Excel VBA are easily portable to other VBA applications, and can be placed into Visual Basic 5 or 6 code with no (or minimal) modifications and compiled into ActiveX DLLs or EXEs. This allows your objects to be used in applications outside of Excel.

Use of classes allows for the design of robust, reusable objects. It requires more forethought and planning, but you receive the benefits of code that is usually more reliable and easier to maintain.

Class modules are inserted into your project by choosing Insert ➤ Class Module or by right-clicking an object in the Project Explorer and choosing Insert ➤ Class Module from the pop-up menu.

Sample Class and Usage

Let's re-create the `Employee` user-defined data type that we looked at in a previous example as an object. Custom data types are a great way to store more than one related value for an item, but they have a few shortcomings. They don't do any validation, they cannot perform actions (methods or functions), and they cannot by themselves trigger events. Classes allow you to do all of these.

The cEmployee Class

Let's take a quick look at the `Employee` data type from our previous example:

```
Type Employee
    ID As Long
    Name As String
    Title As String
    Phone As String
End Type
```

The first thing we will do is create properties for each value type. In Visual Basic 5/6.0 and VBA, you must create methods for getting and setting the values of a property. These are known as `Property Let` and `Property Get` methods. A third method is available if your property will return or set an object. This is known as the `Property Set` method, and it works in a similar manner to the `Property Let` method.

1. In a new workbook open the VBE and insert a class module (choose Insert ➤ Class Module).

2. In the Property Sheet, rename the class module cEmployee.

3. In the code pane, enter the following code:

```
Dim m_lngID As Long
Dim m_sName As String
Dim m_sTitle As String
Dim m_sPhoneNumber As String
```

These module-level variables will contain the values for our object.

4. Next, enter the `Property Let` and `Get` functions for each property:

```
Property Get ID() As Long
    ID = m_lngID
End Property

Property Let ID(newID As Long)
    m_lngID = newID
End Property
```

```
Property Get Name() As String
    Name = m_sName
End Property

Property Let Name(newName As String)
    m_sName = newName
End Property

Property Get Title() As String
    Title = m_sTitle
End Property

Property Let Title(newTitle As String)
    m_sTitle = newTitle
End Property

Property Get PhoneNumber() As String
    PhoneNumber = m_sPhoneNumber
End Property

Property Let PhoneNumber(newPhoneNumber As String)
    m_sPhoneNumber = newPhoneNumber
End Property
```

Note that the module-level variables are used within each Property Let or Get method, and are either being returned (Get) or assigned a value (Let).

```
Property Get ID() As Long
    ID = m_lngID
End Property

Property Let ID(newID As Long)
    m_lngID = newID
End Property
```

Another advantage class modules give us is the ability to initialize the values of the module-level variables when an object is instantiated from the class.

5. Choose Class from the Object box in the code pane, as shown in Figure 1-29.

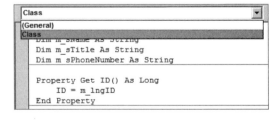

Figure 1-29. *Selecting Class from the VBA code window Object box*

6. The VBE inserts the `Class_Initialize` method for you. Add code to set the default values for the `Employee` class, as shown in Listing 1-4.

Listing 1-4. *Class Initialization Code—Here It's Set to Nonsense Values Useful in Determining What Properties Have or Have Not Been Set.*

```
Private Sub Class_Initialize()
    m_lngID = 0
    m_sName = "NOG"
    m_sTitle = "NOG"
    m_sPhoneNumber = "0000000000"
End Sub
```

There are two methods included with each class module, the `Class_Initialize` and the `Class_Terminate` methods. It's always a good idea to initialize your values so that any clients of your class have a value to work with.

The `Initialize` method is a great place to set default values, to open any data sources or files your class may need, or to perform any other setup that your object may need to do its job.

The `Terminate` method, although not always used, is important because it gives you a place to clean up any data connections or recordsets (or any other objects your class may use) and close any files you've opened.

Using the cEmployee Class

We can test our `cEmployee` class using the Immediate window in the VBE:

1. Open the Immediate window by choosing View ➤ Immediate Window or by pressing the Ctrl+G key combination.

2. In the Immediate window, type - **Set emp = New cEmployee**, and press Enter.

3. Type - **?emp.Name** and press Enter.

Your screen should look like Figure 1-30.

Figure 1-30. *Instantiating the cEmployee object in the Immediate window. Property values have not been set yet.*

We've returned our nonsense value from the class initialization code. Now let's assign values to our properties. Type the following commands into the Immediate window, pressing Enter after each. The first group of commands will set the cEmployee object's properties and the second will retrieve and display them.

```
emp.ID = 15
emp.Name = "John Doe"
emp.Title = "Analyst"
emp.PhoneNumber = "8885555555"
?emp.name
?emp.ID
?emp.title
?emp.phonenumber
set emp = Nothing
```

Your Immediate window should look like Figure 1-31.

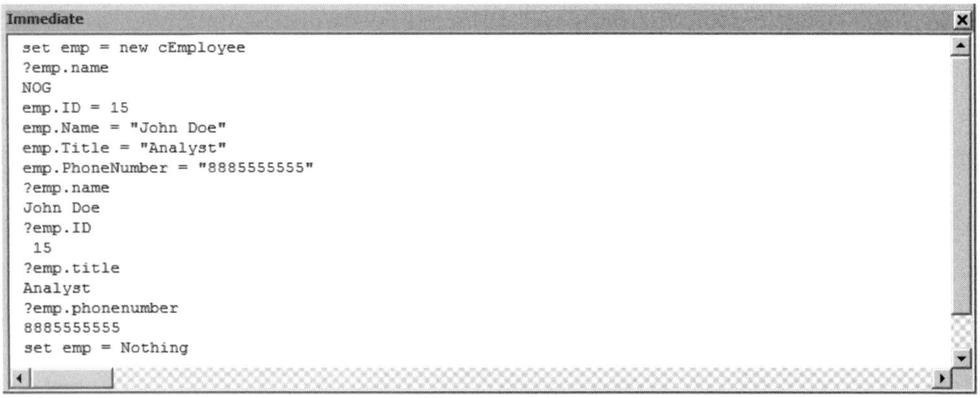

```
Immediate                                                              ×
set emp = new cEmployee
?emp.name
NOG
emp.ID = 15
emp.Name = "John Doe"
emp.Title = "Analyst"
emp.PhoneNumber = "8885555555"
?emp.name
John Doe
?emp.ID
 15
?emp.title
Analyst
?emp.phonenumber
8885555555
set emp = Nothing
```

Figure 1-31. *cEmployee object with property values set and returned*

Let's take a look at what's going on here. The first line of code instantiates (or creates) the employee object:

```
Set emp = New cEmployee
```

When that object is created, the Class_Initialize method fires and the default values are set. As mentioned earlier, this is where you would set up any activities or objects your class needs to have in place.

Next, a quick check of the Name property is done to see that it is holding your default value—in this case the nonsense value NOG.

The next four lines set all of the properties of the Employee object with real values:

```
emp.ID = 15
emp.Name = "John Doe"
emp.Title = "Analyst"
emp.PhoneNumber = "8885555555"
```

Each time you pressed the Enter key, the `Property Let` method fired for each property and assigned the value you passed in to the module-level variable for each property. Then you typed in commands to show that the `cEmployee` object was indeed storing the values entered previously.

```
?emp.name
John Doe
?emp.ID
 15
?emp.title
Analyst
?emp.phonenumber
8885555555
```

Each time you pressed the Enter key, the `Property Get` method fired and retrieved the value currently stored in the module-level variable for each property.

The final line of code removes the object from memory. Any attempt to write or retrieve a value after the object is destroyed will result in an error.

```
set emp = Nothing
```

When the object is set to `Nothing`, any code placed in the `Class_Terminate` method will run. As previously noted, this is where you will perform any necessary cleanup before the object is destroyed.

The Class-y Way of Thinking

Our `cEmployee` class, while extremely simple in content and functionality, does serve the purpose of showing some of the benefits of writing class-based code.

Let's assume for a moment that we had written validation and formatting code into the `Property Lets` and `Gets` of the class, as well as some business rules; or that we had added methods to export the employee data to a delimited string or set of XML tags for import into an external system. It would be very easy for us to export the class module for use in someone else's Excel project, or an Access database or even a Word document.

The key to successfully implementing classes is to keep the code as generic as possible. Of course, if you are creating a class for one specific task, this is an acceptable exception to the rule, but in general, keeping code generic provides great reuse opportunities.

Classes also provide an excellent example of self-documentation via IntelliSense. Anytime you reference an object variable in your code and type the `.` operator, you'll see a complete list of the object's functionality (just like the built-in VBA objects, such as ADO) as shown in Figure 1-32.

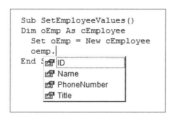

Figure 1-32. *Class objects provide documentation via IntelliSense.*

We will focus heavily on classes and object-oriented development as we move on in this text. The ease of maintenance and high probability of reuse are well worth the extra planning required to build applications using these techniques. Once you are comfortable with these concepts, there really won't be much additional thought or planning required. It will be your natural process to work in an OOP fashion.

UserForms

Excel provides us with UserForms as a means to provide a user interface (UI) to our Excel applications. UserForms are similar to Access or Visual Basic forms. They are containers for input and display controls. Both the forms and controls have properties, methods, and events that we can code against. Excel names new forms UserForm1, UserForm2, and so on, as they are added. They can be renamed as needed.

UserForms are inserted into your project by choosing Insert ➤ UserForm or by right-clicking an object in the Project Explorer and choosing Insert ➤ UserForm from the pop-up menu, as shown in Figure 1-33.

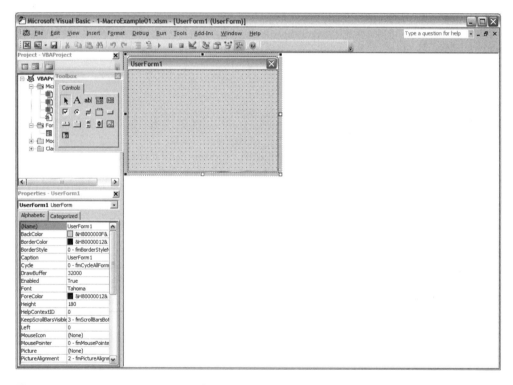

Figure 1-33. *A new UserForm inserted in the VBE*

When a new UserForm is inserted, the Toolbox window is also displayed. The Toolbox identifies the different controls that you can add to your forms.

■**Note** If the Toolbox is not displayed, click View ➤ Toolbox to display it.

The Toolbox (Figure 1-34) is customizable. The following are some of the customization options you have:

- Adding pages to the Toolbox

- Moving controls from one page to another

- Renaming pages

- Adding other controls, including ActiveX controls, to the Toolbox

- Copying customized controls from the form into the Toolbox

■**Tip** The OK and Cancel buttons are special cases of a command button. If you add OK and Cancel templates to the Toolbox, you can quickly add them to other forms.

Figure 1-34. *The Toolbox window*

Toolbox Window Elements

The Toolbox window contains the following controls:

Select Objects: This is the only item in the Toolbox that doesn't draw a control. When you select it, you can only resize or move a control that has already been placed on a form.

Label: This displays text that the user cannot change, such as a form heading.

TextBox: This allows entry or modification of text.

ComboBox: The ComboBox is a combination list box and text box. Users can either choose an item from the list or enter a value in the text box.

ListBox: This is used to display a list of items from which the user can choose. The list can be scrolled if it has more items than can be displayed at one time.

CheckBox: This creates a box that the user can click to select or deselect an item or to show a true or false value.

OptionButton: This displays multiple choices from which the user can choose only one.

ToggleButton: This button is used for toggling on and off.

Frame: This is a graphical or functional grouping for controls. To group controls, draw the frame first, and then place option buttons or check box controls inside the frame.

CommandButton: This creates a button the user can click to carry out a command.

TabStrip: This allows you to define multiple pages for the same area of a window or dialog box in your application.

MultiPage: This presents multiple screens of information as a single set.

ScrollBar: This provides a tool for quickly navigating through a long list of items or a large amount of information. It is also useful for indicating the current position on a scale, or as an input device or indicator of speed or quantity.

SpinButton: This is used in conjunction with another control to increment and decrement numbers. It can also be used to scroll back and forth through a range of values or a list of items.

Image: This displays an image from a graphics file on your form.

RefEdit: This allows the user to type or click and drag range references into its text area. It is similar to Excel's `Set Print Area` input function.

Figure 1-35 shows an example of an Excel 2007 UserForm.

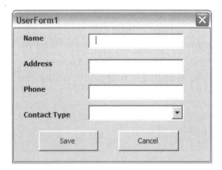

Figure 1-35. *Sample UserForm with controls added*

Object-Oriented Programming: An Overview

I decided early on in the process of writing this book that I would concentrate my efforts on providing guidance in the creation of class-based solutions to Excel VBA coding problems where possible. I have found through programming in Access, VB 6, and then VB.NET that using OOP techniques has helped me visualize my applications more clearly, helped me to better organize my code, and has been invaluable in making my code easier to maintain. Standard code modules and procedural programming allow us to write code anywhere we like. Although programmers always try to group related code in the same well-named module, it's not always possible and not always done. Using objects, you will find that you always create functionality related to the object and that there's really no room for unrelated code. Imagine you're creating the cEmployee class shown earlier. You'd never think of adding a Part Number property or a CalculateHorsepower method in an Employee class. The object defines its interface. These are words to live by. Classes initially built for Access applications were moved to VB 6 with little or no modification (and the reverse is also true). The same is true of bringing those classes into Excel applications. Of course, the .NET world with its new syntax changes that, but the concepts still apply (which helps to make a more effective transition to the .NET environment). That said, the classes provided in this book should work in almost any Microsoft Office environment (prerequisites and differences in component or Office versions notwithstanding). That's the beauty of using class-based code. Objects are defined as an instance of a class. Objects have properties (nouns) and methods (verbs), and can fire events. Each object instance holds its own values for its properties (private instance variables). Objects are responsible for providing a certain behavior (or functionality), and they can collaborate with other objects to perform their tasks. Classes hide their inner workings so we can simply bring an existing class into a project and begin using the functionality it provides. This is known as *encapsulation*, and is one of the fundamental concepts of OOP. A FileReader class may have the ability to open and parse an XML file and return various nodes to me through its interface. I do not need to concern myself with the details of how it accomplishes this. I call the GetNodes method and I've got the nodes I need to work with. Another basic concept to OOP is *polymorphism*. Polymorphism is the ability of objects of different types to respond to calls to methods with the same name. Imagine creating a cEmployee class and a PurchaseOrder class that both make database calls. Each class can contain a SaveData method. Each will perform its function differently, yet the functionality for each is the same. We don't need to know how either one does its job, which brings us back to . . . encapsulation!

OOP purists would tell you that this is an incomplete implementation of polymorphism, and they would be correct. True polymorphism should also include the ability to overload methods. This means that an object can have more than one implementation of a method. For example, my aforementioned SaveData method could have multiple footprints within the same class:

```
Sub SaveData(Name As String, ID As Long)
'code here
End Sub
```

```
Sub SaveData(Name As String, ID As Long, Title As String, Photo As Object)
'code here
End Sub
```

The two SaveData methods take different arguments and are valid in a development environment that supports polymorphism, such as Visual Studio .NET. VBA does not support polymorphism, but you can program in Visual Studio .NET and use those components in your Excel applications. We'll explore that later.

OOP: Is It Worth the Extra Effort?

Of course it is. For the effort of making it through the slight learning curve, you will reap the benefits of object-oriented development. When you let objects do your work, your UI code will be much cleaner. Your business logic will reside in objects, and the UI will send data to and from them. Your data layer will be compartmentalized and reusable between applications. Any workflow can be stored in classes and used in any application that needs it. You'll develop code libraries that will provide easy access to your object-based functionality. How do you transport this functionality from application to application? Simply import the class!

If you create a lot of Excel applications, you may even find yourself building a reusable framework from which you can create new applications that will already contain your base functionality.

Summary

In Chapter 1, you looked at the Excel 2007 Macro Recorder and learned how to use it to let Excel generate code for you. This is useful when learning the Excel 2007 object model, and it can also be used to generate base code that you can then edit to suit your purpose.

You worked with the Excel Visual Basic Editor (VBE), where you created macros to enter and format data. The VBE is similar to the VB 6 code editor, and includes many of the same tools for debugging your code, such the Immediate window, the Locals window, and the Watch window. You were introduced to Excel's Object Browser, which contains tools that let you examine the libraries in your project and investigate an object's methods and properties.

You also looked at standard code modules. Standard code modules contain subroutines, functions, and type statements. You saw how to build your own subroutines to perform tasks and learned that subroutines do not return a value. When you need a routine to return a value, you create functions. Functions can also perform tasks just like subroutines. Type statements allow you to create complex custom data types, such as the Employee type created in this chapter. Types are similar to classes but without the ability to contain code within their data elements.

You then explored class modules. Class modules allow you to create custom objects. These objects can contain properties and methods to perform any task the object needs.

Finally, you looked at the Excel 2007 UserForm object and its Toolbox. UserForms allow you to create data entry forms and data display screens from within the Excel VBE. The Toolbox contains many common controls that you can use on the UserForm, including text boxes, combo boxes, and command buttons. It's similar to the Toolbox in Microsoft Access.

You are equipped with a very powerful set of development tools in Excel 2007. In Chapter 2, we are going to look at the many ways to bring data in and out of an Excel 2007 workbook project.

CHAPTER 2

■■■

Data In, Data Out

Excel 2007 provides us with a number of methods to bring in data. We can import or link to many different data sources, including Microsoft Access databases, SQL Server databases, text files, ODBC databases, and XML files, to name a few.

Excel's Data Import Tools

Excel 2007 has a rich set of data handling tools. On the Developer ribbon, you'll find quick access to Microsoft Access databases, web tables, and text files. Excel also includes data access to SQL Server and OLAP databases, XML data, and ODBC data sources.

By recording macros, you can see how Excel connects us to various data sources. From there, you'll begin writing your own data access routines.

■**Note** The first few examples will run under Windows 2000 or Windows XP as is. Windows Vista still supports Visual Basic 6.0 (and by extension VBA), but does not ship with all of the data access components of its predecessors. To run the examples under Windows Vista, check the following link to Microsoft's Support Statement for Visual Basic 6.0 on Windows Vista: http://msdn2.microsoft.com/en-us/vbrun/ms788708.aspx.

Importing Access Data

Let's look at how Excel brings in external data by recording a quick macro to import data from an Access database.

Create a new macro named GetAccessData. We're going to import the Extended Employees list (query) from the Northwind 2007 database onto Sheet1 in a new Excel workbook.

1. Select the Data ribbon.

2. Select From Access from the Get External Data section of the Data ribbon.

3. Navigate to wherever you have the Northwind database stored.

■Note   The files for these examples can be found in the Source Code/Download section of this book's home page at www.apress.com.

■Note   There is a new version of Northwind in Access 2007 that uses a file extension of *.accdb for Access databases.

4. In the Select Table dialog box, choose Employees Extended, and click OK.

5. In the Import Data dialog box, you have choices of how you want to view the data (table, PivotTable, or PivotChart) and where you want to put the data, as well as advanced options. For now, just accept the defaults by clicking the OK button.

The code generated from this looks like Listing 2-1.

Listing 2-1. *Macro-Generated Data Access Code*

```
Sub GetAccessData()
'
' GetAccessData Macro
' Code created by Excel 2007 Macro Recorder

'
    With ActiveSheet.ListObjects.Add(SourceType:=0, Source:=Array( ➡
        "OLEDB;Provider=Microsoft.ACE.OLEDB.12.0;Password=""""";User ID=Admin;" ➡
        & "Data Source=C:\projects\Excel2007Book\Files\Northwind 2007.accdb;Mod" ➡
        , ➡
        "e=Share Deny Write;Extended Properties=""""";" ➡
        & "Jet OLEDB:System database=""""";Jet OLEDB:Registry Path=""""";" ➡
        & "Jet OLEDB:Database Password=""""" ➡
        , ➡
        ";Jet OLEDB:Engine Type=6;Jet OLEDB:Database Locking Mode=0;" ➡
        & "Jet OLEDB:Global Partial Bulk Ops=2;Jet OLEDB:Global Bulk Transaction" ➡
        , ➡
        "s=1;Jet OLEDB:New Database Password=""""";" ➡
        & "Jet OLEDB:Create System Database=False;" ➡
        & "Jet OLEDB:Encrypt Database=False;Jet OLEDB:Don't C" ➡
        , ➡
        "opy Locale on Compact=False;" ➡
        & "Jet OLEDB:Compact Without Replica Repair=False;Jet OLEDB:SFP=False;" ➡
        & "Jet OLEDB:Support Complex Data=Fa" ➡
        , "lse"), Destination:=Range("$A$1")).QueryTable
        .CommandType = xlCmdTable
        .CommandText = Array("Employees Extended")
```

```
        .RowNumbers = False
        .FillAdjacentFormulas = False
        .PreserveFormatting = True
        .RefreshOnFileOpen = False
        .BackgroundQuery = True
        .RefreshStyle = xlInsertDeleteCells
        .SavePassword = False
        .SaveData = True
        .AdjustColumnWidth = True
        .RefreshPeriod = 0
        .PreserveColumnInfo = True
        .SourceDataFile = "C:\projects\Excel2007Book\Files\Northwind 2007a.accdb"
        .ListObject.DisplayName = "Table_Northwind_2007a.accdb"
        .Refresh BackgroundQuery:=False
    End With
End Sub
```

The SourceType and Source settings of the ListObject.Add method tell whether the data is from an Excel sheet (xlSrcRange = 1) or an external source (xlSrcExternal = 0). When the SourceType is external, the source is an array of string values specifying a connection to the source data.

Buried at the end of our lengthy source data string is this line of code:

```
Destination:=Range("$A$1")).QueryTable
```

A QueryTable object is a worksheet table that is created any time data is returned from an external data source like an Access or SQL Server database. Table 2-1 lists the members of the QueryTable object and describes them.

Table 2-1. *QueryTable Object Members*

QueryTable Object Members	Description
CommandType	Returns/sets one of the xlCmdType constants. The xlCommandType constants define whether an SQL statement, cube, or OLE DB data source will be requested. The default value is xlCmdSQL.
CommandText	Returns/sets the command string for the data source.
RowNumbers	True if row numbers are added as the first column of the query table.
FillAdjacentFormulas	True if formulas to the right of the query table are automatically updated whenever the query table is refreshed.
PreserveFormatting	True if formatting common to the first five rows of data are applied to new rows in the query table.
RefreshOnFileOpen	True if the PivotTable cache or query table is automatically updated whenever the workbook is opened.
BackgroundQuery	True if queries for the query table are performed in the background.
RefreshStyle	Returns/sets the way rows on the specified worksheet are added or deleted to accommodate the number of rows in a recordset (returned by a query).

Continued

Table 2-1. *Continued*

QueryTable Object Members	Description
SavePassword	True if password information in an ODBC connection string is saved with the query. False if the password is removed.
SaveData	True if data for the query table report is saved with the workbook. False if the report definition is saved and nothing else.
AdjustColumnWidth	True if the column widths are automatically adjusted for the best fit each time you refresh the specified query table. False if they are not.
RefreshPeriod	Returns/sets the number of minutes between refreshes.
PreserveColumnInfo	True if column sorting, filtering, and layout information is preserved when a query table is refreshed. Default value is False.
SourceDataFile	Returns/sets a String value that indicates the source data file for a query table.
ListObject.DisplayName	Property of ListObject. Creates or returns a named range for the inserted data.
Refresh	Causes Excel to connect to the data source, execute the SQL query again, and return data to the range that contains the QueryTable object. The QueryTable object doesn't communicate with the data source once data is inserted unless this method is called.

Simplifying the Code

The code Excel generates, while accurate, is certainly not something one would want to maintain. And you can forget about flexibility. The Array function used to pass in the connection string and database information is one scary looking piece of code. One of the first things we can do to simplify this is to create our own connection string and store it in a variable. This will give us the advantage of easier maintenance. Create a new function in Module1 and name it GetAccessData2. Paste the code from GetAccessData into it, and then add the following declaration and code (be sure to change the path to the Northwind 2007 database to your location):

```
Dim sConnString As String

    sConnString = "OLEDB;Provider=Microsoft.ACE.OLEDB.12.0;Password="""";" ➥
    & "User ID=Admin;" ➥
    & "Data Source=C:\projects\Excel2007Book\Files\Northwind 2007.accdb;" ➥
    & "Mode=Share Deny Write;Extended Properties="""";" ➥
    & "Jet OLEDB:System database="""";" ➥
    & "Jet OLEDB:Registry Path="""";Jet OLEDB:Database Password="""";" ➥
    & "Jet OLEDB:Engine Type=6;Jet OLEDB:Database Locking Mode=0;" ➥
    & "Jet OLEDB:Global Partial Bulk Ops=2;Jet OLEDB:Global Bulk Transactions=1;" ➥
    & "Jet OLEDB:New Database Password="""";" ➥
    & "Jet OLEDB:Create System Database=False;" ➥
    & "Jet OLEDB:Encrypt Database=False;" ➥
    & "Jet OLEDB:Don't Copy Locale on Compact=False;" ➥
    & "Jet OLEDB:Compact Without Replica Repair=False;Jet OLEDB:SFP=False;" ➥
    & "Jet OLEDB:Support Complex Data=False"
```

This code is much more readable and there is less danger of breaking our code if we ever need to point to another Access data source.

Now we just need to change the Source property of the ListObjects.Add method to refer to the connection string in place of the array:

```
With ActiveSheet.ListObjects.Add(SourceType:=0, Source:=sConnString, ➥
        Destination:=Range("$A$1")).QueryTable
```

With a couple of quick and easy changes, we've made the Macro Recorder–generated code much easier to read and modify. Let's import the same data onto Sheet2 in the workbook:

1. Navigate to Sheet2 in the workbook.

2. Run the GetAccessData2 macro.

Oops, we've generated an error (see Figure 2-1).

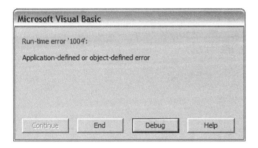

Figure 2-1. *Macro code generates error*

Why should there be an error? Excel generated this code itself (with the exception of your addition of a string variable). Click the Debug button, and the VBE should show us the errant line of code (see Figure 2-2).

```
            .SourceDataFile = "C:\projects\Excel2007Book\Files\Northwind 2007a.accdb"
            .ListObject.DisplayName = "Table_Northwind_2007a.accdb"
            .Refresh BackgroundQuery:=False
        End With
    End Sub
```

Figure 2-2. *DisplayName property fires error*

The ListObject.DisplayName property creates a named range on the worksheet. Even though we're working on Sheet2, a range named Table_Northwind_2007a.accdb already exists in this workbook. Easy enough to fix:

1. Click Debug.

2. Remove or change the a before the file extension, or simply choose another name entirely.

3. Press F5 to continue running the code.

There is still a lot of code stored on our sConnString variable. Many of the Jet database property values default to False, since we did a simple import of data. We can remove them from our connection string and leave just the essential information required to access our Northwind database. Create one last new method and name it GetAccessData3. Paste the code from GetAccessData2 into it and make the following changes:

```
sConnString = "OLEDB;Provider=Microsoft.ACE.OLEDB.12.0;Password="""";" ➥
       & "User ID=Admin;" ➥
       & "Data Source=C:\projects\Excel2007Book\Files\Northwind 2007.accdb;"
```

We could also remove any property call from the QueryTable object's instantiation as well, to further simplify the code—but we'll leave that alone for now.

The GetAccessData, GetAccessData2, and GetAccessData3 subroutines show all three versions of this code with each version becoming more succinct than the last.

Importing Text Data

Before we begin writing our own code to import data, let's record one more macro to see some of the settings available when we bring in data from a text file.

1. Create a new workbook and name it DataAccessSample02.xlsm.

2. Create a new macro and name it GetTextData.

3. On the Data ribbon, choose From Text.

4. Navigate to the myfilepath\maillist.csv file, and then choose the Import command. The Text Import wizard will open, as shown in Figure 2-3.

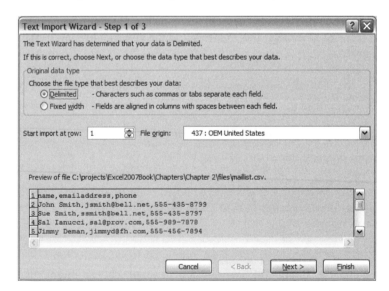

Figure 2-3. *The Text Import wizard*

The file is comma-delimited (the default selection in the Original Data Type section), so just click Next.

On Step 2 of the Text Import wizard, the default delimiter is Tab. The "Data preview" section should show us our columns separated by vertical lines. Since our file is not tab-delimited, the preview shows our raw data file (see Figure 2-4).

Figure 2-4. *View of maillist.csv with Tab selected as delimiter*

Select Comma from the Delimiters options. The data preview now shows your data in the correct columnar display (see Figure 2-5).

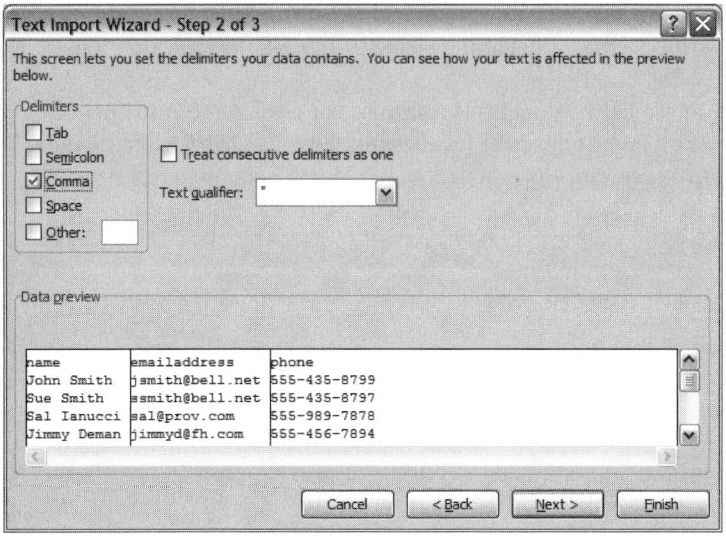

Figure 2-5. *View of maillist.csv with Comma selected as delimiter*

Click Next to continue to Step 3 of the wizard (see Figure 2-6), where we can choose the data type for each column of data.

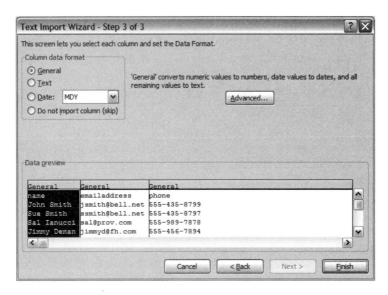

Figure 2-6. *Step 3 lets you choose data types for each column.*

The onscreen prompt tells us that the General format will convert numeric values to numbers, date values to dates, and so on. We will choose each column in turn, and choose the Text data type for our data. The Phone Number column contains numbers, but we want Excel to treat them as text. The column heading in the "Data preview" window shows us the data type selected for each column.

Click Finish after applying the Text data type to all columns (see Figure 2-7).

Click OK to let Excel place the data beginning in cell A1 (see Figure 2-8).

Click cell A1, and then stop the Macro Recorder. Figure 2-9 shows the data after it has been imported from the CSV file.

On the Developer ribbon, click the Visual Basic command or press Alt+F11 to open the Visual Basic window. Let's take a look at the code Excel generated for us. We'll examine the differences between importing Access data and text data in the Macro Recorder.

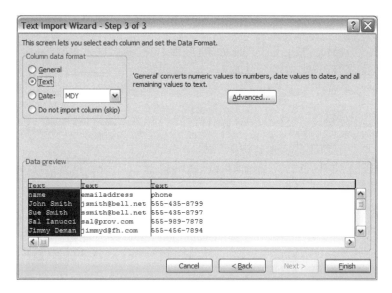

Figure 2-7. *"Data preview" window after applying the Text data type to all columns*

Figure 2-8. *Entering a location for the data*

	A	B	C	
1	name	emailaddress	phone	
2	John Smith	jsmith@bell.net	555-435-8799	
3	Sue Smith	ssmith@bell.net	555-435-8797	
4	Sal Ianucci	sal@prov.com	555-989-7878	
5	Jimmy Deman	jimmyd@fh.com	555-456-7894	
6				

Figure 2-9. *Data imported from maillist.csv*

Macro Recorder–Generated Text Import Code

After we stop the Macro Recorder, we are left with code that looks like Listing 2-2.

Listing 2-2. *Macro-Generated Text Data Import Code*

```
Sub GetTextData()
'
' GetTextData Macro
'
```

```
'
    With ActiveSheet.QueryTables.Add(Connection:= _
        "TEXT;C:\projects\Excel2007Book\Chapters\Chapter 2\files\maillist.csv", ➡
        Destination:=Range("$A$1"))
        .Name = "maillist"
        .FieldNames = True
        .RowNumbers = False
        .FillAdjacentFormulas = False
        .PreserveFormatting = True
        .RefreshOnFileOpen = False
        .RefreshStyle = xlInsertDeleteCells
        .SavePassword = False
        .SaveData = True
        .AdjustColumnWidth = True
        .RefreshPeriod = 0
        .TextFilePromptOnRefresh = False
        .TextFilePlatform = 437
        .TextFileStartRow = 1
        .TextFileParseType = xlDelimited
        .TextFileTextQualifier = xlTextQualifierDoubleQuote
        .TextFileConsecutiveDelimiter = False
        .TextFileTabDelimiter = False
        .TextFileSemicolonDelimiter = False
        .TextFileCommaDelimiter = True
        .TextFileSpaceDelimiter = False
        .TextFileColumnDataTypes = Array(2, 2, 2)
        .TextFileTrailingMinusNumbers = True
        .Refresh BackgroundQuery:=False
    End With
    Application.Goto Reference:="maillist"
    Range("A1").Select
End Sub
```

One of the first differences to notice about this code when compared to the Access data import is how simple the connection string is. There is no complex Source string, and there are no Command object properties (CommandType and CommandText) to set. We simply tell Excel we're connecting to a text file, and then provide the path to the file and add it to the QueryTables collection via the Add method.

Then there are some common properties, such as the FillAdjacentFormulas and SavePassword properties. After the RefreshPeriod property, we begin to see a lot of text file–specific commands. We can set properties that define the type of text file we're working with by setting the TextFileParse type to xlFixedWidth if our data is arranged in columns of fixed widths, or xlDelimited if we have a character-delimited file. If we set this to xlDelimited, we can then set one or more of the following properties to True:

- TextFileTabDelimiter

- TextFileSemicolonDelimiter

- TextFileCommaDelimiter

- TextFileSpaceDelimiter

TextFileColumnDataTypes Property

The Macro Recorder generated this line of code:

```
.TextFileColumnDataTypes = Array(2, 2, 2)
```

Setting this property to 2 for all columns tells Excel to format the columns as text. These values correspond to the xlTextFormat constant in Table 2-2. If you enter more values into this array than there are columns in your data, the additional values are ignored. To see the numeric equivalent for Excel constants like these, type the name into the Immediate window (go to View ➤ Immediate Window or press Ctrl+G) in the VBE, preceded by the ? output character. You can use the xlColumnDataType constants listed in Table 2-2 to specify the column data types used or the actions taken during a data import.

Table 2-2. *TextFileColumnDataTypes Enums*

Constant	Description	Value
xlGeneralFormat	General	1
xlTextFormat	Text	2
xlSkipColumn	Skip column	9
xlDMYFormat	Day-month-year date format	4
xlDYMFormat	Day-year-month date format	7
xlEMDFormat	EMD date	10
xlMDYFormat	Month-day-year date format	3
xlMYDFormat	Month-year-day date format	6
xlYDMFormat	Year-day-month date format	8
xlYMDFormat	Year-month-day date format	5

A quick way to find the value of any of Excel 2007's built-in constants or enumerations is to type it into the Immediate window, preceded by a ? character. This will display the value as shown in Figure 2-10.

Figure 2-10. *Viewing constant values in the Immediate window*

We've seen that Excel's Macro Recorder is a fast and easy way to explore some of the properties and methods available when bringing data into Excel. Let's write a little of our own code and explore some flexible methods of data transfer. These methods will work in Excel or any other VB- or VBA-enabled application, making them relatively portable and reusable.

Using DAO in Excel 2007

Data Access Objects (or DAO, as it's commonly known) has been around Microsoft Office for many versions, going back to 1992, when Jet was introduced. DAO was the first data access tool available to VB and VBA programmers, and can still be used to manipulate data in older versions of Office and ODBC-compliant database systems.

DAO is very easy to use, and you've probably encountered DAO code if you've done any work in versions of Access preceding the 2000 release, when it was the default data access tool. In Office 2000, Microsoft made ADO the default data access method, which caused programmers who used DAO heavily to learn to use explicit references to their data access model.

You can use DAO to access SQL data via ODBC, and Microsoft Access data via Jet. Jet is no longer a part of the Microsoft Data Access Components (MDAC) with the 2007 release. Office 2007 introduces a new version of the Jet engine called ACE (Access Engine).

The DAO object model is shown in Figure 2-11, and its common objects are described in Table 2-3, which follows.

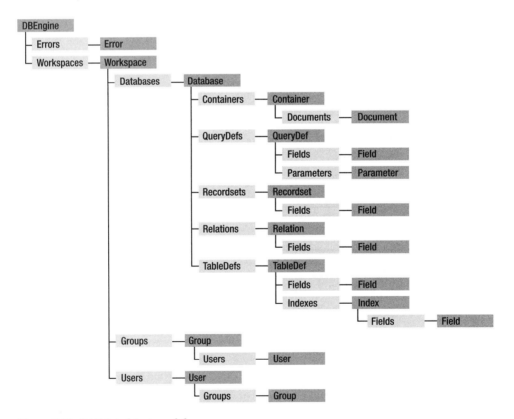

Figure 2-11. *DAO Jet object model*

Table 2-3. *Common DAO Objects*

Object	Description
DBEngine	The top-level object in the DAO object hierarchy
Workspace	An active DAO session
Connection	The network connection to an ODBC database
Database	An open database
Error	Data access error information
Field	A field in a database object
TableDef	Saved table information in a database
QueryDef	Saved query information in a database
Recordset	A set of records defined by a table or query
Index	Table index
User	A user account in the current workgroup
Parameter	Query parameter
Property	Property of an object

Let's take a look at how easy DAO is to use by bringing data from the Northwind 2007 database into an Excel worksheet using DAO.

DAO Example 1: Importing Access Data Using Jet

Open a new workbook and name it DataAccessSample03.xlsm. Be sure to use the .xlsm extension so your workbook is macro-enabled.

Open the VBE by choosing the Visual Basic command from the Developer ribbon or by pressing Alt+F11.

Before we can retrieve data using DAO, we must add a reference to the DAO library in our project.

1. Select Tools ➤ References in the VBE.

2. Find the Microsoft DAO 3.6 Object library in the list, and select it, as shown in Figure 2-12.

3. Click OK.

4. Insert a new standard module by selecting Insert ➤ Module.

5. Create a new subroutine called GetDAOAccessJet().

6. Add the following variable declarations:

```
Dim db As DAO.Database
Dim rs As DAO.Recordset
Dim xlSheet As Worksheet
Dim i As Integer
Dim arr_sPath(1) As String
```

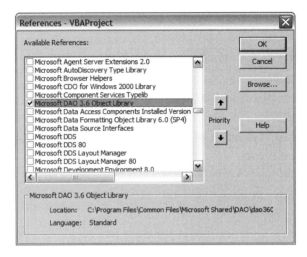

Figure 2-12. *Adding a reference to the DAO library*

We're declaring the db and rs variables to hold our database and recordset objects. The
xlSheet variable will provide a simpler way to refer to the worksheet we'll be populating with
data. We're going to store the path to two versions of the Northwind database—the new version with the .accdb extension and the Access 2000 version with the .mdb extension—to
compare how DAO works with these.

Add the following code to set up the file paths and Excel worksheet (be sure to change
the paths to the database files to reflect your location):

```
arr_sPath(0) = "C:\projects\Excel2007Book\Files\northwind 2007.accdb"
arr_sPath(1) = "C:\projects\Excel2007Book\Files\northwind.mdb"

Set xlSheet = Sheets("Sheet1")
xlSheet.Activate
Range("A1").Activate
Selection.CurrentRegion.Select
Selection.ClearContents
Range("A1").Select
```

We're assigning the Sheet1 object from our workbook to the variable xlSheet to provide
easier access to that sheet. This eliminates the need to type Sheets("Sheet1") whenever we
need to reference the worksheet we're manipulating.

Next we'll instantiate our database and recordset objects:

```
Set db = Workspaces(0).OpenDatabase(arr_sPath(0), ReadOnly:=True)
Set rs = db.OpenRecordset("Employees")
```

This code creates the default Jet workspace and fills a recordset with the information in
the Employees table in the Northwind 2007 database.

Now we'll fill the first row in the worksheet with the field names from the recordset and
add bold formatting to the column headings:

```
For i = 0 To rs.Fields.Count - 1
    xlSheet.Cells(1, i + 1).Value = rs.Fields(i).Name
Next i

xlSheet.Range(xlSheet.Cells(1, 1), xlSheet.Cells(1, rs.Fields.Count)) ➡
    .Font.Bold = True
```

Rather than create a loop to walk through the recordset and populate the sheet row by row and column by column, we'll use Excel's CopyFromRecordset method to fill the sheet with data:

```
xlSheet.Range("A2").CopyFromRecordset rs
```

The last thing we'll do before inserting our cleanup code is adjust the column widths to show the full text values (using the AutoFit method):

```
xlSheet.Select
Range("A1").Select
Selection.CurrentRegion.Select
Selection.Columns.AutoFit
Range("A1").Select
```

The first call to Range("A1").Select puts the cursor within the region we want to work with (in case there's more than one area with data on your worksheet). The next line, Selection.CurrentRegion.Select, selects any contiguous area of cells based on the current cursor location. Next comes our AutoFit command, followed by the selection of a single cell (to remove the selection from the entire range).

The entire function should now look like Listing 2-3.

Listing 2-3. *GetDAOAccessJet Method*

```
Sub GetDAOAccessJet()
Dim db As DAO.Database
Dim rs As DAO.Recordset
Dim xlSheet As Worksheet
Dim i As Integer
Dim arr_sPath(1) As String

    'store path to Access 2007 and 2000 versions of Northwind db
    arr_sPath(0) = "C:\projects\Excel2007Book\Files\northwind 2007.accdb"
    arr_sPath(1) = "C:\projects\Excel2007Book\Files\northwind.mdb"

    Set xlSheet = Sheets("Sheet1")
    xlSheet.Activate
    Range("A1").Activate
    Selection.CurrentRegion.Select
    Selection.ClearContents
    Range("A1").Select
```

```
    Set db = Workspaces(0).OpenDatabase(arr_sPath(0), ReadOnly:=True)
    Set rs = db.OpenRecordset("Employees")

  For i = 0 To rs.Fields.Count - 1
      xlSheet.Cells(1, i + 1).Value = rs.Fields(i).Name
  Next i

  xlSheet.Range(xlSheet.Cells(1, 1), xlSheet.Cells(1, rs.Fields.Count)) ➡
        .Font.Bold = True

  xlSheet.Range("A2").CopyFromRecordset rs

  xlSheet.Select
  Range("A1").Select
  Selection.CurrentRegion.Select
  Selection.Columns.AutoFit
  Range("A1").Select

    rs.Close
    db.Close

    Set xlSheet = Nothing
    Set rs = Nothing
    Set db = Nothing
End Sub
```

Let's run our code and see the result on Sheet1.

1. On the Developer ribbon, choose the Macros command.

2. Select the GetDAOAccessJet macro from the list, and click the Run button. DAO generates an error, as shown in Figure 2-13.

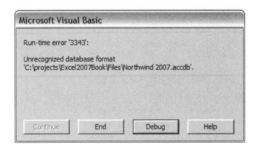

Figure 2-13. *Unrecognized database format error*

3. Click the Debug button, and notice that our attempt to instantiate our DAO.Database object is failing (see Figure 2-14).

```
Set db = Workspaces(0).OpenDatabase(arr_sPath(0), ReadOnly:=True)
Set rs = db.OpenRecordset("Employees")
```

Figure 2-14. *OpenDatabase method fires error*

DAO Jet, it seems, does not support the new Access database format. Does this mean we cannot use DAO with *.accdb files? No, it does not. In a short while, we'll take a look at how we can access data from Access 2007 using DAO with ODBC. For now, let's continue with Jet.

To make this code work, all we have to do is change the array index in our arr_sPath variable from 0 to 1.

```
Set db = Workspaces(0).OpenDatabase(arr_sPath(1), ReadOnly:=True)
```

Rerun the code, and your worksheet should look like Figure 2-15.

	A	B	C	D	E	F	G	H	I	J
1	EmployeeID	LastName	FirstName	Title	TitleOfCourtesy	BirthDate	HireDate	Address	City	Region
2	1	Davolio	Nancy	Sales Representative	Ms.	12/8/1968	5/1/1992	507 - 20th Ave. E.⊡ Apt. 2A	Seattle	WA
3	2	Fuller	Andrew	Vice President, Sales	Dr.	2/19/1952	8/14/1992	908 W. Capital Way	Tacoma	WA
4	3	Leverling	Janet	Sales Representative	Ms.	8/30/1963	4/1/1992	722 Moss Bay Blvd.	Kirkland	WA
5	4	Peacock	Margaret	Sales Representative	Mrs.	9/19/1958	5/3/1993	4110 Old Redmond Rd.	Redmond	WA
6	5	Buchanan	Steven	Sales Manager	Mr.	3/4/1955	10/17/1993	14 Garrett Hill	London	
7	6	Suyama	Michael	Sales Representative	Mr.	7/2/1963	10/17/1993	Coventry House⊡ Miner Rd.	London	
8	7	King	Robert	Sales Representative	Mr.	5/29/1960	1/2/1994	Edgeham Hollow⊡ Winchester Way	London	
9	8	Callahan	Laura	Inside Sales Coordinator	Ms.	1/9/1958	3/5/1994	4726 - 11th Ave. N.E.	Seattle	WA
10	9	Dodsworth	Anne	Sales Representative	Ms.	7/2/1969	11/15/1994	7 Houndstooth Rd.	London	

Figure 2-15. *The Employees table from the Access 2000 version of the Northwind database*

■**Note** According to the help file, the Range.CopyFromRecordset method will fail if the DAO (or ADO) recordset contains an OLE object. This seems to be true only sometimes. In the preceding example, we filled a DAO recordset object with the entire contents of the Employees table from the Access 2000 version of the Northwind database. This table includes a field named Photo that *does* contain an OLE object and is included in the data returned to us.

Using the CopyFromRecordset method is much more efficient and more performant than looping through a recordset to retrieve the entire contents.

■**Note** When using the `Range.CopyFromRecordset` method, copying begins at the current row of the recordset object. After copying is completed, the `EOF` property of the recordset object is `True`. If you need to reuse your recordset, you must call its `MoveFirst` method (if the type of recordset you've created is not using a forward-only cursor).

DAO Example 2: Importing Access Data Using ODBC

In the previous example, you saw that Jet 4 does not support the `*.accdb` format, and you learned that it is no longer a part of the MDAC. How can you use DAO to access data in the new Access database format? The answer is ODBC (Open Database Connectivity).

The DAO ODBC object model is shown in Figure 2-16.

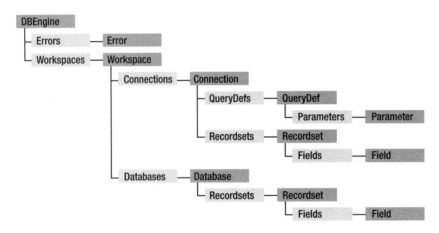

Figure 2-16. *DAO ODBC object model*

The method for importing data using DAO ODBC is somewhat different than using Jet. In Jet, we could use a database object to refer to our Access database. Using ODBC, we have to create `Workspace` and `Connection` objects that we'll use to connect to the database and retrieve a recordset of data.

In the VBE, on the same code module, add a subroutine called `GetDAOAccess2007ODBC()`. Add the following variable declarations:

```
Dim wrk As DAO.Workspace
Dim cnn As DAO.Connection
Dim rs As DAO.Recordset
Dim sConn As String
Dim xlSheet As Worksheet
Dim iFieldCount As Integer
Dim i As Integer
Dim arr_sPath(1) As String
```

This looks very similar to our last example, but let's look at the differences. We've added variables to hold our Workspace and Connection objects, as previously noted. We've also added the sConn variable to hold our connection string. This is where we'll tell our Connection object where to find the data we require. The last difference is that we've added a variable, iFieldCount, to hold the number of fields in our Recordset object.

Copy and paste the path string and worksheet setup code from the previous example:

```
'store path to Access 2007 and 2000 versions of Northwind db
arr_sPath(0) = "C:\projects\Excel2007Book\Files\northwind 2007.accdb"
arr_sPath(1) = "C:\projects\Excel2007Book\Files\northwind.mdb"

Set xlSheet = Sheets("Sheet1")
xlSheet.Activate
Range("A1").Activate
Selection.CurrentRegion.Select
Selection.ClearContents
Range("A1").Select
```

Set the connection string:

```
sConn = "ODBC;Driver={Microsoft Access Driver (*.mdb, *.accdb)};" ➥
           & "DBQ=" & arr_sPath(0)
```

Instantiate the Workspace and Connection objects:

```
Set wrk = CreateWorkspace("", "", "", dbUseODBC)
Set cnn = wrk.OpenConnection("", , , sConn)
```

We use the Workspace object's OpenConnection method to create the Connection object.

Next we'll use the Connection object's OpenRecordset method to fill our recordset with data from the Employees table:

```
Set rs = cnn.OpenRecordset("SELECT * FROM Customers", dbOpenDynamic)
```

Insert our column headings using the iFieldCount variable:

```
iFieldCount = rs.Fields.Count
For i = 1 To iFieldCount
    xlSheet.Cells(1, i).Value = rs.Fields(i - 1).Name
Next i

xlSheet.Range(xlSheet.Cells(1, 1), _
                xlSheet.Cells(1, rs.Fields.Count)).Font.Bold = True
```

Our first example used a zero-based counter to do this job:

```
For i = 0 To rs.Fields.Count - 1
   xlSheet.Cells(1, i + 1).Value = rs.Fields(i).Name
Next i
```

The only real difference in this code is that we've assigned the rs.Fields.Count property to a variable in the new version. This is a bit more efficient because it eliminates the need to query the Recordset object for its Fields.Count with each pass through the loop. It does, however, change the way we reference our index values. In the first example, our loop refers to Fields.Count - 1; in the second, it simply refers to Fields.Count; and so on.

The remainder of the code is the same as the first example, with the addition of cleanup code for our new Workspace and Connection objects. The entire new subroutine looks like Listing 2-4.

Listing 2-4. *Retrieving Access 2007 Code via ODBC*

```
Sub GetDAOAccess2007ODBC()
Dim wrk As DAO.Workspace
Dim cnn As DAO.Connection
Dim rs As DAO.Recordset
Dim sConn As String
Dim xlSheet As Worksheet
Dim iFieldCount As Integer
Dim i As Integer
Dim arr_sPath(1) As String

    'store path to Access 2007 and 2000 versions of Northwind db
    arr_sPath(0) = "C:\projects\Excel2007Book\Files\northwind 2007.accdb"
    arr_sPath(1) = "C:\projects\Excel2007Book\Files\northwind.mdb"

    Set xlSheet = Sheets("Sheet1")
    xlSheet.Activate
    Range("A1").Activate
    Selection.CurrentRegion.Select
    Selection.ClearContents
    Range("A1").Select

    sConn = "ODBC;Driver={Microsoft Access Driver (*.mdb, *.accdb)};" ➥
            & "DBQ=" & arr_sPath(0)

    Set wrk = CreateWorkspace("", "", "", dbUseODBC)
    Set cnn = wrk.OpenConnection("", , , sConn)

    Set rs = cnn.OpenRecordset("SELECT * FROM Customers", dbOpenDynamic)


    iFieldCount = rs.Fields.Count
    For i = 1 To iFieldCount
        xlSheet.Cells(1, i).Value = rs.Fields(i - 1).Name
    Next i
```

```
xlSheet.Range(xlSheet.Cells(1, 1), ➥
                xlSheet.Cells(1, rs.Fields.Count)).Font.Bold = True

xlSheet.Cells(2, 1).CopyFromRecordset rs

xlSheet.Select
Range("A1").Select
Selection.CurrentRegion.Select
Selection.Columns.AutoFit
Range("A1").Select

'close workspace
wrk.Close

'release objects
Set xlSheet = Nothing
Set rs = Nothing
Set wrk = Nothing
Set cnn = Nothing

End Sub
```

Let's run this code from Sheet1 and see what it does.

1. Choose the Macros command from the Developer ribbon.

2. Select the DAOAccess2007ODBC macro from the list, and click Run. This should generate an error, as shown in Figure 2-17.

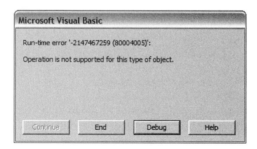

Figure 2-17. *DAO ODBC runtime error*

3. Click the Debug button, and let's see where the code is stopping (see Figure 2-18).

```
    xlSheet.Cells(2, 1).CopyFromRecordset rs
```

Figure 2-18. *CopyFromRecordset stops the code.*

Now we run into the error that I mentioned in the previous example. Excel's CopyFromRecordset method doesn't like the data type of a field or fields that we're returning in the recordset being passed to it. A look at the Northwind 2007 Customers table in Design view (Figure 2-19) will show us the data types in use here.

Field Name	Data Type
Job Title	Text
Business Phone	Text
Home Phone	Text
Mobile Phone	Text
Fax Number	Text
Address	Memo
City	Text
State/Province	Text
ZIP/Postal Code	Text
Country/Region	Text
Web Page	Hyperlink
Notes	Memo
Attachments	Attachment

Figure 2-19. *Northwind Customers table Design view*

Figure 2-19 shows us that most of these fields use the Text data type, but we see a few that do not. You'll recall me mentioning that the Excel help file noted that OLE fields would cause the CopyFromRecordset method to fail, yet there are no OLE fields present here. The Memo, Hyperlink, and Attachment data types will all cause the CopyFromRecordset method to fail. To check, you could change your SQL statement in the OpenRecordset call to any of these:

```
SELECT Address FROM Customers
```

or

```
SELECT [Web Page] FROM Customers
```

or

```
SELECT Attachments FROM Customers
```

A recordset that includes any of these filters will cause our subroutine to fail. So let's then modify our SQL statement to include only those fields that are not of these data types.

```
Set rs = cnn.OpenRecordset("SELECT ID, Company, [Last Name]," ➥
                    & " [First Name], [E-mail address], [Job title]," ➥
                    & " [Business Phone], [Mobile Phone], [Fax Number]," ➥
                    & " city, [state/province], [zip/postal code]," ➥
                    & " [country/region] " ➥
                    & "FROM Customers Order By Company", dbOpenDynamic)
```

Run the code, and your result should look like that in Figure 2-20.

	A	B	C	D	E	F	G
1	ID	Company	Last Name	First Name	E-mail address	Job title	Business Phone
2	1	Company A	Bedecs	Anna		Owner	(123)555-0100
3	27	Company AA	Toh	Karen		Purchasing Manager	(123)555-0100
4	2	Company B	Gratacos Solsona	Antonio		Owner	(123)555-0100
5	28	Company BB	Raghav	Amritansh		Purchasing Manager	(123)555-0100
6	3	Company C	Axen	Thomas		Purchasing Representative	(123)555-0100
7	29	Company CC	Lee	Soo Jung		Purchasing Manager	(123)555-0100
8	4	Company D	Lee	Christina		Purchasing Manager	(123)555-0100
9	5	Company E	O'Donnell	Martin		Owner	(123)555-0100
10	6	Company F	Pérez-Olaeta	Francisco		Purchasing Manager	(123)555-0100
11	7	Company G	Xie	Ming-Yang		Owner	(123)555-0100
12	8	Company H	Andersen	Elizabeth		Purchasing Representative	(123)555-0100
13	9	Company I	Mortensen	Sven		Purchasing Manager	(123)555-0100
14	10	Company J	Wacker	Roland		Purchasing Manager	(123)555-0100
15	11	Company K	Krschne	Peter		Purchasing Manager	(123)555-0100
16	12	Company L	Edwards	John		Purchasing Manager	(123)555-0100
17	13	Company M	Ludick	Andre		Purchasing Representative	(123)555-0100
18	14	Company N	Grilo	Carlos		Purchasing Representative	(123)555-0100
19	15	Company O	Kupkova	Helena		Purchasing Manager	(123)555-0100
20	16	Company P	Goldschmidt	Daniel		Purchasing Representative	(123)555-0100
21	17	Company Q	Bagel	Jean Philippe		Owner	(123)555-0100
22	18	Company R	Autier Miconi	Catherine		Purchasing Representative	(123)555-0100
23	19	Company S	Eggerer	Alexander		Accounting Assistant	(123)555-0100
24	20	Company T	Li	George		Purchasing Manager	(123)555-0100
25	21	Company U	Tham	Bernard		Accounting Manager	(123)555-0100

Figure 2-20. *DAO ODBC result from Northwind 2007 Customers table*

Can you access data in other versions of Access using DAO ODBC? Yes, you can. With a simple edit to the GetDAOAccess2007ODBC subprocedure, you could use an ODBC call.

Change the connection string to reference the Access 2000 version file path by changing the 0 to 1 in the arr_sPath array:

```
sConn = "ODBC;Driver={Microsoft Access Driver (*.mdb, *.accdb)};" ➥
            & "DBQ=" & arr_sPath(1)
```

Then use the original SQL statement in the call to OpenRecordset:

```
Set rs = cnn.OpenRecordset("SELECT * FROM Customers", dbOpenDynamic)
```

The Access 2000 version of the Northwind Customers table does not contain any of these issue-bearing data types, so we are able to query using Select * syntax.

DAO Example 3: Importing SQL Data Using ODBC

The final example of using DAO to bring data into your Excel project will focus on getting data from an SQL server (or other ODBC-compliant database). The process is identical to what we just did in our previous example, with the exception of a new connection string:

```
sConn = "ODBC;DATABASE=msdb;DSN=mySQL"
```

We're still using the ODBC reference in the string, but now we're passing in the database name and the DSN name. Here's the complete code. (You must reference a valid database and DSN for this to provide you with output.)

```
Sub GetDAOSQLODBC()
Dim wrk As DAO.Workspace
Dim cnn As DAO.Connection
Dim rs As DAO.Recordset
Dim sConn As String
Dim xlSheet As Worksheet
Dim iFieldCount As Integer
Dim i As Integer

    Set xlSheet = Sheets("Sheet1")
    xlSheet.Activate
    Range("A1").Activate
    Selection.CurrentRegion.Select
    Selection.ClearContents
    Range("A1").Select

    sConn = "ODBC;DATABASE=msdb;DSN=mySQL"

    Set wrk = CreateWorkspace("", "", "", dbUseODBC)
    Set cnn = wrk.OpenConnection("", , , sConn)
    Set rs = cnn.OpenRecordset("SELECT * FROM msdbms", dbOpenDynamic)

    iFieldCount = rs.Fields.Count
    For i = 1 To iFieldCount
        xlSheet.Cells(1, i).Value = rs.Fields(i - 1).Name
    Next i

    xlSheet.Cells(2, 1).CopyFromRecordset rs

    xlSheet.Select
    Range("A1").Select
    Selection.CurrentRegion.Select
    Selection.Columns.AutoFit
    Range("A1").Select


    'close workspace
    wrk.Close

    'release objects
    Set xlSheet = Nothing
    Set rs = Nothing
    Set wrk = Nothing
    Set cnn = Nothing
End Sub
```

Using ADO in Excel 2007

ActiveX Data Objects (ADO) was introduced by Microsoft in 1996 and has become the successor to DAO. Its database access technology is OLE DB (Object Linking and Embedding Database), which is the successor to ODBC.

The latest version of ADO is ADO 2.8. ADO lets us access, edit, and update data from many data sources by interfacing to these data sources via OLE DB providers. OLE DB providers speak to the database engine more directly than ODBC, and provide us with better performance.

In the examples in the previous section, we used DAO to interact with an Access 2007 database and an SQL database. You'll recall we could not interface with Access 2007 directly with Jet, but we could interact using ODBC. In both cases, DAO goes through Jet, then from Jet to ODBC, and then to the data engine. Then our data comes back. As you might imagine, this may not be the speediest route to your data. ADO, on the other hand, talks directly to your OLE DB provider, which speaks directly to the data engine, and vice versa. This is a much more direct route and provides better performance. ADO also gives us many settings to help fine-tune how we interact with our data. We can choose to run our cursor on the server (in a connected environment) or on the client (if the database supports it, in a disconnected environment).

I mentioned my use of explicit reference to DAO and ADO in my variable declarations earlier. This is due to the fact that Microsoft made ADO the default data mechanism with the release of Access 2000. Up until that time, `Dim rs As Recordset` meant a DAO recordset object to Access and nothing else. After the release of Access 2000, that same line of code referred to an ADO recordset. Having started out in life as an Access developer, I relied heavily on DAO in many of my applications. After upgrading to Access 2000 and beginning to use ADO (along with DAO), I learned to make my declarations complete to avoid confusing the compiler (not to mention debugging!).

In any application that uses both access protocols, explicitly creating your objects eliminates any confusion. Your application will always know the difference between an object declared as `DAO.Recordset` and one declared as `ADODB.Recordset`. If you do not explicitly declare your DAO or ADO objects, whichever object is higher in the references list will get priority. If the ADO 2.8 library is listed above the DAO 3.6 library, then any object declared as type `Recordset` will default to the ADO library.

ADO Example 1: Importing SQL Data

For our first ADO example, we're going to use the AdventureWorks sample database provided by Microsoft. You can install a copy of the AdventureWorks database by running the file `AdventureWorksDB.msi`.

You will be using SQL Server 2005 Management Studio Express to view the various database objects. To install Management Studio Express, run `SQLServer2005_SSMSEE.msi`.

1. Open a new workbook and name it `DataAccessSample04.xlsm`.

2. Before we begin using ADO in Excel 2007, we must add a reference to the ADO 2.8 library (see Figure 2-21).

a. In the VBE, choose Tools ➤ References.

b. Select the Microsoft ActiveX Data Objects 2.8 library.

c. Click OK.

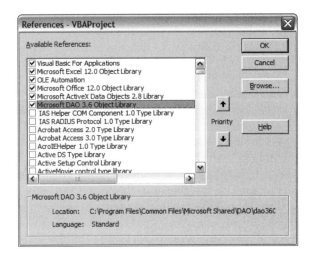

Figure 2-21. *Adding a reference to the ADO 2.8 library*

If you have SQL Server 2005 installed on your machine, you can use that instead of SQL Server 2005 Management Studio Express.

For our first example, we'll be using a parameterized stored procedure to return a list of AdventureWorks employees for a selected manager. We'll enter the manager's employee ID and retrieve a list of that manager's direct and indirect reports.

The AdventureWorks database contains a stored procedure called uspGetManagerEmployees. If we expand that item in the Stored Procedures tree, we see that it takes one parameter, ManagerID, which is of the Integer data type (as shown in Figure 2-22).

Figure 2-22. *Parameterized stored procedure in AdventureWorks database, as viewed in SQL Server 2005 Management Studio Express*

1. In the VBE, add a standard module.

2. Create a new subroutine called `GetManagerEmployeeListSQL`.

3. Add the following variable declarations:

```
Dim cnn As ADODB.Connection
Dim cmd As ADODB.Command
Dim param As ADODB.Parameter
Dim xlSheet As Worksheet
Dim rs As ADODB.Recordset
Dim sConnString As String
Dim i As Integer
```

We're using a few ADO objects to retrieve our data: an ADO `Connection` object to connect to the data, an ADO `Command` object to run our stored procedure, an ADO `Parameter` object to pass the `ManagerID` data to the stored procedure, and an ADO `Recordset` object to hold the results of our stored procedure.

In this example we are going to use cell A1 to hold the `ManagerID` information for our stored procedure's parameter. Let's add a modified version of the code we've been using to set up and clear our Excel worksheet:

```
Set xlSheet = Sheets("Sheet1")
xlSheet.Activate
Range("A3").Activate
Selection.CurrentRegion.Select
Selection.ClearContents
Range("A1").Select
```

Although this looks very similar to the code used in the DAO examples, the third line, `Range("A3").Activate`, has changed. The DAO examples activated cell A1 to clear the entire current region on the worksheet. Since we're using cell A1 as input to our stored procedure in this example, we want to start clearing the contiguous range beginning at cell A3 instead.

Let's open our connection and assign it to a `Command` object:

```
Set cnn = New ADODB.Connection
sConnString = "Provider=SQLNCLI;Server=MyServerName\SQLEXPRESS;" ➥
              & "Database=AdventureWorks;Trusted_Connection=yes;"
cnn.Open sConnString

Set cmd = New ADODB.Command
cmd.ActiveConnection = cnn
```

■**Note** To connect to a named instance of SQL Server, the convention is to use a server name of the format `<servername>\<instancename>`. Note the way the `Server` property is set in our previous example: `Server=MyServerName\SQLEXPRESS`.

Now let's create our `Parameter` object, fill some of its properties, and add it to our `Command` object.

```
Set param = New ADODB.Parameter
With param
    .Name = "ManagerID"
    .Type = adInteger
    .Value = ActiveSheet.Range("A1").Value
End With

With cmd
    .CommandType = adCmdStoredProc
    .CommandText = "uspGetManagerEmployees"
    .Parameters.Append param
End With
```

We are setting the `Parameter` object's `Name` property to `ManagerID`, as called for by the stored procedure, and telling it to use the `Integer` data type. Finally, we set its `Value` property to whatever value is contained in the active sheet's cell A1.

Once that's done, we set up our `Command` object by telling it what kind of command we need (stored procedure), and the name of the stored procedure. Then we append our `Parameter` object to the `Command` object's `Parameters` collection.

Table 2-4 gives a list of ADO data type enums, along with their actual values and the corresponding Access and SQL data types they refer to.

Table 2-4. *ADO Data Types*

Data Type	Value	Access	SQL Server
adBigInt	20		BigInt (SQL Server 2000 +)
adBinary	128		Binary TimeStamp
adBoolean	11	YesNo	Bit
adChar	129		Char
adCurrency	6	Currency	Money SmallMoney
adDate	7	Date	DateTime
adDBTimeStamp	135	DateTime (Access 97 [ODBC])	DateTime SmallDateTime
adDecimal	14		
adDouble	5	Double	Float
adGUID	72	ReplicationID (Access 97 [OLEDB]), (Access 2000 [OLEDB])	UniqueIdentifier (SQL Server 7.0 +)
adIDispatch	9		

Continued

Data Type	Value	Access	SQL Server
adInteger	3	AutoNumber Integer Long	Identity (SQL Server 6.5) Int
adLongVarBinary	205	OLEObject	Image
adLongVarChar	201	Memo (Access 97) Hyperlink (Access 97)	Text
adLongVarWChar	203	Memo (Access 2000 [OLEDB]) Hyperlink (Access 2000 [OLEDB])	NText (SQL Server 7.0 +)
adNumeric	131	Decimal (Access 2000 [OLEDB])	Decimal Numeric
adSingle	4	Single	Real
adSmallInt	2	Integer	SmallInt
adUnsignedTinyInt	17	Byte	TinyInt
adVarBinary	204	ReplicationID (Access 97)	VarBinary
adVarChar	200	Text (Access 97)	VarChar
adVariant	12		Sql_Variant (SQL Server 2000 +)
adVarWChar	202	Text (Access 2000 [OLEDB])	NVarChar (SQL Server 7.0 +)
adWChar	130		NChar (SQL Server 7.0 +)

The remainder of our code is basically identical to our previous examples. Listing 2-5 shows what the finished subroutine looks like.

Listing 2-5. *Calling Parameterized SQL in VBA*

```
Sub GetManagerEmployeeListSQL()
Dim cnn As ADODB.Connection
Dim cmd As ADODB.Command
Dim param As ADODB.Parameter
Dim xlSheet As Worksheet
Dim rs As ADODB.Recordset
Dim sConnString As String
Dim i As Integer

    Set xlSheet = Sheets("Sheet1")
    xlSheet.Activate
    Range("A3").Activate
    Selection.CurrentRegion.Select
    Selection.ClearContents
    Range("A1").Select
```

```
Set cnn = New ADODB.Connection
sConnString = "Provider=SQLNCLI;Server=MyServerName\SQLEXPRESS;" ➦
              & "Database=AdventureWorks;Trusted_Connection=yes;"
cnn.Open sConnString

Set cmd = New ADODB.Command
cmd.ActiveConnection = cnn

Set param = New ADODB.Parameter
With param
    .Name = "ManagerID"
    .Type = adInteger
    .Value = ActiveSheet.Range("A1").Value
End With

With cmd
    .CommandType = adCmdStoredProc
    .CommandText = "uspGetManagerEmployees"
    .Parameters.Append param
End With

Set rs = New ADODB.Recordset
Set rs = cmd.Execute

For i = 1 To rs.Fields.Count
    ActiveSheet.Cells(3, i).Value = rs.Fields(i - 1).Name
Next i

xlSheet.Range(xlSheet.Cells(3, 1), _
    xlSheet.Cells(3, rs.Fields.Count)).Font.Bold = True

ActiveSheet.Range("A4").CopyFromRecordset rs

xlSheet.Select
Range("A3").Select
Selection.CurrentRegion.Select
Selection.Columns.AutoFit
Range("A1").Select

rs.Close
cnn.Close
```

```
Set cmd = Nothing
Set param = Nothing
Set rs = Nothing
Set cnn = Nothing
Set xlSheet = Nothing

End Sub
```

Note that our cleanup code also refers to cell A3 when setting up the worksheet with the AutoFit method.

We can test this code out by entering a ManagerID in cell A1 on Sheet1 and running the GetManagerEmployeeListSQL method from the macro list.

1. Enter **16** in cell A1.

2. Choose GetManagerEmployeeListSQL from the macro list and run the code. The results are shown in Figure 2-23.

	A	B	C	D	E	F	G
1	16						
2							
3	RecursionLevel	ManagerID	ManagerFirstName	ManagerLastName	EmployeeID	FirstName	LastName
4	0	16 Jo		Brown	1	Guy	Gilbert
5	0	16 Jo		Brown	57	Annik	Stahl
6	0	16 Jo		Brown	80	Rebecca	Laszlo
7	0	16 Jo		Brown	89	Margie	Shoop
8	0	16 Jo		Brown	129	Mark	McArthur
9	0	16 Jo		Brown	137	Britta	Simon
10	0	16 Jo		Brown	157	Brandon	Heidepriem
11	0	16 Jo		Brown	162	Jose	Lugo
12	0	16 Jo		Brown	175	Suchitra	Mohan
13	0	16 Jo		Brown	213	Chris	Okelberry
14	0	16 Jo		Brown	235	Kim	Abercrombie
15	0	16 Jo		Brown	247	Ed	Dudenhoefer

Figure 2-23. *Result of GetManagerEmployeeListSQL code*

3. Enter a manager ID of **21** in cell A1 and run the code again. You'll see a longer list of employees since this is a higher-level manager.

4. Enter a manager ID of **16** again to see the setup code at work, clearing the used cells for the next round of data import.

EXCEL 97 AND ADO RECORDSETS

For efficiency and performance, CopyFromRecordset is the preferred method of filling cells with data from an ADO recordset. Because Excel 97 supports only DAO recordsets with CopyFromRecordset, if you attempt to pass an ADO recordset to CopyFromRecordset with Excel 97, you receive the following error:

```
Run-time error 430:
Class does not support Automation or does not support expected interface.
```

In the code sample, you can avoid this error by checking Excel's version using the ExcelVersionShort property from the cExcelUtils class in the codeLib.xlsm workbook included on the CD so that you do not use CopyFromRecordset for the 97 version.

```
Property Get ExcelVersionShort() As String
Dim xlApp As Object
Dim sExcelVersionShort As String

    Set xlApp = CreateObject("Excel.Application")
    sExcelVersionShort = Mid(xlApp.Version, 1, InStr(1, xlApp.Version, ".") - 1)

    Set xlApp = Nothing
    ExcelVersionShort = sExcelVersionShort
End Property

Property Get ExcelVersion() As String
Dim xlApp As Object
Dim sExcelVersion As String

    Set xlApp = CreateObject("Excel.Application")
    sExcelVersion = xlApp.Version

    Set xlApp = Nothing
    ExcelVersion = sExcelVersion
End Property
```

If Excel 97 is detected, use the GetRows method of the ADO recordset to copy the recordset into an array. If you assign the array returned by GetRows to a range of cells in the worksheet, the data goes across the columns instead of down the rows. For example, if the recordset has two fields and ten rows, the array appears as two rows and ten columns. Therefore, you need to transpose the array using your TransposeDim() function before assigning the array to the range of cells.

ADO Example 2: Importing SQL Data Based on a Selection

In this exercise, we'll see how we can use Excel to generate a list, and how by making a selection from that list we can view detailed information about the selected item.

Adventure Works management wants to see a quick view of their reporting tree by manager. We're going to create a list of managers and then add code that will show the selected manager's reporting structure.

On Module1, add a new subroutine and name it `GetManagerList`. Add the following variable declarations:

```
Dim cnn As ADODB.Connection
Dim rs As ADODB.Recordset
Dim xlSheet As Worksheet
Dim sConnString As String
Dim sSQL As String
```

Our setup code is very similar to our last example, except that we are going to put our list of managers on Sheet2. Our opening line of setup code will now look like this:

```
Set xlSheet = Sheets("Sheet2")
```

The remainder of the code is the same, with the obvious exception of the SQL statement. The SQL statement to generate our manager list looks like this:

```
sSQL = "SELECT HumanResources.Employee.EmployeeID, Person.Contact.FirstName," ➡
    & " Person.Contact.LastName FROM Person.Contact" ➡
    & " INNER JOIN HumanResources.Employee" ➡
    & " ON Person.Contact.ContactID = HumanResources.Employee.ContactID" ➡
    & " WHERE (((HumanResources.Employee.EmployeeID) In" ➡
    & " (SELECT  HumanResources.Employee.ManagerID" ➡
    & " FROM HumanResources.Employee)));"
```

Let's dissect this SQL statement a bit. Our manager list will show the employee ID as well as the first and last name for each manager. As you can see, the data is stored in two tables. The HumanResources.Employee table stores the EmployeeID field and the Person.Contact table stores the name fields.

The two tables have a common field, `ContactID`, that is used to join the tables in this query. Notice the `WHERE` clause, which contains a `SELECT` statement within it. This is known as nested SQL or an SQL subquery. Essentially, it says, "Only show us those employees whose employee ID can be found in the result of the subquery that contains only manager IDs." Subqueries such as this are a nice way to avoid creating temporary tables or individual queries to narrow down our search.

Here's the complete `GetManagerList` code:

```
Sub GetManagerList()
Dim cnn As ADODB.Connection
Dim rs As ADODB.Recordset
Dim xlSheet As Worksheet
Dim sConnString As String
Dim sSQL As String
```

```
    Set xlSheet = Sheets("Sheet2")
    xlSheet.Activate
    Range("A1").Activate
    Selection.CurrentRegion.Select
    Selection.ClearContents
    Range("A1").Select

    Set cnn = New ADODB.Connection
    sConnString = "Provider=SQLNCLI;Server=MyServerName\SQLEXPRESS;" ➡
                    & "Database=AdventureWorks;Trusted_Connection=yes;"

    cnn.Open sConnString

    sSQL = "SELECT HumanResources.Employee.EmployeeID, Person.Contact.FirstName," ➡
            & " Person.Contact.LastName FROM Person.Contact" ➡
            & " INNER JOIN HumanResources.Employee" ➡
            & " ON Person.Contact.ContactID = HumanResources.Employee.ContactID" ➡
            & " WHERE (((HumanResources.Employee.EmployeeID) In" ➡
            & " (SELECT  HumanResources.Employee.ManagerID" ➡
            & " FROM HumanResources.Employee)));"

    Set rs = New ADODB.Recordset

    rs.Open sSQL, cnn, adOpenDynamic

    Sheets("Sheet2").Activate
    Range("A1").CopyFromRecordset rs

    xlSheet.Select
    Range("A1").Select
    Selection.CurrentRegion.Select
    Selection.Columns.AutoFit
    Range("A1").Select

    rs.Close
    cnn.Close

    Set rs = Nothing
    Set cnn = Nothing
    Set xlSheet = Nothing
End Sub
```

Run the code, and your result on Sheet2 should look like Figure 2-24.

	A	B	C
1	3	Roberto	Tamburello
2	6	David	Bradley
3	7	JoLynn	Dobney
4	12	Terri	Duffy
5	14	Taylor	Maxwell
6	16	Jo	Brown
7	18	John	Campbell
8	21	Peter	Krebs
9	25	Zheng	Mu
10	30	Paula	Barreto de Mattos
11	38	Jinghao	Liu
12	41	Peng	Wu
13	42	Jean	Trenary
14	44	A. Scott	Wright
15	49	Christian	Kleinerman
16	51	Reuben	D'sa
17	64	Cristian	Petculescu
18	71	Wendy	Kahn
19	74	Kok-Ho	Loh
20	85	Pilar	Ackerman
21	87	David	Hamilton
22	90	Zainal	Arifin
23	108	Eric	Gubbels
24	109	Ken	Sánchez
25	123	Jeff	Hay

Figure 2-24. *The manager list displayed*

Now that we have our list of managers, let's write the code to show the selected manager's staff.

Add a new subroutine to Module1 and name it GetSelectedManagerEmployeeListSQL.

Since this code is very similar to GetManagerEmployeeListSQL, take a look at Listing 2-6, which shows the entire code set, and we'll review the differences.

Listing 2-6. *GetSelectedManagerEmployeeListSQL Subroutine*

```
Sub GetSelectedManagerEmployeeListSQL()
Dim cnn As ADODB.Connection
Dim cmd As ADODB.Command
Dim param As ADODB.Parameter
Dim rs As ADODB.Recordset
Dim xlSheet As Worksheet
Dim sConnString As String
Dim iMgrID As Integer
Dim sMgrName As String
Dim i As Integer
```

```
Set xlSheet = Sheets("Sheet3")
xlSheet.Activate
Range("A3").Activate
Selection.CurrentRegion.Select
Selection.ClearContents
Range("A1").Select
Sheets("Sheet2").Activate 'make sure we're on the right sheet

Set cnn = New ADODB.Connection
sConnString = "Provider=SQLNCLI;Server=MyServerName\SQLEXPRESS;" ➥
              & "Database=AdventureWorks;Trusted_Connection=yes;"

cnn.Open sConnString

Set cmd = New ADODB.Command
cmd.ActiveConnection = cnn

iMgrID = GetMgrID
sMgrName = GetMgrName

Set param = New ADODB.Parameter
With param
    .Name = "ManagerID"
    .Type = adInteger
    .Value = iMgrID
End With

With cmd
    .CommandType = adCmdStoredProc
    .CommandText = "uspGetManagerEmployees"
    .Parameters.Append param
End With

Set rs = New ADODB.Recordset
Set rs = cmd.Execute

xlSheet.Activate 'activate the display sheet
Range("A1").Value = "Employee List for: " & sMgrName
Range("A1").Font.Bold = True

For i = 1 To rs.Fields.Count
    ActiveSheet.Cells(3, i).Value = rs.Fields(i - 1).Name
Next i

xlSheet.Range(xlSheet.Cells(3, 1), _
    xlSheet.Cells(3, rs.Fields.Count)).Font.Bold = True
```

```
    ActiveSheet.Range("A4").CopyFromRecordset rs

    xlSheet.Select
    Range("A3").Select
    Selection.CurrentRegion.Select
    Selection.Columns.AutoFit
    Range("A1").Select

    rs.Close
    cnn.Close

    Set cmd = Nothing
    Set param = Nothing
    Set rs = Nothing
    Set cnn = Nothing
    Set xlSheet = Nothing
End Sub
```

When a manager is selected and this code is run, it will generate the employee list on Sheet3. The manager's name will appear at the top of the page in cell A1, and the employee list will populate below it. We've added a couple of variables to our declarations:

```
Dim iMgrID As Integer
Dim sMgrName As String
```

These will hold the ID for our search and the name for our display.
We're setting our xlSheet variable to refer to Sheet3:

```
Set xlSheet = Sheets("Sheet3")
```

And we're pointing back to Sheet2 to get our selected manager information:

```
Sheets("Sheet2").Activate
```

We've added calls to two helper functions, GetMgrID and GetMgrName. These functions refer to the active sheet, so this line of code is important. We could optionally have made explicit references to Sheet2 in our functions or passed in the worksheet as an argument to the functions.

Add these functions to Module1.

```
Function GetMgrID() As Integer
Dim iReturn As Integer
Dim rngMgrID As Range

    Set rngMgrID = Cells(ActiveCell.Row, 1)
    iReturn = rngMgrID.Value
    Set rngMgrID = Nothing

    GetMgrID = iReturn
End Function
```

```
Function GetMgrName() As String
Dim sReturn As String
Dim iRow As Integer

    iRow = ActiveCell.Row
    sReturn = Cells(iRow, 2).Value & " " & Cells(iRow, 3).Value

    GetMgrName = sReturn
End Function
```

These functions illustrate two methods for referring to cells on Sheet2. GetMgrID uses a variable of type Range to refer to the cell in the current row and column 1. GetMgrName uses direct references to the cells by using the Cells object.

Let's test the code. On Sheet2, put your cursor in any column on a row containing manager information, as in Figure 2-25.

5	14	Taylor	Maxwell
6	16	Jo	Brown
7	18	John	Campbell
8	21	Peter	Krebs

Figure 2-25. *Selecting a manager*

In the Macro window, run the GetSelectedManagerEmployeeListSQL subroutine, the results of which are shown in Figure 2-26.

	A	B	C	D	E	F	G
1	Employee List for: John Campbell						
2							
3	RecursionLevel	ManagerID	ManagerFirstName	ManagerLastName	EmployeeID	FirstName	LastName
4	0	18	John	Campbell	53	David	Ortiz
5	0	18	John	Campbell	174	Steve	Masters
6	0	18	John	Campbell	208	Jay	Adams
7	0	18	John	Campbell	219	Charles	Fitzgerald
8	0	18	John	Campbell	226	Karan	Khanna
9	0	18	John	Campbell	243	Maciej	Dusza
10	0	18	John	Campbell	254	Michael	Zwilling
11	0	18	John	Campbell	255	Randy	Reeves

Figure 2-26. *Results of manager's employee search*

ADO Example 3: Updating SQL Data

Now it's time to let Excel 2007 do some real work. We've seen a few different methods of retrieving data. Let's see what we can do to provide some updating capabilities to our worksheets.

In this example, we will import a list of employees with some personal data ("personal data" as defined by the AdventureWorks database; I don't know that many of us would agree that this meets our definition). Once we have that list, we'll create a routine that lets us update any information that has changed.

1. Open a new workbook and name it `DataAccessSample05.xlsm`.

2. In the VBE, add a new standard module.

3. Create a function named `GetEmpList`.

4. Add the following code:

```
Sub GetEmpList()
Dim cnn As ADODB.Connection
Dim rs As ADODB.Recordset
Dim xlSheet As Worksheet
Dim sConnString As String
Dim sSQL As String
Dim i As Integer

    Set xlSheet = Sheets("Sheet1")
    xlSheet.Activate
    Range("A1").Activate
    Selection.CurrentRegion.Select
    Selection.ClearContents
    Range("A1").Select

    Set cnn = New ADODB.Connection
    sConnString = "Provider=SQLNCLI;Server=MYSERVERNAME\SQLEXPRESS;" ➥
                  & "Database=AdventureWorks;Trusted_Connection=yes;"

    cnn.Open sConnString
    sSQL = "SELECT emp.EmployeeID, Person.Contact.FirstName, " ➥
         & "Person.Contact.LastName, emp.NationalIDNumber, " ➥
         & "emp.BirthDate, emp.MaritalStatus, emp.Gender " ➥
         & "FROM HumanResources.Employee AS emp " ➥
         & "INNER JOIN Person.Contact ON emp.ContactID = " ➥
         & "Person.Contact.ContactID"

    Set rs = New ADODB.Recordset
    rs.Open sSQL, cnn, adOpenDynamic

    For i = 1 To rs.Fields.Count
        ActiveSheet.Cells(1, i).Value = rs.Fields(i - 1).Name
    Next i

    xlSheet.Range(xlSheet.Cells(1, 1), _
        xlSheet.Cells(1, rs.Fields.Count)).Font.Bold = True

    ActiveSheet.Range("A2").CopyFromRecordset rs
```

```
        xlSheet.Select
        Range("A1").Select
        Selection.CurrentRegion.Select
        Selection.Columns.AutoFit
        Range("A1").Select


        rs.Close
        cnn.Close

        Set rs = Nothing
        Set cnn = Nothing
    End Sub
```

This should be fairly standard code by now. We're setting up our worksheet, opening our ADO Connection object, filling a recordset with employee personal data from our SQL statement, and then displaying it on the worksheet.

■**Note** All of our examples require a reference to the Microsoft ActiveX Data Objects 2.8 library.

---

5. Run the code and show the employee personal information data (see Figure 2-27).

	A	B	C	D	E	F	G
1	EmployeeID	FirstName	LastName	NationalIDNumber	BirthDate	MaritalStatus	Gender
2	1	Guy	Gilbert	14417807	5/15/1972	M	M
3	2	Kevin	Brown	253022876	6/3/1977	S	M
4	3	Roberto	Tamburello	509647174	12/13/1964	M	M
5	4	Rob	Walters	112457891	1/23/1965	S	M
6	5	Thierry	D'Hers	480168528	8/29/1949	M	M
7	6	David	Bradley	24756624	4/19/1965	S	M
8	7	JoLynn	Dobney	309738752	2/16/1946	S	F
9	8	Ruth	Ellerbrock	690627818	7/6/1946	M	F
10	9	Gail	Erickson	695256908	10/29/1942	M	F
11	10	Barry	Johnson	912265825	4/27/1946	S	M

Figure 2-27. *Employee personal data list*

The AdventureWorks database comes with a stored procedure called HumanResources. uspUpdateEmployeePersonalInfo that will update this information (see Figure 2-28).

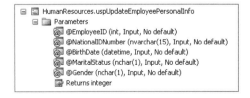

Figure 2-28. *uspUpdateEmployeePersonalInfo and parameters*

We are going to write a procedure called `UpdateEmpPersonalInfo` that will call this stored procedure and update the database with the information from the currently selected row in our Excel worksheet.

Before we begin coding this procedure, note that this stored procedure has five input parameters. Our earlier `GetSelectedManagerEmployeeListSQL` procedure called a stored procedure that took one parameter, which we instantiated and filled, and then appended to a `Command` object within the procedure, like so:

```
Dim param As ADODB.Parameter
'Code omitted...

    Set param = New ADODB.Parameter
    With param
        .Name = "ManagerID"
        .Type = adInteger
        .Value = iMgrID
    End With

    With cmd
        .CommandType = adCmdStoredProc
        .CommandText = "uspGetManagerEmployees"
        .Parameters.Append param
    End With
```

We could declare five variables of `ADODB.Parameter` type and repeat the `Set param =...` and the `With...End With` block five times from within our procedure—but that would make the code for this otherwise simple subroutine somewhat lengthy (the coders dictate of keeping routines to what can be seen on one monitor screen comes into play here). What we can do instead is use a VBA `Collection` object that we'll fill with `Parameter` objects (through a helper function), and that will then be appended to an ADO `Command` object.

1. On Module1, create a new subroutine named `UpdateEmpPersonalInfo`.

2. Add the following variable declarations:

    ```
    Dim cnn As ADODB.Connection
    Dim cmd As ADODB.Command
    Dim colParams As Collection
    Dim sConnString As String
    Dim i As Integer
    ```

3. Insert the following code to activate the data worksheet and set up the `Connection` and `Command` objects:

    ```
    Sheets("Sheet1").Activate 'make sure we're on the data sheet

    Set cnn = New ADODB.Connection
    sConnString = "Provider=SQLNCLI;Server=MYSERVERNAME\SQLEXPRESS;" ➥
                & "Database=AdventureWorks;Trusted_Connection=yes;"
    ```

```
        cnn.Open sConnString

        Set cmd = New ADODB.Command
        cmd.ActiveConnection = cnn
```

4. Next, fill the colParams collection with ADODB.Parameter objects:

```
        Set colParams = SetParams(ActiveCell.Row)
```

The SetParams function returns a filled collection and looks like this:

```
Function SetParams(RowNum As Integer) As Collection
'returns a collection of filled ADO Parameter objects
Dim colReturn As Collection
Dim prm As ADODB.Parameter

    Set colReturn = New Collection
    Set prm = New ADODB.Parameter
    With prm
        .Name = "EmployeeID"
        .Type = adInteger
        .Value = Cells(RowNum, 1).Value
    End With
    colReturn.Add prm

    Set prm = New ADODB.Parameter 'wipe prm and start over; best way to ➥
                            prevent leftover data
    With prm
        .Name = "NationalIDNumber"
        .Type = adLongVarWChar
        .Size = 15
        .Value = Cells(RowNum, 4).Value
    End With

    colReturn.Add prm

    Set prm = New ADODB.Parameter
    With prm
        .Name = "BirthDate"
        .Type = adDBTimeStamp
        .Value = Cells(RowNum, 5).Value
    End With
    colReturn.Add prm
```

```
    Set prm = New ADODB.Parameter
    With prm
        .Name = "MaritalStatus"
        .Type = adWChar
        .Size = 1
        .Value = Cells(RowNum, 6).Value
    End With
    colReturn.Add prm

    Set prm = New ADODB.Parameter
    With prm
        .Name = "Gender"
        .Type = adWChar
        .Size = 1
        .Value = Cells(RowNum, 7).Value
    End With
    colReturn.Add prm

    Set prm = Nothing
    Set SetParams = colReturn
End Function
```

There is nothing really fancy going here, although we have called upon a new property of the `Parameter` object. We're instantiating the `Parameter` object with this line of code:

```
    Set prm = New ADODB.Parameter
```

Then we are setting various properties. You might have noticed when looking at the parameters list in SQL Server that some parameters were numeric and others were various flavors of char (nchar and nvarchar, to be exact). These parameters require an additional property setting, the `Parameter.Size` property. You also have other properties available, such as the `Direction` property, which you can set to determine whether a value is for input or output.

```
    With prm
        .Name = "EmployeeID"
        .Type = adInteger
        .Value = Cells(RowNum, 1).Value
    End With
    colReturn.Add prm
```

Once the properties are set, we add the `prm` variable to our `colReturn` collection.

We reuse the `prm` variable by reinstantiating it before setting the next set of properties and adding to the collection. This is an effective way of reusing an object and ensures you don't have any "leftover" property settings lingering.

This process is repeated for each input parameter that `uspUpdateEmployeePersonalInfo` requires us to provide. Finally, we set the function's return value to the internal collection object:

```
Set SetParams = colReturn
```

Next, we'll finish setting up the `Command` object and loop through the collection of
`Parameter` objects, appending each to the `Command` object's `Parameters` collection:

```
With cmd
    .CommandType = adCmdStoredProc
    .CommandText = "HumanResources.uspUpdateEmployeePersonalInfo"
    For i = 1 To colParams.Count
        .Parameters.Append colParams(i)
    Next i

End With

cmd.Execute
```

We end by calling the `Command.Execute` method to send the updated data to the database.
Before we run this command, let's take a look at the entire procedure. It should look like this:

```
Sub UpdateEmpPersonalInfo()
Dim cnn As ADODB.Connection
Dim cmd As ADODB.Command
Dim colParams As Collection
Dim sConnString As String
Dim i As Integer

    Sheets("Sheet1").Activate 'make sure we're on the data sheet

    Set cnn = New ADODB.Connection
    sConnString = "Provider=SQLNCLI;Server=MYSERVERNAME\SQLEXPRESS;" ➥
                   & "Database=AdventureWorks;Trusted_Connection=yes;"

    cnn.Open sConnString

    Set cmd = New ADODB.Command
    cmd.ActiveConnection = cnn

    Set colParams = SetParams(ActiveCell.Row)

    With cmd
        .CommandType = adCmdStoredProc
        .CommandText = "HumanResources.uspUpdateEmployeePersonalInfo"
        For i = 1 To colParams.Count
            .Parameters.Append colParams(i)
        Next i

    End With

    cmd.Execute
    cnn.Close
```

```
    Set colParams = Nothing
    Set cmd = Nothing
    Set cnn = Nothing

    MsgBox "Record has been updated", vbOKOnly, "Record Processed"

End Sub
```

Now we'll modify some data and run the procedure. Figure 2-29 shows the data before we make any changes.

1	EmployeeID	FirstName	LastName	NationalIDNumber	BirthDate	MaritalStatus	Gender
2	1	Guy	Gilbert	14417807	5/15/1972	M	M
3	2	Kevin	Brown	253022876	6/3/1977	S	M

Figure 2-29. *Employee data before update*

Kevin Brown, EmployeeID 2, has been recently married. Change his marital status to **M**, and then move the cursor to save the change. Run the UpdateEmpPersonalInfo routine, making sure the cursor is in the row containing Kevin's record. The "Record has been updated" message will appear.

To test your success, select and delete all the data from Sheet1 (or just change Kevin's marital status to any character), and run the GetEmpList subroutine again. Your display should look like Figure 2-30.

1	EmployeeID	FirstName	LastName	NationalIDNumber	BirthDate	MaritalStatus	Gender
2	1	Guy	Gilbert	14417807	5/15/1972	M	M
3	2	Kevin	Brown	253022876	6/3/1977	M	M

Figure 2-30. *Employee data after update*

Of Excel, Data, and Object Orientation

Earlier in this book, I promised that we'd see object-oriented solutions to our coding problems in Excel 2007. Let's take our manager list–creation code and the code that lists a manager's staff, and convert them to classes. Normally, this is the way I would directly approach a solution, but up to this point we've been exploring some of the VBA possibilities in Excel 2007.

Open DataAccessSample04.xlsm and save it as DataAccessSample06.xlsm.

Open Module1 in the VBE and review the GetManagerList subroutine. We can break its functionality down to just a few items. The problem with that is it's doing a number of unrelated things. It's setting up the worksheet for data import, opening a connection to the database, getting data, putting it on the worksheet, and then formatting and cleaning up the worksheet.

When we build our objects, we will pay strict attention to the separation of functionality. The rule of thumb is that objects should do only one well-defined job. Of course there are exceptions, but if you plan carefully, you will develop objects that provide a clearly defined set of methods and properties, providing a focused set of functionality.

The first thing we're doing in our original code is setting up the worksheet by activating it and then clearing a contiguous region in preparation for importing our data:

```
Set xlSheet = Sheets("Sheet2")
xlSheet.Activate
Range("A1").Activate
Selection.CurrentRegion.Select
Selection.ClearContents
Range("A1").Select
```

Then we're instantiating and opening a connection to our data:

```
Set cnn = New ADODB.Connection
sConnString = "Provider=SQLNCLI;Server=MYSERVERNAME\SQLEXPRESS;" ➥
              & "Database=AdventureWorks;Trusted_Connection=yes;"

cnn.Open sConnString
```

Next, we get our data into an ADO recordset and place it on our worksheet:

```
sSQL = "SELECT HumanResources.Employee.EmployeeID, Person.Contact.FirstName," ➥
       & " Person.Contact.LastName FROM Person.Contact" ➥
       & " INNER JOIN HumanResources.Employee" ➥
       & " ON Person.Contact.ContactID = HumanResources.Employee.ContactID" ➥
       & " WHERE (((HumanResources.Employee.EmployeeID) In" ➥
       & " (SELECT  HumanResources.Employee.ManagerID" ➥
       & " FROM HumanResources.Employee)));"

Set rs = New ADODB.Recordset

rs.Open sSQL, cnn, adOpenDynamic

Sheets("Sheet2").Activate
Range("A1").CopyFromRecordset rs
```

And finally, we do a quick bit of formatting the sheet by using the AutoFit command to resize the data columns:

```
xlSheet.Select
Range("A1").Select
Selection.CurrentRegion.Select
Selection.Columns.AutoFit
Range("A1").Select
```

These are four simple units of functionality that we can provide in a very generic and reusable object-oriented solution.

In the VBE, add a new class module and name it cData. Add a second new class module and name it cExcelSetup. These will contain the code that will provide all of the functionality provided in our standard code module.

Let's work with cExcelSetup first, and create an object that can provide our worksheet setup and cleanup functionality.

Add three module-level variables:

```
Private m_xlSheet As Worksheet
Private m_rngInitialCellSelect As Range
Private m_rngDataRegionStart As Range
```

These are the private variables that will hold key property values for us. Next we'll create read/write properties to set and retrieve our property values:

```
Public Property Get Worksheet() As Worksheet
    Set Worksheet = m_xlSheet
End Property

Public Property Set Worksheet(newSheet As Worksheet)
    Set m_xlSheet = newSheet
End Property

Public Property Get InitialCellSelection() As Range
    Set InitialCellSelection = m_rngInitialCellSelect
End Property

Public Property Set InitialCellSelection(newCell As Range)
    Set m_rngInitialCellSelect = newCell
End Property

Public Property Get DataRegionStart() As Range
    Set DataRegionStart = m_rngDataRegionStart
End Property

Public Property Set DataRegionStart(newCellAddress As Range)
    Set m_rngDataRegionStart = newCellAddress
End Property
```

The GetInitialCellSelection and DataRegionStart properties both return Range objects. We'll be using the GetInitialCellSelection property to determine where our cursor will be after our code runs. The DataRegionStart property sets and returns the cell that begins our data region. This is used when we clear the sheet at the start of our procedures and when we perform our autofit during cleanup.

Even though we've got Property Get and Set functions for these two properties, we're going to create an initialization function that allows us to set them both at once. This give us the advantage of using less client code to accomplish the task of setting two properties, yet gives us the flexibility of using the property settings directly if we need to.

```
Public Sub SetKeyCells(InitialCell As Range, DataRegionStart As Range)
    Set m_rngInitialCellSelect = InitialCell
    Set m_rngDataRegionStart = DataRegionStart
End Sub
```

Now that we've got our key properties laid out, we can concentrate on adding our setup and cleanup code.

Add a new subroutine called SetupWorksheet, and add the following code:

```
Public Sub SetupWorksheet()
    Me.Worksheet.Activate
    ClearRegion
    Me.InitialCellSelection.Select
End Sub
```

This code corresponds to our original code from our standard module:

```
Set xlSheet = Sheets("Sheet2")
xlSheet.Activate
Range("A1").Activate
Selection.CurrentRegion.Select
Selection.ClearContents
Range("A1").Select
```

The first and last lines of the SetupWorksheet routine correspond to the first and last lines of our original code. There is a call to a private method called ClearRegion that does the work of the remaining original code:

```
Private Sub ClearRegion()
    m_xlSheet.Activate
    Me.DataRegionStart.Activate
    Selection.CurrentRegion.Select
    Selection.ClearContents
End Sub
```

Add one last function to do our autofit cell formatting, and clean up the worksheet:

```
Public Sub DoAutoFit()
    Me.Worksheet.Select
    Me.DataRegionStart.Select
    Selection.CurrentRegion.Select
    Selection.Columns.AutoFit
    Me.InitialCellSelection.Select
End Sub
```

By now, I'm sure you've noticed that this code is very similar to the original code in our standard module. The major difference is that rather than referring to specific cells, we are using internal class properties such as Me.DataRegionStart.Select.

That's all there is to our cExcelSetup class. Let's create our cData class to populate our worksheet with data. Add the following private module-level variables:

```
Private m_cnn As ADODB.Connection
Private m_rs As ADODB.Recordset
Private m_sConnString As String
Private m_sSQL As String
```

These are the same tools we've been using all along to connect to our data and return sets of data from the AdventureWorks database. We're going to create properties to hold our connection string and SQL statement. We'll also create methods (functions) to open and close our ADO connections and recordsets.

Add the following `Property Get/Lets`:

```
Public Property Get ConnectString() As String
    ConnectString = m_sConnString
End Property

Public Property Let ConnectString(newString As String)
    m_sConnString = newString
End Property

Public Property Get SQL() As String
    SQL = m_sSQL
End Property

Public Property Let SQL(newSQL As String)
    m_sSQL = newSQL
End Property
```

Next we are going to add methods to open and close our ADO `Connection` object:

```
Function OpenConnection()
    If m_sConnString <> "" Then
        m_cnn.Open m_sConnString
    Else
        MsgBox "Cannot open connection", vbOKOnly, "cData: OpenConnection Error"
    End If
End Function

Function CloseConnection()
    m_cnn.Close
End Function
```

Note that the `OpenConnection` method is using the private variable `m_sConnString` to return the connection string to the AdventureWorks database.

Next we'll create a new function called `GetData` and add the following code:

```
Function GetData() As ADODB.Recordset
    m_rs.Open m_sSQL, m_cnn, adOpenDynamic

    Set GetData = m_rs
End Function
```

This function returns a dataset based on an SQL statement passed in from the private variable `m_sSQL`, and uses the private connection object to connect to the database. In reality, this is a very simplistic method. In the real world, we would probably add arguments or properties for the cursor type, location, and other key settings, but for our example this will suffice.

Our last order of business for this class is setting its initialization and termination methods. It is good practice to initialize any internal objects and data variables, and the `Class_Initialize` method is the place to do it. When using internal objects like the ADO objects, using the `Class_Terminate` method allows us a place to clean them up when the object goes out of scope in our client code.

```
Private Sub Class_Initialize()
    m_sConnString = ""
    m_sSQL = ""
    Set m_cnn = New ADODB.Connection
    Set m_rs = New ADODB.Recordset
    Set m_prm = New ADODB.Parameter
    Set m_cmd = New ADODB.Command
End Sub

Private Sub Class_Terminate()
    Set m_cnn = Nothing
    Set m_rs = Nothing
    Set m_prm = Nothing
    Set m_cmd = Nothing
End Sub
```

Let's take a look at both classes in their entirety (shown in Listings 2-7 and 2-8). Then we'll create client code to use these objects and compare them to the original code in Module1.

Listing 2-7. *cExcelSetup Class Code*

```
Option Explicit

Private m_xlSheet As Worksheet
Private m_rngInitialCellSelect As Range
Private m_rngDataRegionStart As Range
'

Public Property Get Worksheet() As Worksheet
    Set Worksheet = m_xlSheet
End Property

Public Property Set Worksheet(newSheet As Worksheet)
    Set m_xlSheet = newSheet
End Property

Public Property Get InitialCellSelection() As Range
    Set InitialCellSelection = m_rngInitialCellSelect
End Property
```

```
Public Property Set InitialCellSelection(newCell As Range)
    Set m_rngInitialCellSelect = newCell
End Property

Public Property Get DataRegionStart() As Range
    Set DataRegionStart = m_rngDataRegionStart
End Property

Public Property Set DataRegionStart(newCellAddress As Range)
    Set m_rngDataRegionStart = newCellAddress
End Property

Public Sub SetKeyCells(InitialCell As Range, DataRegionStart As Range)
    Set m_rngInitialCellSelect = InitialCell
    Set m_rngDataRegionStart = DataRegionStart
End Sub

Public Sub SetupWorksheet()
    Me.Worksheet.Activate
    ClearRegion
    Me.InitialCellSelection.Select
End Sub

Private Sub ClearRegion()
    m_xlSheet.Activate
    Me.DataRegionStart.Activate
    Selection.CurrentRegion.Select
    Selection.ClearContents
End Sub

Public Sub DoAutoFit()
    Me.Worksheet.Select
    Me.DataRegionStart.Select
    Selection.CurrentRegion.Select
    Selection.Columns.AutoFit
    Me.InitialCellSelection.Select
End Sub
```

Listing 2-8. *cData Class Code*

```
Option Explicit

Private m_cnn As ADODB.Connection
Private m_rs As ADODB.Recordset
Private m_sConnString As String
Private m_sSQL As String
'
```

```
Public Property Get ConnectString() As String
    ConnectString = m_sConnString
End Property

Public Property Let ConnectString(newString As String)
    m_sConnString = newString
End Property

Public Property Get SQL() As String
    SQL = m_sSQL
End Property

Public Property Let SQL(newSQL As String)
    m_sSQL = newSQL
End Property

Function OpenConnection()
    If m_sConnString <> "" Then
        m_cnn.Open m_sConnString
    Else
        MsgBox "Cannot open connection", vbOKOnly, "cData: OpenConnection Error"
    End If
End Function

Function CloseConnection()
    m_cnn.Close
End Function

Function GetData() As ADODB.Recordset
    m_rs.Open m_sSQL, m_cnn, adOpenDynamic

    Set GetData = m_rs
End Function

Private Sub Class_Initialize()
    m_sConnString = ""
    m_sSQL = ""
    Set m_cnn = New ADODB.Connection
    Set m_rs = New ADODB.Recordset
End Sub

Private Sub Class_Terminate()
    Set m_cnn = Nothing
    Set m_rs = Nothing
End Sub
```

Using the cExcelSetup and cData Objects

Now that we've created the objects we need, let's put them to use in client code.

In the VBE, add a new standard module and name it basManagers. Add two module-level variables to hold our cExcelSetup and cData objects:

```
Dim m_cData As cData
Dim m_cXL As cExcelSetup
```

These are placed at module level in case we need to use the objects across function calls. Create a new subroutine and name it GetManagers. Add the following code:

```
Dim sConnString As String
Dim sSQL  As String
    Set m_cXL = New cExcelSetup
    Set m_cData = New cData
    sConnString = "Provider=SQLNCLI;Server=MyServerName\SQLEXPRESS;" ➥
                  & "Database=AdventureWorks;Trusted_Connection=yes;"
    sSQL = "SELECT HumanResources.Employee.EmployeeID, Person.Contact.FirstName," ➥
           & " Person.Contact.LastName FROM Person.Contact" ➥
           & " INNER JOIN HumanResources.Employee" ➥
           & " ON Person.Contact.ContactID = HumanResources.Employee.ContactID" ➥
           & " WHERE (((HumanResources.Employee.EmployeeID) In" ➥
           & " (SELECT  HumanResources.Employee.ManagerID" ➥
           & " FROM HumanResources.Employee)));"
```

Here we are instantiating our cExcelSetup and cData objects, and preparing variables to set up the cData class.

When we analyzed the original code, we found we needed to have three sets of functionality, prepare the worksheet for data import, get and display the data, and resize the columns for the data. We are going to create helper functions to do most of this work.

Add a new subroutine to basManagers and name it DoClearSheet(). Add the following code:

```
    With m_cXL
        Set .Worksheet = Sheets("Sheet1")
        .SetKeyCells .Worksheet.Range("A1"), .Worksheet.Range("A3")
        .SetupWorksheet
    End With
```

Note that we're using our cExcelSetup object's SetKeyCells method, allowing us to assign values to the InitialCellSelection and DataRegionStart properties with one line of code.

Add another subroutine called GetData. This procedure will take two arguments: the connection string and the SQL statement. Here is the code for the GetData method:

```
Sub GetData(ConnString As String, which As String)
    With m_cData
        .ConnectString = ConnString
        .OpenConnection
        .SQL = which
```

```
        m_cXL.Worksheet.Range("A1").CopyFromRecordset .GetData
        .CloseConnection
    End With
End Sub
```

Both of these methods use only our `cExcelSetup` and `cData` objects with no external code.

Let's finish our `GetManagers` procedure by adding calls to these methods, and also adding some cleanup code. The entire `GetManagers` subroutine should look like this:

```
Sub GetManagers()
Dim sConnString As String
Dim sSQL  As String
    Set m_cXL = New cExcelSetup
    Set m_cData = New cData
    sConnString = "Provider=SQLNCLI;Server=MyServerName\SQLEXPRESS;" ➥
                  & "Database=AdventureWorks;Trusted_Connection=yes;"
    sSQL = "SELECT HumanResources.Employee.EmployeeID, Person.Contact.FirstName," ➥
           & " Person.Contact.LastName FROM Person.Contact" ➥
           & " INNER JOIN HumanResources.Employee" ➥
           & " ON Person.Contact.ContactID = HumanResources.Employee.ContactID" ➥
           & " WHERE (((HumanResources.Employee.EmployeeID) In" ➥
           & " (SELECT  HumanResources.Employee.ManagerID" ➥
           & " FROM HumanResources.Employee)));"
    DoClearSheet
    GetData sConnString, sSQL
    m_cXL.DoAutoFit
    Set m_cData = Nothing
    Set m_cXL = Nothing
End Sub
```

I mentioned a moment ago that neither of our helper methods made any direct VBA calls. The same is true of the `GetManagers` method. All of our work is being done by our objects from start to finish. The beauty of this is that we can drop these classes in any Excel project and have this functionality available instantly.

In our current Excel project, we can change the database and/or SQL statement and import any data we need via the `cData` object.

Summary

In this chapter, you've taken a look at some of the many data access methods you can use in Excel. You've seen how to use DAO to get data into an Excel workbook. DAO, while old technology, is certainly still a viable alternative for Windows 2000 or XP users. It's easy to use and very fast if you're working with local data sources like an Access database stored on your hard drive. But what if you need to work with remote data? Or what if you need to work with data in a disconnected fashion? In the next section, we began using ActiveX Data Objects (ADO), a technology that addresses these issues and more.

You've also explored various methods of importing data into your Excel workbooks. You've pulled data from Access databases to text files to ODBC and OLE DB data sources. You've also taken a look at how to think of functionality from an object-oriented point of view. Taking existing code that you reuse often or rewrite in a similar manner is a great way to start moving into OOP practices.

As you move into the next chapter and begin looking at some of the XML features of Excel 2007, you'll continue developing objects to do your work for you. Some will provide a level of reusability; some may be one-offs. There is no rule that says all of your code must be reusable. In fact, you might find that you write a lot of code for an application that is specific to that application. This is perfectly acceptable. Reusability is not the only advantage to programming custom objects. Ease of maintenance is another by-product of OOP, and is just as valuable as code reuse.

CHAPTER 3

■ ■ ■

Using XML in Excel 2007

The XML file format was introduced with Excel 2003 (XML support was introduced in Excel 2000). Excel 2007 has new XML file formats. The `*.xlsx` format represents a workbook that does not and cannot contain macros. The `*.xlsm` format represents a workbook that can or does contain macros. This separation is a security enhancement that lets the user know in advance of opening a document that there may be code inside. Remember the "This document may contain harmful code" warnings in previous Microsoft Office versions? With these, you would not be aware of the possibility of code until you opened the file. Now, your users will know in advance if they are opening a workbook containing code.

The Excel XML format is compatible with Microsoft Office 2003, Office XP, and Office 2000 with the addition of a file format converter patch, available from Microsoft Office Online and Microsoft Update. Users of Office 2003, Office XP, and Office 2000 can open, edit, and save files using the new Excel XML format.

By providing the XML file format, Microsoft has given us the ability to create Excel files (and Word and PowerPoint files as well) on machines that do not have these applications installed. Navigating the Excel DOM, some of which we worked with in the previous chapter, is no longer the only method to access Excel data and/or create Excel files.

XML also gives us the advantage of using XSL to transform external XML to Excel format and from Excel format to many other formats.

Importing XML in Excel 2007

Importing XML data into an Excel workbook is a fairly straightforward process. The `Workbook` object has a method called `XmlImport` that does the work for us.

Open a new workbook and save it with an `.xlsm` format file extension. Open the VBE, add a standard module, and create a new function named `GetXMLData()`:

```
Sub GetXMLData()
  ActiveWorkbook.XmlImport URL:= ➡
    "C:\projects\Excel\cds.xml", ImportMap:= ➡
    Nothing, Overwrite:=True, Destination:=Range("$A$1")
End Sub
```

Caution Be sure to adjust the file path to reflect your location for the XML file.

The ActiveWorkbook object is actually a property of the Application object that returns a Workbook object type, and therefore contains all the properties and methods of the Workbook object.

Figure 3-1 shows the ActiveWorkbook object as it appears in the Visual Basic Object Browser. Figure 3-2 shows the Workbook object and its properties and methods. The ActiveWorkbook object *has all the properties and methods of the* Workbook *object.*

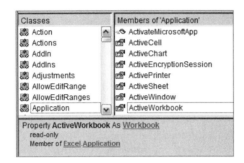

Figure 3-1. *ActiveWorkbook property of Application object*

If you try double-clicking the ActiveWorkbook property, you will not find any properties or methods associated with it in the Object Browser. Click the Workbook link in the description section of the Object Browser, however, and you will see the Workbook object's properties and methods listed, as shown in Figure 3-2. Since a reference to the ActiveWorkbook is actually returning a Workbook, you can access all of these properties and methods.

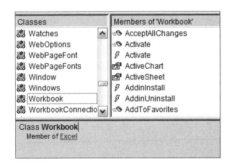

Figure 3-2. *Workbook object and class members*

I'll present you with a quick example to show that the two objects contain the same class members. Following are two screenshots. Figure 3-3 contains the Immediate window showing IntelliSense for the Workbook object, and Figure 3-4 shows IntelliSense for the ActiveWorkbook object.

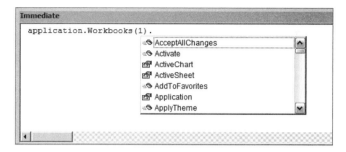

Figure 3-3. *IntelliSense for Workbook object*

Figure 3-4. *IntelliSense for ActiveWorkbook object*

So if you find yourself examining an object in the Object Browser and you don't see any class members, check to see if it's a property of another object and look at that object's class members.

Before we run the code, let's take a look at the XmlImport function and see what it does (see Figure 3-5).

Figure 3-5. *XmlImport function arguments*

The XmlImport function takes four arguments, as shown in Table 3-1.

Table 3-1. *XmlImport Function Argument Descriptions*

Name	Required (Y/N)	Data Type	Description
URL	Y	String	Path to an XML data file.
ImportMap	Y	XMLMap	The XML map to apply when importing the file.
Overwrite	N	Variant	Specifies whether or not to overwrite data that has been mapped to the schema map specified in the ImportMap parameter. Set to True to overwrite the data or False to append the new data to the existing data.
Destination	N	Variant	Specifies the top-left cell of the range that will display the data.

The XmlImport function returns a value of type XlXmlImportResult, which is an enum showing the success or failure of the call. Figure 3-6 shows the available options displayed in the Object Browser window.

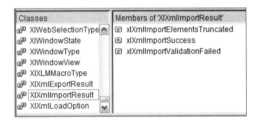

Figure 3-6. *XlXmlImportResult members*

Let's run our GetXMLData procedure and see what we get.

If no schema exists for this data, Excel will create one for you, as shown in Figure 3-7.

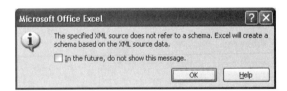

Figure 3-7. *XML Schema dialog box*

Excel refers to these schemas as XML maps. Click the check box so you won't see this message any longer, and let the import continue. When the import is finished, the data should look like that in Figure 3-8.

	A	B	C
1	artist	title	releasedate
2	Nirvana	Nevermind	1991
3	Nirvana	In Utero	1993
4	Alice In Chains	Facelift	1990
5	Alice In Chains	Dirt	1992
6	Alice In Chains	Unplugged	1996
7	Tool	Undertow	1993
8	Tool	Aenima	1996
9	Pearl Jam	Ten	1992

Figure 3-8. *Imported XML file*

Our call to XmlImport sets the arguments like this:

```
ActiveWorkbook.XmlImport URL:= _
    "C:\projects\Excel\cds.xml", ImportMap:= ➥
    Nothing, Overwrite:=True, Destination:=Range("$A$1")
```

The URL argument is pointing to a file named cds.xml, which contains discography information. The ImportMap argument is set to Nothing for now because we do not have an existing schema for this data. We are setting Overwrite to True to overwrite any existing data, and the Destination range is setting cell A1 as the target for the start of our data range.

If we try to rerun this code as is, we will generate an error, as shown in Figure 3-9.

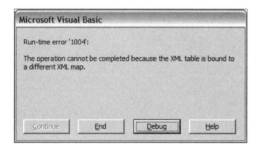

Figure 3-9. *XML map error*

This is due to the fact that the first time we ran the code, Excel created a map for us and bound our data table to it. To view that map, right-click anywhere in the data range and choose XML ➤ XML Source (Figures 3-10 and 3-11).

Figure 3-10. *XML menu*

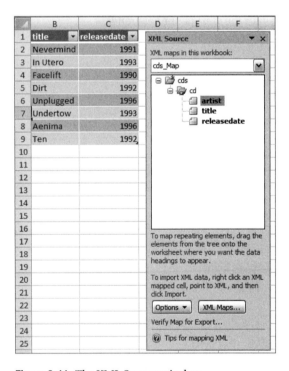

Figure 3-11. *The XML Source window*

Figure 3-11 shows the XML Source window with the artist element selected. Selecting an element in the XML Source window selects the associated (or mapped) data range. Above the XML map is a drop-down list that contains all of the XML maps in the currently active workbook. The XML map in this project is called cds_Map.

The second time the code is run, we run into trouble because Excel automatically creates a new map for the data that is mapped to destination cell A1. Excel will not allow you to bind your data to more than one XML map. If you change the destination cell, the procedure runs fine, however. So how do we refresh our data if a source file is updated?

The XMLMaps collection has a DataBinding property that has a Refresh method. Using this method, we can read in any changes to the XML file that our data range is mapped to.

Before we begin, let's copy our GetXMLData function into a standard code module in a new workbook and save it. Run the GetXMLData macro from the Developer ribbon.

Open the cds.xml file and add a new title to the list by adding the following set of nodes at the top of the XML file:

```
<cd>
   <artist>Nirvana</artist>
   <title>Greatest Hits</title>
   <releasedate>2000</releasedate>
</cd>
```

Save the file. Add the following function to the standard module:

```
Sub RefreshXML()
    Range("A1").Select
    ActiveWorkbook.XmlMaps("cds_Map").DataBinding.Refresh
End Sub
```

Run the code by pressing the F5 key with the insertion point inside the RefreshXML subroutine. The data range is expanded to include the new data, as shown in Figure 3-12.

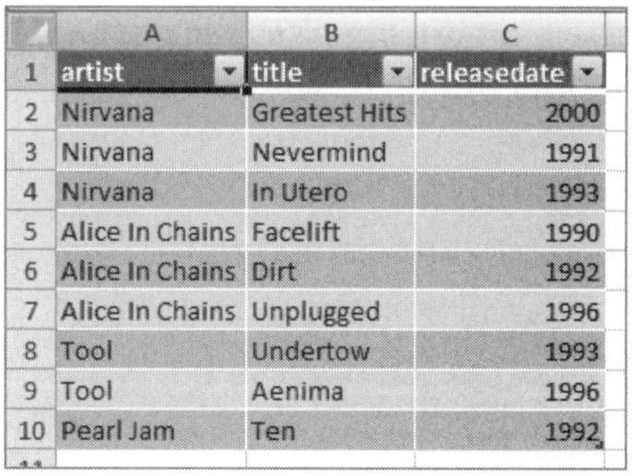

	A	B	C
1	artist	title	releasedate
2	Nirvana	Greatest Hits	2000
3	Nirvana	Nevermind	1991
4	Nirvana	In Utero	1993
5	Alice In Chains	Facelift	1990
6	Alice In Chains	Dirt	1992
7	Alice In Chains	Unplugged	1996
8	Tool	Undertow	1993
9	Tool	Aenima	1996
10	Pearl Jam	Ten	1992

Figure 3-12. *XML data refreshed*

Remove the new set of nodes and run the RefreshXML method again, and the table will be resized to display only the data from the XML file.

Excel 2007 provides other methods to remove and load XML map settings. The DataBinding.ClearSettings method unbinds the data in a range from the XML file.

```
ActiveWorkbook.XmlMaps("cds_Map").DataBinding.ClearSettings
```

The DataBindings.LoadSettings method takes the file path or URL as an argument to load the mapping from the specified XML file.

```
ActiveWorkbook.XmlMaps("cds_Map").DataBinding.LoadSettings ➥
    "C:\projects\Excel\cds.xml"
```

Appending XML Data

Both the Excel Workbook object and the XmlMaps collection contain methods for appending or overwriting XML data in a workbook. The Workbook.XmlImport method and the Xmlmaps. Import method provide functionality to do either. Both methods take Overwrite arguments, which when set to False will append data to any existing data. The XmlImport method, however, will *not* append data when Overwrite is set to False if the optional Destination argument is used. In this case, nothing will happen (the append is cancelled).

We're going to append data from another XML file containing more discography information that we've received. We'll use the ActiveWorkbook's XmlImport method to do the append. Add a function to a standard module and name it AppendXMLData. The code looks like this:

```
Sub AppendXMLData()
Dim map As XmlMap
  Set map = ActiveWorkbook.XmlMaps("cds_Map")
  ActiveWorkbook.XmlImport URL:= ➥
    "C:\projects\Excel\cds02.xml", ImportMap:= ➥
    map, Overwrite:=False
End Sub
```

Run the AppendXMLData() method on the same worksheet that you imported the original XML discography information on. The data should look like that shown in Figure 3-13.

	A	B	C
1	artist	title	releasedate
2	Nirvana	Nevermind	1991
3	Nirvana	In Utero	1993
4	Alice In Chains	Facelift	1990
5	Alice In Chains	Dirt	1992
6	Alice In Chains	Unplugged	1996
7	Tool	Undertow	1993
8	Tool	Aenima	1996
9	Pearl Jam	Ten	1992
10	Aerosmith	Aerosmith	1973
11	Aerosmith	Get Your Wings	1974
12	Rush	2112	1976
13			

Figure 3-13. *XML data appended*

Using the XmlMaps collection's Import method, the same call might look like this:

```
Sub AppendXMLIntoExistingMap()
Dim sNewData As String
  sNewData = "C:\projects\Excel\cds02.xml"

  ActiveWorkbook.XmlMaps("cds_Map").Import sNewData, False
End Sub
```

The Overwrite argument is set to False, causing the data to be appended to the end of your data range. Set it to True to write over the data.

```
Sub ImportXMLIntoExistingMap()
Dim sNewData As String
  sNewData = "C:\projects\Excel\cds.xml"

  ActiveWorkbook.XmlMaps("cds_Map").Import sNewData, True
End Sub
```

Saving XML Data

Saving your data back to the existing XML file or a new file is as simple as a call to the Workbook object's SaveAsXMLData method. The SaveAsXMLData method takes two arguments, the file name to save to and the XML map object to retrieve the file schema from. Figure 3-14 shows the SaveAsXMLData method displayed in the Visual Basic Immediate window with its arguments shown via IntelliSense.

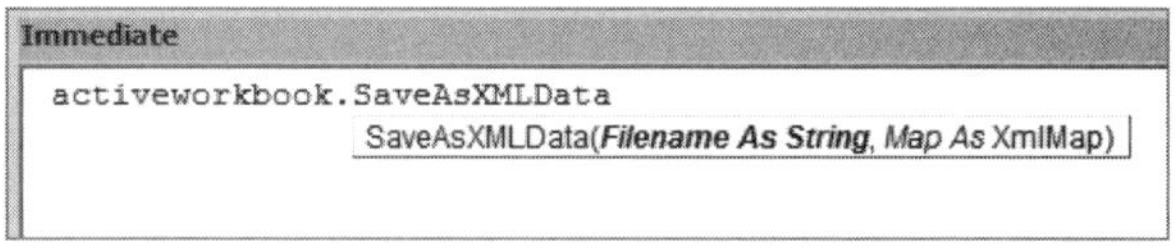

Figure 3-14. *SaveAsXMLData method*

Add a new procedure to the standard module you've been working with, and name it SaveXML.

```
Sub SaveXML()
Dim ExportMap As XmlMap
  Set ExportMap = ActiveWorkbook.XmlMaps("cds_Map")

  If ExportMap.IsExportable Then
    ActiveWorkbook.SaveAsXMLData ➥
      "C:\projects\Excel\cds_XML_out.xml", ExportMap
  Else
    MsgBox ExportMap.Name & " cannot be used to export XML"
  End If
End Sub
```

Before persisting your data, it's a good idea to ensure that the XML is exportable. The XMLMaps collection contains a read-only IsExportable method that returns True if any lists that refer to the map are exportable. A map is not exportable if an invalid value for an element is present or if required fields are not supplied.

Run the SaveXML macro from the Macros dialog box, accessible from the Developer ribbon. Figure 3-15 shows the XML generated by the SaveXML subroutine.

```
<?xml version="1.0" encoding="UTF-8" standalone="yes" ?>
- <cds xmlns:xsi="http://www.w3.org/2001/XMLSchema-instance">
  - <cd>
      <artist>Nirvana</artist>
      <title>Nevermind</title>
      <releasedate>1991</releasedate>
    </cd>
  - <cd>
      <artist>Nirvana</artist>
      <title>In Utero</title>
      <releasedate>1993</releasedate>
    </cd>
  - <cd>
      <artist>Alice In Chains</artist>
      <title>Facelift</title>
      <releasedate>1990</releasedate>
    </cd>
  + <cd>
  + <cd>
  + <cd>
  + <cd>
  + <cd>
  + <cd>
  + <cd>
  + <cd>
  - <cd>
      <artist>Dream Theater</artist>
      <title>Images and Words</title>
      <releasedate>1992</releasedate>
    </cd>
  </cds>
```

Figure 3-15. *Exported XML file*

When saving an XML map to a file, Excel adds the processing instructions. Our original file was very basic and did not include them (of course, there's no harm in including them).

Building an XML Data Class

Now that we've got an idea of what XML data services Excel provides us, let's build a class that will give us an easy-to-use interface to this functionality. Before we begin, though, let's think about what we'd like our class to do:

- We want it to bring in data from various XML data sources.

- We want the ability to refresh the data in case the source file is updated (either manually or through an automated process).

- We want to append data from another file that conforms to the same XML schema.

- We want to be able to clear and reset the data bindings.

- We want to be able to persist the data back to the original file or to a new file.

Those are some basic functions we'd expect from this object, but what else might a class of this type do for us?

- Check for the existence of XML maps?

- Enumerate XML maps?

- Rename an XML map?

- Add or delete XML maps?

Open a new workbook and add a new class module in the VBE. Name the class cXML.

Before we do any importing of XML data, it's a good idea to see if a map exists for our data. Add a new public property and call it HasMaps. Normally, I would add a module-level variable to hold the contents of this property, but the HasMaps property will be read-only. Creating a module-level variable presents us with the option of accessing that variable directly in our code. I'm suggesting leaving it out to prevent that possibility.

Add the following code to the HasMaps property:

```
Public Property Get HasMaps() As Boolean
Dim blnReturn As Boolean

  blnReturn = ActiveWorkbook.XmlMaps.Count >= 1
  HasMaps = blnReturn
End Property
```

My preference is to keep my code as concise as possible without sacrificing readability. I'm using one line of code in place of an If...Else block. The long form, if you prefer it, looks like this.

```
Dim blnReturn As Boolean

  If ActiveWorkbook.XmlMaps.Count >= 1 Then
    blnReturn = True
  Else
    blnReturn = False
  End If

  HasMaps = blnReturn
```

Add a property to store the name of the XML file to import plus a few additional setup properties:

```
Public Property Get XMLSourceFile() As String
  XMLSourceFile = m_sXMLSourceFile
End Property
```

```
Public Property Let XMLSourceFile(newXMLSourceFile As String)
  m_sXMLSourceFile = newXMLSourceFile
End Property

Public Property Get DataRange() As Excel.Range
  Set DataRange = m_oRange
End Property

Public Property Set DataRange(newRange As Excel.Range)
  Set m_oRange = newRange
End Property

Property Get Overwrite() As Boolean
  Overwrite = m_blnOverwrite
End Property

Property Let Overwrite(newOverwrite As Boolean)
  m_blnOverwrite = newOverwrite
End Property

Public Property Get MapName() As String
  MapName = m_sMapName
End Property
```

We've added a property to store and retrieve the DataRange into which we'll put our data (remember, it's the top-left cell reference in the range). We've also added an overwrite flag and a read-only property to retrieve the name of the XML map for this object.

The module-level declarations section should now look like this:

```
Dim m_sXMLSourceFile As String
Dim m_blnOverwrite As Boolean
Dim m_oRange As Excel.Range
Dim m_sMapName As String
```

Now let's start getting some work done. We are going to build, import, append, refresh, and save functions for our XML data. The first step is to get data from the XML file into the worksheet. We have a few scenarios in which to put data on our worksheet:

- Bringing in data from an XML file

- Overwriting existing XML data with a file that shares the same schema

- Appending XML data to our existing XML data

We'll start out by building a function that gives a developer who might be using this class in a project the ability to bring in new data (thereby creating an XML map) and a function to add additional data to previously imported XML data (or overwrite it if desired). These will be declared as private functions within the class. We will create a wrapper method to let our code make the decision as to which process we are calling. We'll also add a method to provide a direct call to an append function.

In the cXML class module, add a private method named GetNewXMLData. The code for this method will look very familiar:

```
Private Function GetNewXMLData()
  ActiveWorkbook.XmlImport m_sXMLSourceFile, Nothing, m_blnOverwrite, m_oRange
  m_sMapName = ActiveWorkbook.XmlMaps(ActiveWorkbook.XmlMaps.Count).Name
End Function
```

We are making the same call to the XmlImport method of the ActiveWorkbook object as we did in the examples that we created in standard code modules—but rather than directly setting its arguments, we are referring to the internal variables of our cXML class.

The GetNewXMLData method is actually doing two jobs for us. The first, of course, is getting the data into our worksheet. Remember that a call to the XmlImport method brings in data and creates an XML map. The second line of code in this method is setting our class's MapName property for us:

```
m_sMapName = ActiveWorkbook.XmlMaps(ActiveWorkbook.XmlMaps.Count).Name
```

This will come in handy when we need to add data or overwrite the current set of data. By checking the XmlMaps.Count property, we can get the latest addition to the collection that was added by the XmlImport method.

Now we'll add a second private function that will append or overwrite data for an existing XML map. Add a new private function and name it GetXMLForExistingMap. Add the following code:

```
Private Function GetXMLForExistingMap(DoOverwrite As Boolean)
  ActiveWorkbook.XmlMaps(m_sMapName).Import m_sXMLSourceFile, DoOverwrite
End Function
```

This function takes one argument, which is used to flag whether we want to append or overwrite our existing data. The single line of code should again be familiar. We are using the XmlMaps collection's Import method to get our data. Notice that we're using the internal m_sMapName variable to determine which XML map the data corresponds to.

Now let's add that wrapper method and let our class decide how to handle the data retrieval. Add a public function to the cXML class and name it GetXMLData. Add the following code:

```
Public Function GetXMLData(Optional DoOverwrite As Boolean = True)
  If (m_sMapName = "") Or (Not Me.HasMaps) Then
    GetNewXMLData
  Else
  'must set XMLSourceFile Property before appending if necessary
    GetXMLForExistingMap DoOverwrite
  End If
End Function
```

The GetXMLData method has one optional argument, which is used to set an overwrite flag for the incoming data. This argument has a default value of True, remaining consistent with Excel's built-in object interfaces.

The code begins with branching logic to determine whether our object already contains a reference to an XML map or whether the workbook does not contain any XML maps.

Once that's determined, the code will either bring in new data and create an XML map via the private GetNewXMLData function or it will call GetXMLForExistingMap, where, depending on how the overwrite flag is set, it will either append or overwrite the data in the existing mapping. The second branch also contains a comment noting that the XMLSourceFile property should be set before calling this function to perform an append.

Before we create client code to test this, remember that the original GetXMLData function that we wrote in our standard module in a previous example generated an error if it was run two times in a row (against a data table that was already mapped). We are going correct that error in our cXML class. Our private GetNewXMLData method is almost identical to that original code. This was done this way to show the relationship of the standard code to the class code.

We can use the XPath property of the Range object to determine if our destination cell (which is set when we instantiate our cXML object) already belongs to a mapping. If it belongs to a mapping, we'll perform a data refresh using the XmlMaps collection; if not, we'll import the data and create a new XML map. We are also going to validate the import using the XlXmlImportResult data type as the return value of our XmlImport call.

The first thing we need to do is return the name of the destination range's map if it has one. Add the following private function to the cXML class:

```
Private Function CurrentMapName() As String
Dim strReturn As String
  On Error GoTo Err_Handle
  If Me.HasMaps Then
    strReturn = m_oRange.XPath.map.Name
  Else
     strReturn = ""
  End If

Exit_Function:
  CurrentMapName = strReturn
  Exit Function
Err_Handle:
'not in a cell in the mapped table - treat as new mapping
  strReturn = ""
  Resume Exit_Function
End Function
```

This code first checks to see if the workbook has any XML maps. If it does, it returns the map name for the class's destination range. If not, it returns an empty string. The error handler is there in case the destination range is set to a location outside an XML-mapped area. It returns an empty string in that case, and treats it like a new mapping.

Now we'll modify the private method, GetNewXMLData, to use CurrentMapName and to give us a return value on our import. And while we're at it, we'll add a result output to GetXMLForExistingMap, and finally, the GetXMLData method will respond to those results with a message to the user. The finished code for all three methods looks like this:

```
Private Function GetNewXMLData() As XlXmlImportResult
Dim sCurrMap As String
Dim result As XlXmlImportResult
'check to see if data range is already bound to a map
  sCurrMap = CurrentMapName
  If sCurrMap = "" Then
    result = ActiveWorkbook.XmlImport(m_sXMLSourceFile, Nothing, ➥
             m_blnOverwrite, m_oRange)
    m_sMapName = ActiveWorkbook.XmlMaps(ActiveWorkbook.XmlMaps.Count).Name
  Else
    m_sMapName = sCurrMap
    ActiveWorkbook.XmlMaps(m_sMapName).DataBinding.Refresh
    result = xlXmlImportSuccess
  End If

  GetNewXMLData = result
End Function


Private Function GetXMLForExistingMap(DoOverwrite As Boolean) As XlXmlImportResult
'calling this function to append data requires ➥
                            setting the XMLSourceFile Property
Dim result As XlXmlImportResult
  result = ActiveWorkbook.XmlMaps(m_sMapName).Import(m_sXMLSourceFile, DoOverwrite)

  GetXMLForExistingMap = result
End Function


Public Function GetXMLData(Optional DoOverwrite As Boolean = True)
Dim result As XlXmlImportResult
  If (m_sMapName = "") Or (Not Me.HasMaps) Then
    result = GetNewXMLData
  Else
  'must set XMLSourceFile Property before appending if necessary
    result = GetXMLForExistingMap(DoOverwrite)
  End If

  Select Case result
  Case xlXmlImportSuccess
    MsgBox "XML data import complete"
  Case xlXmlImportValidationFailed
    MsgBox "Invalid document could not be processed"
  Case xlXmlImportElementsTruncated
    MsgBox "Data too large. Some data was truncated"
  End Select
End Function
```

Let's create some client code to test our cXML class out as we build it.

Add a standard module to the workbook, and declare a module-level variable:

```
Dim oEmpDept As cXML
```

Add a new procedure and name it GetEmpDept. Add the following code:

Note Be sure to change the file path to where you have the XML file stored.

```
Public Sub GetEmpDept()
  Set oEmpDept = New cXML

  oEmpDept.XMLSourceFile = ➥
    "C:\Chapter 3\EmpDept.xml"
  Set oEmpDept.DataRange = Sheets(1).Range("A1")
  oEmpDept.GetXMLData
End Sub
```

Before running the client code, save your work. We are going to import some test data, and then we'll close the workbook without saving to remove the data and XML maps between each test. This is an easy way to reset the project without deleting worksheets and XML maps between tests.

Our data file contains a listing of Adventure Works employees and their department and job information. Since the object is just being instantiated here and its MapName property is empty, the code will fall into the first branch of the If statement and call the GetNewXMLData method.

Run the GetEmpDept procedure. Figure 3-16 shows the last few rows of the imported XML data.

	EmployeeID	FirstName	MiddleName	LastName	JobTitle	Department
282	281	Shu	K	Ito	Sales Representative	Sales
283	282	José	Edvaldo	Saraiva	Sales Representative	Sales
284	283	David	R	Campbell	Sales Representative	Sales
285	284	Amy	E	Alberts	European Sales Manager	Sales
286	285	Jae	B	Pak	Sales Representative	Sales
287	286	Ranjit	R	Varkey Chudukatil	Sales Representative	Sales
288	287	Tete	A	Mensa-Annan	Sales Representative	Sales
289	288	Syed	E	Abbas	Pacific Sales Manager	Sales
290	289	Rachel	B	Valdez	Sales Representative	Sales
291	290	Lynn	N	Tsoflias	Sales Representative	Sales

Figure 3-16. *Last few rows of Adventure Works employee XML file*

Run the GetEmpDept procedure once again. This time, the data is just refreshed. If you need to see the proof, put a breakpoint in the GetEmpDept procedure before you run it the second time. Figure 3-17 shows the code in break mode when being run a second time. Figure 3-18 shows the code falling into the Else statement and calling the RefreshXML method instead when the XML map already exists.

```
Private Function GetNewXMLData () As XlXmlImportResult
Dim sCurrMap As String
Dim result As XlXmlImportResult
'check to see if data range is already bound to a map
  sCurrMap = CurrentMapName
  If sCurrMap = "" Then
    result = ActiveWorkbook.XmlImport(m_sXMLSourceFile, Nothing, _
             m_blnOverwrite, m_oRange)
    m_sMapName = ActiveWorkbook.XmlMaps(ActiveWorkbook.XmlMaps.Count).Name
  Else
    m_sMapName = sCurrMap
    Me.RefreshXML
    result = xlXmlImportSuccess
  End If

  GetNewXMLData = result
End Function
```

Figure 3-17. *First time importing EmpDept.xml*

```
Private Function GetNewXMLData () As XlXmlImportResult
Dim sCurrMap As String
Dim result As XlXmlImportResult
'check to see if data range is already bound to a map
  sCurrMap = CurrentMapName
  If sCurrMap = "" Then
    result = ActiveWorkbook.XmlImport(m_sXMLSourceFile, Nothing, _
             m_blnOverwrite, m_oRange)
    m_sMapName = ActiveWorkbook.XmlMaps(ActiveWorkbook.XmlMaps.Count).Name
  Else
    m_sMapName = sCurrMap
    Me.RefreshXML
    result = xlXmlImportSuccess
  End If

  GetNewXMLData = result
End Function
```

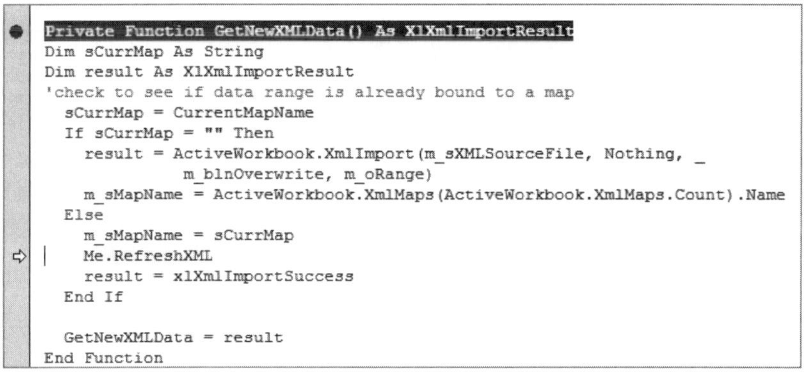

Figure 3-18. *Second time importing EmpDept.xml*

Close the file without saving it, and then reopen it. Let's append some data contained in another XML file that conforms to the same XML schema. In the same standard module, add another method and name it GetAdditionalEmpDeptInfo.

```
Public Sub GetAdditionalEmpDeptInfo()
'appends data from files sent in from field offices.
  If oEmpDept Is Nothing Then
    Set oEmpDept = New cXML
  End If

  oEmpDept.XMLSourceFile = ➡
    "C:\Chapter 3\EmpDeptAdd.xml"
  Set oEmpDept.DataRange = Sheets(1).Range("A1")
  oEmpDept.GetXMLData False
End Sub
```

Save the file after adding this code.

This function might be used to append data from files you receive on a regular basis. Run the GetEmpDept macro once again. Open the Macro dialog and run the GetAdditionalEmpDeptInfo subroutine to append the new data.

Let's take a look at what this code is doing. First we check to see that we have created an oEmpDept object, and if not, create one. Then we set the XMLSourceFile property to the location of the file containing the additional XML data (otherwise, we'll just append the same data to our list). Once that's done, we call the GetXMLData method again, but this time we pass in the Overwrite flag with a value of False to tell the method to append the data.

Remember to not save the file after importing the data so that you can easily reset the file. Figure 3-19 shows the new XML data appended to our existing worksheet.

	EmployeeID	FirstName	MiddleName	LastName	JobTitle	Department
284	283	David	R	Campbell	Sales Representative	Sales
285	284	Amy	E	Alberts	European Sales Manager	Sales
286	285	Jae	B	Pak	Sales Representative	Sales
287	286	Ranjit	R	Varkey Chudukatil	Sales Representative	Sales
288	287	Tete	A	Mensa-Annan	Sales Representative	Sales
289	288	Syed	E	Abbas	Pacific Sales Manager	Sales
290	289	Rachel	B	Valdez	Sales Representative	Sales
291	290	Lynn	N	Tsoflias	Sales Representative	Sales
292	291	Guy	R	Bert	Production Technician - WC60	Production
293	292	Kevin	F	Greene	Marketing Assistant	Marketing
294	293	Roberto		Tambur	Engineering Manager	Engineering
295	294	Rob		Edwards	Senior Tool Designer	Tool Design
296	295	Terry	B	D'Amico	Tool Designer	Tool Design

Figure 3-19. *New rows appended to Adventure Works employee information*

There may be a case where you do not want to change the XMLSourceFile property but still need to append data. Let's create a method in our class that allows us to point to the data file directly.

First reset the file by closing without saving. Then reopen the file.

In the cXML class, add a method called AppendFromFile. We'll pass in the file name as an argument and use the XmlMaps collection's Import method to append the data. The finished method will look like this:

```
Public Function AppendFromFile(FileName As String)
'calling this function to append data will not modify the XMLSourceFile Property
  ActiveWorkbook.XmlMaps(m_sMapName).Import FileName, False
End Function
```

Once again, this line of code is identical to the code in our earlier experiments, with the exception of calling on the class's internal variable for the XML map name. We can quickly test this method. Add a new subroutine to the standard module called AppendEmpDeptInfo. Add the following code:

```
Public Sub AppendEmpDeptInfo()
'sample routine to get additional XML data w/o modifying XMLSourceFile Property
  oEmpDept.AppendFromFile ➡
    "C:\Chapter 3\EmpDeptAdd.xml"
End Sub
```

Run the GetEmpDept macro to get the initial data on the worksheet. Then run the AppendEmpDeptInfo procedure from the Macro dialog box. The result is identical, but the XMLSourceFile property was not modified.

In case the contents of the file you're reading will be updated from time to time by external sources, the XmlMaps collection has the ability to refresh the data source.

Add a new method to the cXML class called RefreshXML. Here is the code for the RefreshXML method:

```
Public Function RefreshXML()
    ActiveWorkbook.XmlMaps(m_sMapName).DataBinding.Refresh
End Function
```

Now that we have our XML data in a worksheet, we can modify it or add records. We need to add one last bit of functionality to our class: the ability to save the data back to XML. Reset your project by closing without saving and reopening it.

Add a new method to the cXML class called SaveToFile. The finished SaveToFile method will look like this:

```
Public Function SaveToFile(Optional SaveAsFileName As String = "FileNotSet")
'if no SaveAsFileName is provided the current XMLSourceFile will be overwritten
Dim ExportMap As XmlMap

  If SaveAsFileName = "FileNotSet" Then
    SaveAsFileName = m_sXMLSourceFile
  End If

  Set ExportMap = ActiveWorkbook.XmlMaps(m_sMapName)
  If ExportMap.IsExportable Then
    ActiveWorkbook.SaveAsXMLData SaveAsFileName, ExportMap
  Else
    MsgBox ExportMap.Name & " cannot be used to export XML"
  End If
End Function
```

We've included an optional argument for the file name of the saved document and passed in a default nonsense value. If we want to save the data back to the file from which it came, we simply call the method with no argument. The code will use whatever file is stored in the XMLSourceFile property. If we want to write the data out to a new file, we pass in the new file name. As in our original example, we're checking to ensure the map is exportable, and then we're calling the ActiveWorkbook object's SaveAsXMLData method.

A Final Test

There is one last test to perform that will show just how using objects can compartmentalize your code and provide easy-to-reuse functionality. In our HR workbook, we will create two objects from the cXML class. Each will store its own mappings and property settings.

The following code shows the contents of the standard module containing the client code for using the cXML class:

```
Dim oEmpDept As cXML
Dim oHREmployees As cXML
'

Sub GetHREmployees()
  Set oHREmployees = New cXML

oHREmployees.XMLSourceFile = ➡
 "C:\Chapter 3\HREmployees.xml"
Set oHREmployees.DataRange = Sheets(1).Range("A1")
oHREmployees.GetXMLData
End Sub

Public Sub GetEmpDept()
  Set oEmpDept = New cXML

  oEmpDept.XMLSourceFile = ➡
    "C:\Chapter 3\EmpDept.xml"
  Set oEmpDept.DataRange = Sheets(2).Range("A1")
  oEmpDept.GetXMLData
End Sub

Public Sub GetAdditionalEmpDeptInfo()
'appends data from files sent in from field offices.
  If oEmpDept Is Nothing Then
    Set oEmpDept = New cXML
  End If

oEmpDept.XMLSourceFile = ➡
    "C:\Chapter 3\EmpDeptAdd.xml"
Set oEmpDept.DataRange = Sheets(2).Range("A1")
oEmpDept.GetXMLData False
End Sub

Public Sub AppendEmpDeptInfo()
'sample routine to get additional XML data w/o modifying XMLSourceFile Property
  oEmpDept.AppendFromFile _
    "C:\Chapter 3\EmpDeptAdd.xml"
End Sub

Public Sub RefreshEmps()
 oEmpDept.RefreshXML
End Sub

Public Sub RefreshHR()
  oHREmployees.RefreshXML
End Sub
```

```
Public Sub SaveEmps()
  oEmpDept.SaveToFile
End Sub

Public Sub SaveEmpsNewFile()
  oEmpDept.SaveToFile ➥
          "C:\Chapter 3\EmpDeptAddNEW.xml"
End Sub

Sub Cleanup()
  Set oEmpDept = Nothing
  Set oHREmployees = Nothing
End Sub
```

To test the code, save the workbook, and then do the following:

1. With Sheet1 active, run the GetEmpDept macro (shows Adventure Works employee department information).

2. With Sheet 2 active, run the GetHREmployees macro (shows employee personal information).

3. With any sheet active, run the GetAdditionalEmpDeptInfo or AppendEmpDeptInfo macro to append new data to the end of the data on Sheet1. The oEmpDept variable knows where the data lives in the workbook due to the internal XML mapping.

4. Open the HREmployees.xml file in any text editor and modify a data element, and then save the file.

5. Run the RefreshHR macro.

6. When the code has finished running, run the Cleanup macro to destroy both objects.

As you can see, we have simultaneous objects of the same type performing similar activities, but each monitoring and controlling its own set of values.

Adding a Custom Ribbon to Your Workbook

Excel 2007 has a whole new XML file format that adds a lot of flexibility to your projects. One neat thing you can do is add a custom ribbon to call your code and to hide the standard Excel ribbons from your users. Before we delve into the mechanism, behind this technique a bit of background on the new file format is in order.

Inside the Excel 2007 XML File Format

Excel 2007 builds on its history of XML support with a new file format called the Office Open XML format. This new format improves file and data management, data recovery, and interoperability. Any application that supports XML can access and work with information in an Excel 2007 workbook. This means it is now possible to work with your Excel data in systems outside of Microsoft Office products as long as they provide XML support.

Additionally, security concerns are reduced, since you now have your Excel data in what is essentially a text file. This allows data to pass through firewalls without difficulty.

The new XML file format is based on the compressed ZIP file format specification. Each ZIP container is made up of numerous XML files containing what Microsoft refers to as "parts." While most parts are XML files describing workbook data, metadata, and document information, non-XML files like binary files representing images or OLE objects may also be included in the ZIP file. There are also relationship parts that describe the relationships between parts, thus providing the structure for the workbook file. The parts are the content of the workbook and the relationships detail how the content parts fit together.

Figure 3-20 shows the Open XML format's file container.

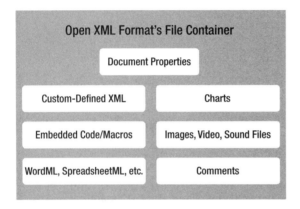

Figure 3-20. *Open XML format's file container*

Viewing the XML

To see what's inside an Excel document, you must change the extension to *.zip.

In the Downloads section for this book on the Apress web site, find the file Chapter 3\ NwindEmps.xlsx, rename it NwindEmps.zip, and copy it to a folder on your PC called unzippedExcelfiles (you'll have to create the folder first). This file contains Northwind employee information that was typed or pasted in (not imported).

Even though we could open the files directly from the ZIP file, we will create a folder into which we'll extract the contents of the ZIP file. Be sure keep "Use folder names" checked in the options list. Figure 3-21 shows the Extract function in WinZip.

You can see the file structure associated with Office documents clearly once the files are extracted (see Figure 3-22). I've created a folder named unzippedExcelfiles to store them in.

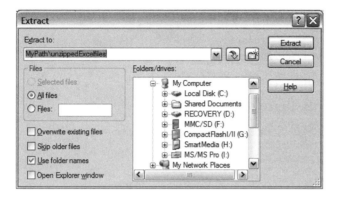

Figure 3-21. *Check "Use folder names" in the Extract dialog.*

Figure 3-22. *Excel's XML file structure*

The _rels Folder

The _rels folder is the first place you should look to see what your Excel file is made of. The _rels folder contains a file named .rels. This file contains the top-level relationships. In your file, they should look like Figure 3-23.

```
<?xml version="1.0" encoding="UTF-8" standalone="yes" ?>
- <Relationships xmlns="http://schemas.openxmlformats.org/package/2006/relationships">
    <Relationship Id="rId3" Type="http://schemas.openxmlformats.org/officeDocument/2006/relationships/extended-properties"
      Target="docProps/app.xml" />
    <Relationship Id="rId2" Type="http://schemas.openxmlformats.org/package/2006/relationships/metadata/core-properties"
      Target="docProps/core.xml" />
    <Relationship Id="rId1" Type="http://schemas.openxmlformats.org/officeDocument/2006/relationships/officeDocument"
      Target="xl/workbook.xml" />
  </Relationships>
```

Figure 3-23. *.rels file contents*

This file contains three relationship items. Table 3-2 describes the relationship attributes.

Table 3-2. *Relationship Attributes*

Attribute	Description
Id	Any string (must be unique in the .rels file)
Type	The type of the relationship
Target	The folder and file that contain the target of the relationship (this is also a part)

Following is a list of the many types of relationships that can be found in an Office document:

- http://schemas.microsoft.com/office/2006/relationships/officeDocument
- http://schemas.microsoft.com/office/2006/relationships/vbaProject
- http://schemas.microsoft.com/office/2006/relationships/userXmlData
- http://schemas.microsoft.com/office/2006/relationships/styleSheet
- http://schemas.microsoft.com/office/2006/relationships/hyperlink
- http://schemas.microsoft.com/office/2006/relationships/comments
- http://schemas.microsoft.com/office/2006/relationships/oleObject
- http://schemas.microsoft.com/office/2006/relationships/e1Object
- http://schemas.microsoft.com/office/2006/relationships/e2Object
- http://schemas.microsoft.com/office/2006/relationships/image
- http://schemas.microsoft.com/office/2006/relationships/sound
- http://schemas.microsoft.com/office/2006/relationships/movie
- http://schemas.microsoft.com/office/2006/relationships/slide
- http://schemas.microsoft.com/office/2006/relationships/layout
- http://schemas.microsoft.com/office/2006/relationships/notesslide
- http://schemas.microsoft.com/office/2006/relationships/slidemaster
- http://schemas.microsoft.com/office/2006/relationships/glossaryDoc
- http://schemas.microsoft.com/office/2006/relationships/chart
- http://schemas.microsoft.com/office/2006/relationships/activeXControl
- http://schemas.microsoft.com/office/2006/relationships/cfChunk
- http://schemas.microsoft.com/office/2006/relationships/dataStoreItem
- http://schemas.microsoft.com/office/2005/relationships/diagram
- http://schemas.microsoft.com/office/2006/relationships/embeddedFont
- http://schemas.microsoft.com/office/2006/relationships/embeddedMetroObject
- http://schemas.microsoft.com/office/2005/relationships/diagramData
- http://schemas.microsoft.com/office/2005/relationships/diagramStyle
- http://schemas.microsoft.com/office/2005/relationships/diagramColorTrans
- http://schemas.microsoft.com/office/2005/relationships/diagramDefinition

- http://schemas.microsoft.com/package/2005/02/md/core-properties

- http://schemas.microsoft.com/office/2006/relationships/docPropsApp

- http://schemas.microsoft.com/office/2006/relationships/docPropsCustom

- http://schemas.microsoft.com/office/2006/relationships/glossaryDoc

- http://schemas.microsoft.com/ office/2006/relationships/documentThumbnail

The relationship in our XML file with an ID attribute of rId1 and a Type of http://
schemas.microsoft.com/office/2006/relationships/officeDocument is the main document
part. Since we're working in Excel, this translates to an Excel workbook (as defined by the target of this relationship item, xl/workbook.xml). If we were working with PowerPoint, this
would be a presentation, and if we were working in Word, it would be a document.

The Application Folder

The next folder to explore is the application folder, whose name will reflect the program used
to create the file. Ours is named xl (for Excel), as displayed in Figure 3-24. The application
folder contains application-specific document files. Some of these files are found in their own
folder, but the root contains the workbook part and the sharedStrings (data) part.

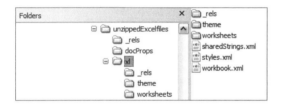

Figure 3-24. *xl folder contents*

The [Content_Types].xml File

Another file of interest is the [Content_Types].xml file found in the root folder we created
(unzippedExcelfiles). It lists the content types for the other parts included in the Excel file
package. *Content types* are the types of parts that can be included in a package. Following is
a list of the content types that can be found in an Office document:

- application/vnd.ms-excel.12application/x-font

- application/vnd.ms-excel.addin.12application/xml

- application/vnd.ms-excel.template.12audio/mp3

- application/vnd.ms-excel.binary.12audio/aiff

- application/vnd.ms-excel.macroEnabled.12audio/basic

- application/vnd.ms-excel.macroEnabledTemplate.12audio/midi

- application/vnd.ms-office.activeX+xmlaudio/x-ms-wax

- application/vnd.ms-office.chartaudio/x-ms-wma
- application/vnd.ms-office.vbaProjectimage/bmp
- application/vnd.ms.powerpoint.template.macroEnabled.12application/x-font
- application/vnd.ms-powerpoint.image/gif
- application/vnd.ms-powerpoint.macroEnabled.12image/jpeg
- application/vnd.ms-powerpoint.main.12+xmlimage/png
- application/vnd.ms-powerpoint.presentation.12image/tiff
- application/vnd.ms-powerpoint.template.12video/avi
- application/vnd.ms-powerpoint.show.12image/xbm
- application/vnd.ms-powerpoint.show.macroEnabled.12image/x-icon
- application/vnd.ms-word.document.12video/mpeg
- application/vnd.ms-word.document.macroEnabled.12video/mpg
- application/vnd.ms-word.document.macroEnabled.main+xmlvideo/x-ivf
- application/vnd.ms-word.document.main+xmlvideo/x-ms-asf
- application/vnd.ms-word.template.12
- application/vnd.ms-word.template.macroEnabled.12
- application/vnd.ms-word.template.macroEnabled.main+xml
- application/vnd.ms-word.fontTable+xmlvideo/x-ms-asf-plugin
- application/vnd.ms-word.listDefs+xmlvideo/x-ms-wm
- application/vnd.ms-word.settings+xmlvideo/x-ms-wmv
- application/vnd.ms-word.styles+xmlvideo/x-ms-wmx
- application/vnd.ms-word.subDoc+xmlvideo/x-ms-wvx
- application/vnd.ms-word.template.main+xml
- application/vnd.ms-metro.core-properties+xmlaudio/mpegurl
- application/vnd.ms-metro.relationships+xmlaudio/wav

The docProps Folder

This folder contains files listing document properties, similar to what you see when you click the Office button and select Prepare ➤ Properties. The docProps folder contains at a minimum a file named app.xml and a file named core.xml. These files contain meta-information about your Excel file, such as the creator name, and modified and creation dates.

Relationships

An Excel 2007 document is made of parts. These parts are "joined" together via relationships as defined in the various XML files we've seen. The connection between a data table and the worksheet it resides in is defined by a relationship.

Our root folder contains a _rels folder that contains a .rels file. This file defines relationships between our document properties files, app.xml and core.xml, and the xl/workbook.xml file. The xl folder itself contains a _rels folder that has a relationship file, workbook.xml.rels. This file defines the relationships of the workbook, data, and formatting parts. Figure 3-25 shows an example of the workbook.xml.rels file.

```xml
<?xml version="1.0" encoding="UTF-8" standalone="yes" ?>
<Relationships xmlns="http://schemas.openxmlformats.org/package/2006/relationships">
    <Relationship Id="rId3" Type="http://schemas.openxmlformats.org/officeDocument/2006/relationships/worksheet"
        Target="worksheets/sheet3.xml" />
    <Relationship Id="rId2" Type="http://schemas.openxmlformats.org/officeDocument/2006/relationships/worksheet"
        Target="worksheets/sheet2.xml" />
    <Relationship Id="rId1" Type="http://schemas.openxmlformats.org/officeDocument/2006/relationships/worksheet"
        Target="worksheets/sheet1.xml" />
    <Relationship Id="rId6" Type="http://schemas.openxmlformats.org/officeDocument/2006/relationships/sharedStrings"
        Target="sharedStrings.xml" />
    <Relationship Id="rId5" Type="http://schemas.openxmlformats.org/officeDocument/2006/relationships/styles"
        Target="styles.xml" />
    <Relationship Id="rId4" Type="http://schemas.openxmlformats.org/officeDocument/2006/relationships/theme"
        Target="theme/theme1.xml" />
</Relationships>
```

Figure 3-25. *Contents of the workbook.xml.rels file*

From the Downloads section of this book's page on the Apress web site, copy the file named NwindEmps01.xlsx to a local folder and rename it to NwindEmps.zip. This file contains the same Northwind employee information as NwindEmps.xlsx, but this data was imported from the Northwind Access database. Note the additional files reflecting the imported data when we open it. I've opened the file using WinZip, as shown in Figure 3-26.

Before we look at these new files, let's check the [Content_Types].xml file (shown in Figure 3-27). Remember that this shows us all the various types of content we'll find in our Excel project.

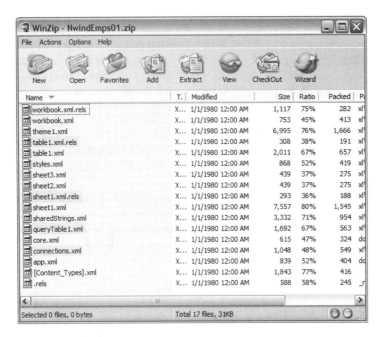

Figure 3-26. *Additional XML files with imported data highlighted*

```
<?xml version="1.0" encoding="UTF-8" standalone="yes" ?>
- <Types xmlns="http://schemas.openxmlformats.org/package/2006/content-types">
    <Override PartName="/xl/queryTables/queryTable1.xml" ContentType="application/vnd.openxmlformats-
        officedocument.spreadsheetml.queryTable+xml" />
    <Override PartName="/xl/theme/theme1.xml" ContentType="application/vnd.openxmlformats-officedocument.theme+xml" />
    <Override PartName="/xl/styles.xml" ContentType="application/vnd.openxmlformats-
        officedocument.spreadsheetml.styles+xml" />
    <Override PartName="/xl/tables/table1.xml" ContentType="application/vnd.openxmlformats-
        officedocument.spreadsheetml.table+xml" />
    <Default Extension="rels" ContentType="application/vnd.openxmlformats-package.relationships+xml" />
    <Default Extension="xml" ContentType="application/xml" />
    <Override PartName="/xl/workbook.xml" ContentType="application/vnd.openxmlformats-
        officedocument.spreadsheetml.sheet.main+xml" />
    <Override PartName="/docProps/app.xml" ContentType="application/vnd.openxmlformats-officedocument.extended-
        properties+xml" />
    <Override PartName="/xl/worksheets/sheet2.xml" ContentType="application/vnd.openxmlformats-
        officedocument.spreadsheetml.worksheet+xml" />
    <Override PartName="/xl/worksheets/sheet3.xml" ContentType="application/vnd.openxmlformats-
        officedocument.spreadsheetml.worksheet+xml" />
    <Override PartName="/xl/connections.xml" ContentType="application/vnd.openxmlformats-
        officedocument.spreadsheetml.connections+xml" />
    <Override PartName="/xl/worksheets/sheet1.xml" ContentType="application/vnd.openxmlformats-
        officedocument.spreadsheetml.worksheet+xml" />
    <Override PartName="/xl/sharedStrings.xml" ContentType="application/vnd.openxmlformats-
        officedocument.spreadsheetml.sharedStrings+xml" />
    <Override PartName="/docProps/core.xml" ContentType="application/vnd.openxmlformats-package.core-properties+xml" />
</Types>
```

Figure 3-27. *New parts in [Content_Types].xml (other parts omitted for clarity)*

New parts are listed for the query table, table, and connections that we know from the previous chapter are associated with a workbook containing imported data. The contents of the \xl\connections.xml file in Figure 3-28 should look very familiar to you by now.

```
<?xml version="1.0" encoding="UTF-8" standalone="yes" ?>
- <connections xmlns="http://schemas.openxmlformats.org/spreadsheetml/2006/main">
- <connection id="1" sourceFile="C:\projects\Excel2007Book\Files\Northwind 2007.accdb" keepAlive="1" name="Northwind 2007"
    type="5" refreshedVersion="3" background="1" saveData="1">
    <dbPr connection="Provider=Microsoft.ACE.OLEDB.12.0;User ID=Admin;Data
    Source=C:\projects\Excel2007Book\Files\Northwind 2007.accdb;Mode=Share Deny Write;Extended Properties="";Jet
    OLEDB:System database="";Jet OLEDB:Registry Path="";Jet OLEDB:Engine Type=6;Jet OLEDB:Database Locking
    Mode=0;Jet OLEDB:Global Partial Bulk Ops=2;Jet OLEDB:Global Bulk Transactions=1;Jet OLEDB:New Database
    Password="";Jet OLEDB:Create System Database=False;Jet OLEDB:Encrypt Database=False;Jet OLEDB:Don't Copy
    Locale on Compact=False;Jet OLEDB:Compact Without Replica Repair=False;Jet OLEDB:SFP=False;Jet OLEDB:Support
    Complex Data=False" command="Employees Extended" commandType="3" />
  </connection>
</connections>
```

Figure 3-28. *Connections.xml contents*

It's the same connect string we used in the code we generated and that Excel generated for us with the Macro Recorder. The id attribute tells us this is connection 1 (in this case, the only connection in the file). The sourceFile attribute tells us where the data came from. The last two attributes of the connection node refer to the ADO Command object and the CommandType.

The xl\queryTables\queryTable1.xml file displayed in Figure 3-29 shows the relationship between the connection and the query table object. The queryTable node has a connectionId attribute of 1, referring to the OLE DB connection we just looked at. Then there are some formatting attributes, followed by a list of field names with queryTableField IDs and tableColumnIds linking the query table to an Excel table (or range).

```
<?xml version="1.0" encoding="UTF-8" standalone="yes" ?>
- <queryTable xmlns="http://schemas.openxmlformats.org/spreadsheetml/2006/main" name="Northwind 2007.accdb"
    connectionId="1" autoFormatId="16" applyNumberFormats="0" applyBorderFormats="0" applyFontFormats="0" applyPatternFormats="0"
    applyAlignmentFormats="0" applyWidthHeightFormats="0">
  - <queryTableRefresh nextId="21">
    - <queryTableFields count="20">
      <queryTableField id="1" name="File As" tableColumnId="1" />
      <queryTableField id="2" name="Employee Name" tableColumnId="2" />
      <queryTableField id="3" name="ID" tableColumnId="3" />
      <queryTableField id="4" name="Company" tableColumnId="4" />
      <queryTableField id="5" name="Last Name" tableColumnId="5" />
      <queryTableField id="6" name="First Name" tableColumnId="6" />
      <queryTableField id="7" name="E-mail Address" tableColumnId="7" />
      <queryTableField id="8" name="Job Title" tableColumnId="8" />
      <queryTableField id="9" name="Business Phone" tableColumnId="9" />
      <queryTableField id="10" name="Home Phone" tableColumnId="10" />
      <queryTableField id="11" name="Mobile Phone" tableColumnId="11" />
      <queryTableField id="12" name="Fax Number" tableColumnId="12" />
      <queryTableField id="13" name="Address" tableColumnId="13" />
      <queryTableField id="14" name="City" tableColumnId="14" />
      <queryTableField id="15" name="State/Province" tableColumnId="15" />
      <queryTableField id="16" name="ZIP/Postal Code" tableColumnId="16" />
      <queryTableField id="17" name="Country/Region" tableColumnId="17" />
      <queryTableField id="18" name="Web Page" tableColumnId="18" />
      <queryTableField id="19" name="Notes" tableColumnId="19" />
      <queryTableField id="20" name="Attachments" tableColumnId="20" />
    </queryTableFields>
  </queryTableRefresh>
</queryTable>
```

Figure 3-29. *queryTable1.xml contents*

We find that there's a new folder in our structure called tables. In this folder is a file named Table1.xml (shown in Figure 3-30). Table1.xml looks very similar to queryTables1.xml. It has the same field mapping information, but also contains information about the range name (Table_Northwind_2007.accdb), cell locations for the data, what data is autofiltered, and whether a totals row is shown.

```
<?xml version="1.0" encoding="UTF-8" standalone="yes" ?>
- <table xmlns="http://schemas.openxmlformats.org/spreadsheetml/2006/main" id="1" name="Table_Northwind_2007.accdb"
    displayName="Table_Northwind_2007.accdb" ref="A1:T10" tableType="queryTable" totalsRowShown="0">
    <autoFilter ref="A1:T10" />
  - <tableColumns count="20">
      <tableColumn id="1" uniqueName="1" name="File As" queryTableFieldId="1" />
      <tableColumn id="2" uniqueName="2" name="Employee Name" queryTableFieldId="2" />
      <tableColumn id="3" uniqueName="3" name="ID" queryTableFieldId="3" />
      <tableColumn id="4" uniqueName="4" name="Company" queryTableFieldId="4" />
      <tableColumn id="5" uniqueName="5" name="Last Name" queryTableFieldId="5" />
      <tableColumn id="6" uniqueName="6" name="First Name" queryTableFieldId="6" />
      <tableColumn id="7" uniqueName="7" name="E-mail Address" queryTableFieldId="7" />
      <tableColumn id="8" uniqueName="8" name="Job Title" queryTableFieldId="8" />
      <tableColumn id="9" uniqueName="9" name="Business Phone" queryTableFieldId="9" />
      <tableColumn id="10" uniqueName="10" name="Home Phone" queryTableFieldId="10" />
      <tableColumn id="11" uniqueName="11" name="Mobile Phone" queryTableFieldId="11" />
      <tableColumn id="12" uniqueName="12" name="Fax Number" queryTableFieldId="12" />
      <tableColumn id="13" uniqueName="13" name="Address" queryTableFieldId="13" />
      <tableColumn id="14" uniqueName="14" name="City" queryTableFieldId="14" />
      <tableColumn id="15" uniqueName="15" name="State/Province" queryTableFieldId="15" />
      <tableColumn id="16" uniqueName="16" name="ZIP/Postal Code" queryTableFieldId="16" />
      <tableColumn id="17" uniqueName="17" name="Country/Region" queryTableFieldId="17" />
      <tableColumn id="18" uniqueName="18" name="Web Page" queryTableFieldId="18" />
      <tableColumn id="19" uniqueName="19" name="Notes" queryTableFieldId="19" />
      <tableColumn id="20" uniqueName="20" name="Attachments" queryTableFieldId="20" />
    </tableColumns>
    <tableStyleInfo name="TableStyleMedium9" showFirstColumn="0" showLastColumn="0" showRowStripes="1" showColumnStripes="0" />
  </table>
```

Figure 3-30. *Table1.xml contents*

There is also table style information in the last node of the file. So how are the queryTable and Table1.xml files associated? In the tables folder is a subfolder named _rels. This folder contains a file named table1.xml.rels (the full path to the file is \xl\table_res.\table1.xml.rels). The contents of table1.xml.rels is shown in Figure 3-31.

```
<?xml version="1.0" encoding="UTF-8" standalone="yes" ?>
- <Relationships xmlns="http://schemas.openxmlformats.org/package/2006/relationships">
    <Relationship Id="rId1" Type="http://schemas.openxmlformats.org/officeDocument/2006/relationships/queryTable"
      Target="../queryTables/queryTable1.xml" />
  </Relationships>
```

Figure 3-31. *table1.xml.rels contents*

As you can see, the tables folder's Relationship element is referring to the relationships/queryTable content item in its Type attribute with a target of the queryTable1.xml file.

Adding a Ribbon to Run Your Custom Macros

So that was quite a bit to take in just to add a ribbon to a project, right? It's really just important background information that will be helpful as you do more and more work with Excel (or other Office products).

Next, let's add a ribbon to our XML data project. We're going to add a ribbon that contains one tab with four groups: one for adding new data, one for appending data, one for refreshing data, and one for saving data.

To do so, we will create a ribbon extensibility customization file with one tab, four groups, and seven buttons. We'll specify a callback event in the buttons to call each macro we've created in the document. Then we will modify the contents of the macro-enabled document container file to point to the ribbon extensibility customization file.

1. Save your XML_Class.xlsm file as XML_Class_Ribbon.xlsm.

2. Open the VBE.

3. In the VBE, double-click ThisWorkbook to open the code window.

4. Type the following VBA subroutines, and then close the VBE:

```
Sub GetEmpDataBtn(ByVal ControlID As IRibbonControl)
    Call GetEmpDept
End Sub

Sub AppendEmpDataBtn(ByVal ControlID As IRibbonControl)
    Call AppendEmpDeptInfo
End Sub

Sub GetHRDataBtn(ByVal ControlID As IRibbonControl)
    Call GetHREmployees
End Sub

Sub RefreshEmpDataBtn(ByVal ControlID As IRibbonControl)
    Call RefreshEmps
End Sub

Sub RefreshHRDataBtn(ByVal ControlID As IRibbonControl)
    Call RefreshHR
End Sub

Sub SaveEmpBtn(ByVal ControlID As IRibbonControl)
    Call SaveEmps
End Sub

Sub SaveEmpNewFileBtn(ByVal ControlID As IRibbonControl)
    Call SaveEmpsNewFile
End Sub
```

These procedures will be mapped to the controls on the custom ribbon via an XML configuration file.

Save the workbook and close it.

Creating the XML File That Contains the Markup to Modify the UI

1. Create a folder called customUI.

2. Open a new file in the text editor of your choice, and save it as customUI.xml in the customUI folder.

3. Add the following code to the customUI.xml file:

```xml
<customUI xmlns="http://schemas.microsoft.com/office/2006/01/customui">
    <ribbon startFromScratch="true">
        <tabs>
            <tab id="DataFunctions" label="XML Data Functions">
                <group id="NewDataControls" label="New Data">
                    <button id="Button1" size="large" label="Get Emps Dept" ➥
                                    onAction="ThisWorkbook.GetEmpDataBtn" />
                    <button id="Button2" size="large" label="Get HR Info" ➥
                                    onAction="ThisWorkbook.GetHRDataBtn" />
                </group>

                <group id="AppendDataControls" label="Append Data">
                    <button id="Button3" size="large" label="Append Emps Dept" ➥
                                    onAction="ThisWorkbook.AppendEmpDataBtn" />
                </group>

                <group id="RefreshDataControls" label="Refresh Data">
                    <button id="Button4" size="large" label="Refresh Emp Dept" ➥
                                    onAction="ThisWorkbook.RefreshEmpDataBtn" />
                    <button id="Button5" size="large" label="Refresh HR Info" ➥
                                    onAction="ThisWorkbook.RefreshHRDataBtn" />
                </group>

                <group id="SaveDataControls" label="Save Data">
                    <button id="Button6" size="large" label="Save Emp Dept" ➥
                                    onAction="ThisWorkbook.SaveEmpBtn" />
                    <button id="Button7" size="large" label="Save Emp Dept As" ➥
                                    onAction="ThisWorkbook.SaveEmpNewFileBtn" />
                </group>

            </tab>
        </tabs>
    </ribbon>
</customUI>
```

4. Save the file.

This XML defines the XML Data Functions tab and its four groups. Within each group, note the reference to each macro we just created in the ThisWorkbook module in our Excel project.

Next, we will modify some of the files contained in the macro-enabled Excel file that we just created.

1. Change the extension of XML_Class_Ribbon.xlsm to .zip, and double-click the file to open it.

2. Add the customization file to the ZIP container by dragging the customUI folder from its location to the ZIP file.

3. Extract the .rels file to a local folder. A _rels folder containing the .rels file is copied to your folder. (If only the file appears, use your ZIP tool's extract function rather than dragging the file from the ZIP window.)

4. Open the .rels file and add the following line between the last Relationship tag and the Relationships tag, as shown in Listing 3-1. This creates a relationship between the workbook file and the customization file.

Listing 3-1. *Adding the CustomUI Relationship to the .rels. File*

```
<Relationships ➥
  xmlns="http://schemas.openxmlformats.org/package/2006/relationships">
    <Relationship Id="rId3" Type="http://schemas.openxmlformats.org/ ➥
      officeDocument/2006/relationships/extended-properties" ➥
      Target="docProps/app.xml" />
    <Relationship Id="rId2" Type="http://schemas.openxmlformats.org ➥
      /package/2006/relationships/metadata/core-properties" ➥
      Target="docProps/core.xml" />
    <Relationship Id="rId1" Type="http://schemas.openxmlformats.org ➥
      /officeDocument/2006/relationships/officeDocument" ➥
      Target="xl/workbook.xml" />
    <Relationship Id="someID" Type="http://schemas.microsoft.com/office/ ➥
      2006/relationships/ui/extensibility" Target="customUI/customUI.xml" />
</Relationships>
```

5. Close and save the file.

6. Add the _rels folder back to the container file by dragging it from its location, over-writing the existing file.

7. Rename the workbook file back to its original name.

8. Open the workbook and notice that the Ribbon UI now displays your XML data functions.

9. Click the buttons to check that the functionality is there and working (shown in Figure 3-32).

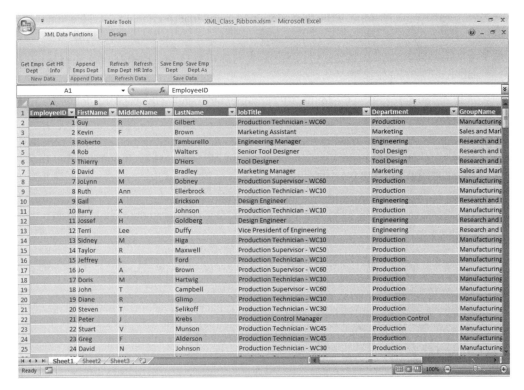

Figure 3-32. *A custom ribbon added using an XML configuration file*

Summary

In this chapter, we explored the various methods of bringing XML data in and out of Excel. We also took an excursion into the new Office Open XML file format. While it looks complicated at first glance, remember that it is all about relationships between parts. Once that's understood, you'll be able to explore its many possibilities.

Finally, we added a custom user interface by modifying the underlying ZIP file format in Excel 2007. By adding a `customUI` XML file describing the ribbon we wanted to add, and by adding a relationship reference to one of Excel's built-in configuration files, we were able to very simply add a custom ribbon.

Very powerful stuff indeed.

CHAPTER 4

■■■

UserForms

As skilled as we developers are at laying out a UI, when working with spreadsheets we find our options may be a bit limited. Depending on what data is being entered, you may find your users scrolling off the screen to the right or bottom of an Excel worksheet window.

UserForms in Excel 2007 allow you to create easy-to-use data entry screens for your users. They can be used to display summary data or data from any data source. They provide us with the tools we need to create "wizard" applications or simple data entry forms.

Creating a Simple Data Entry Form

Let's create a form for quick data entry for a call center doing a one-minute customer contact. The user's task is to call the customer and find out if they've heard of "the Widget" and whether they're interested in finding out more about the product. If the customer is interested, the user will mark that on the form as well so sales can follow up.

■**Note** The example files and source code for this book are available to readers at www.apress.com in the Downloads section of this book's home page.

Designing the Form

From the sample files for this book, open the workbook named UserForm.xlsm. This file contains the Customer Survey database shown in Figure 4-1. Our custom form will collect and save its data to this table.

	A	B	C	D	E	F
1	ID	State	PhoneNum	HeardOfProduct	WantsProduct	FollowupYN
2	100	NJ	201-555-5555	TRUE	FALSE	TRUE
3	101	NY	212-555-6666	FALSE	TRUE	FALSE
4	102	CT	203-456-7890	TRUE	TRUE	TRUE

Figure 4-1. *The Customer Survey database*

Open the VBE, and add a UserForm to the project. You can do this by choosing Insert ➤ UserForm, or you can right-click in the Project Explorer window and choose Insert ➤ UserForm, as shown in Figure 4-2.

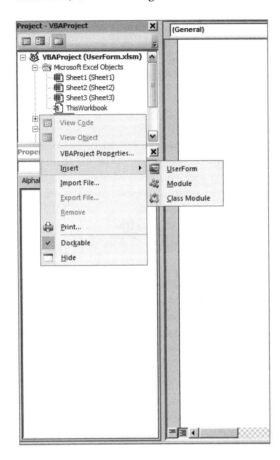

Figure 4-2. *Adding a UserForm to the project*

A new empty UserForm named UserForm1 is added to the project, as shown in Figure 4-3.

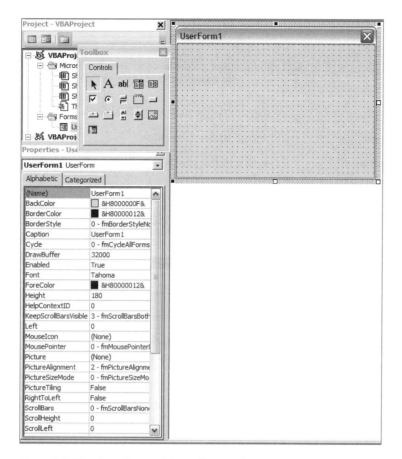

Figure 4-3. *New UserForm with Toolbox and Property Sheet displayed*

Along with the UserForm, you'll see the Toolbox window, which contains a palette of controls to use, and the UserForm Property Sheet, where you can rename your form and modify various settings.

The Toolbox controls are described in Table 4-1.

UserForm Toolbox Controls

Table 4-1. *UserForm Toolbox Objects*

Toolbox Button	Command	Description
	Select Objects	Resizes or moves a control on a form.
	Label	Holds text that is not editable except through code.
	TextBox	Holds text that users can enter or modify.

Continued

Table 4-1. *Continued*

Toolbox Button	Command	Description
	ComboBox	A combination of a list box and a text box. Users can choose an item from a list or enter a value in the text box.
	ListBox	Displays a list of items from which users can choose.
	CheckBox	Indicates a true or false value.
	OptionButton	Presents multiple choices, of which only one can be selected.
	ToggleButton	A button that toggles off and on.
	Frame	A grouping for controls such as option buttons or check boxes. Users can only select one of a group of controls placed inside a Frame control.
	CommandButton	A button the user can click to perform an action.
	TabStrip	Multiple pages in the same form area.
	MultiPage	Multiple screens of information.
	ScrollBar	Provides quick navigation through a long list of items. It is also useful for indicating the current position on a scale, or as an input device or indicator of speed or quantity.
	SpinButton	Increments or decrements a numeric value.
	Image	Presents an image from a bitmap, icon, or metafile.
	RefEdit	Simulates the behavior of the reference edit boxes such as the Range selector in the Print Area section of the Page Setup dialog box.

On UserForm1, add the controls and enter the property settings listed in Table 4-2.

Table 4-2. *UserForm1 Settings and Controls*

Item/Property	Value
UserForm	—
Caption:	Customer Survey Form
Label	—
Caption:	ID
Label	—
Name:	lblID
Caption:	Label1
Label	—
Caption:	State

Item/Property	Value
TextBox	—
Name:	txtState
Label	—
Caption:	Phone Number
TextBox	—
Name:	txtPhone
CheckBox	—
Name:	chkHeard
Caption:	Customer Has Heard of Product
CheckBox	—
Name:	chkInterested
Caption:	Customer Is Interested in Product
CheckBox	—
Name:	chkFollowup
Caption:	Followup Required
CommandButton	—
Name:	cmdSave
Cancel:	False
Caption:	Save
Default:	True
CommandButton	—
Name:	cmdNew
Cancel:	False
Caption:	New
Default:	False
CommandButton	—
Name:	cmdCancel
Cancel:	True
Caption:	Cancel
Default:	False

The finished form should look like Figure 4-4.

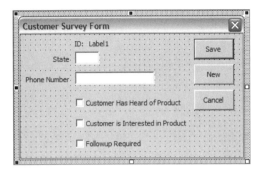

Figure 4-4. *UserForm with controls placed*

As you can see, we're designing a very simple data collection tool. We're going to write a record to the database that is stored on Sheet1 in the UserForm workbook, and we want to do some validation of the data before we save.

Before we begin, we need to think about a couple of functions we might need and how to approach our code design. First, our form needs to know which worksheet to save the data to (in this case, Sheet1 contains our database). It also needs to know the next available ID number and the location of the next available row to place the data when we save the data.

A function that can tell us where the next available row in a worksheet is might be useful in another project as well. Remember the cExcelUtils class we started in Chapter 2? Let's put our function in that class and export it so we can reuse it in other projects.

Open the last project you worked on in Chapter 2, DataAccessSample06.xlsm, and then open the VBE. In the Project Explorer, right-click the cExcelUtils class icon and choose Export File from the shortcut menu, as shown in Figure 4-5.

Figure 4-5. *Exporting a module*

Choose your location and save the *.cls file. Once that's done, you can close the DataAccessSample06.xlsm workbook. Right-click anywhere in the Project Explorer in the UserForm.xlsm project, and choose Import File, as shown in Figure 4-6. Navigate to where you just saved the cExcelUtils.cls file and choose the Open command.

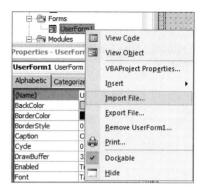

Figure 4-6. *Importing a module*

The cExcelUtils class is now a part of your project. Open the cExcelUtils class in the VBE and add the following method. The FindEmptyRow function returns a Long Integer containing the row number of the next available row on a worksheet.

```
Function FindEmptyRow(ws As Worksheet) As Long
Dim lngReturn As Long

  lngReturn = ws.Cells(Rows.Count, 1).End(xlUp).Offset(1, 0).Row
  FindEmptyRow = lngReturn
End Function
```

This simple bit of code uses the Range object's End property to find the last cell in the region and offsets it by 1. We're passing in a worksheet as an argument so the function will return the next open row in the passed worksheet.

The Working Class

Next we're going to build a class to hold the values for each customer survey. This class will also store the location of the database worksheet and it will perform a data save to the database.

In the VBE, add a new class module and name it cCustSurvey. Add the following module-level variables to hold the various properties:

```
Private m_lngID As Long
Private m_strState As String
Private m_strPhone As String
Private m_blnHeardOfProduct As Boolean
Private m_blnWantsProduct As Boolean
Private m_blnFollowup As Boolean
Private m_xlWksht As Worksheet
Private m_oXL As cExcelUtils
```

The first six items are simply the data we'll enter on our UserForm plus the ID field that we'll generate from the database worksheet. The m_xlWksht variable will hold the location of the database worksheet, which we'll need for a couple of things. The m_oXL variable is how we'll determine where to put any new data.

Let's add the data properties first, and then we'll get into adding some functionality to the class. Add the following properties to the cCustSurvey class module:

```
Property Get ID() As Long
  ID = m_lngID
End Property

Property Get State() As String
  State = m_strState
End Property

Property Let State(newState As String)
  m_strState = newState
End Property

Property Get PhoneNumber() As String
  PhoneNumber = m_strPhone
End Property

Property Let PhoneNumber(newPhoneNumber As String)
  m_strPhone = newPhoneNumber
End Property

Property Get HeardOfProduct() As Boolean
HeardOfProduct = m_blnHeardOfProduct
End Property

Property Let HeardOfProduct(newHeardOf As Boolean)
  m_blnHeardOfProduct = newHeardOf
End Property

Property Get WantsProduct() As Boolean
  WantsProduct = m_blnWantsProduct
End Property

Property Let WantsProduct(newWants As Boolean)
  m_blnWantsProduct = newWants
End Property

Property Get Followup() As Boolean
  Followup = m_blnFollowup
End Property

Property Let Followup(newFollowup As Boolean)
  m_blnFollowup = newFollowup
End Property
```

```
Property Get DBWorkSheet() As Worksheet
  Set DBWorkSheet = m_xlWksht
End Property

Property Set DBWorkSheet(newSheet As Worksheet)
  Set m_xlWksht = newSheet
End Property
```

Notice that our ID property has no Property Let method, so it's read-only. The ID will be pulled from the database as it's needed. Everything else is rather generic until we get to our DBWorksheet property. This is where we are storing the worksheet that contains our database and must be set before the class can work.

We're going to add a GetNextID method to find the last row, grab the value from the first column, and then increment it by 1. This function will set the ID property's internal variable so we can retrieve it from the class once it's set.

Add the following code to the cCustSurvey class module:

```
Public Function GetNextID() As Long
Dim lngReturn As Long
  lngReturn = m_xlWksht.Cells(Rows.Count, 1).End(xlUp).Value + 1
  m_lngID = lngReturn ' set the ID property
  GetNextID = lngReturn
End Function
```

This code is very similar to the FindEmptyRow method in the cExcelUtils class, but it's returning a cell value instead of a row number.

Next, add initialization and cleanup code:

```
Private Sub Class_Initialize()
  Set m_oXL = New cExcelUtils
End Sub

Private Sub Class_Terminate()
  Set m_oXL = Nothing
End Sub
```

■**Tip** As mentioned in previous chapters, the Class_Initialize method is a great place to set up any internal objects used by your custom classes, and the Terminate method is the place to clean these objects up when you're finished using your class.

Now let's make this class do some work. First let's add some validation code. We cannot save the record if the State and PhoneNumber properties do not contain data. Add a new function called ValidateData and type in the following code:

```
Public Function ValidateData() As Boolean
Dim blnReturn As Boolean
  If (Len(Me.PhoneNumber & "") * Len(Me.State & "")) = 0 Then
    blnReturn = False
  Else
    blnReturn = True
  End If


  ValidateData = blnReturn
End Function
```

By multiplying the lengths of the text values State and PhoneNumber, we can determine whether one is missing, because the math will always return 0 if we're multiplying by 0.

Create a new function named Save that returns a success flag. This function needs to know the row number of the next available row for data entry; it needs to know what sheet that row is on; and if there are no errors, it must return a Boolean True value.

Here is the code for the Save method:

```
Public Function Save() As Boolean
Dim lngNewRowNum As Long
Dim blnReturn As Boolean

  If m_xlWksht Is Nothing Then
    blnReturn = False
    GoTo Exit_Function
  End If

  lngNewRowNum = m_oXL.FindEmptyRow(m_xlWksht)

  With m_xlWksht
    .Cells(lngNewRowNum, 1).Value = Me.ID
    .Cells(lngNewRowNum, 2).Value = Me.State
    .Cells(lngNewRowNum, 3).Value = Me.PhoneNumber
    .Cells(lngNewRowNum, 4).Value = Me.HeardOfProduct
    .Cells(lngNewRowNum, 5).Value = Me.WantsProduct
    .Cells(lngNewRowNum, 6).Value = Me.Followup
  End With

  If Err.Number = 0 Then
    blnReturn = True
  End If

Exit_Function:
  Save = blnReturn
  Exit Function
End Function
```

The first thing we're doing is checking to make sure our worksheet object still exists.

```
If m_xlWksht Is Nothing Then 'double check that we still have a valid object
  blnReturn = False
  GoTo Exit_Function
End If
```

If it doesn't, we return a False value and exit the function.

Next we get our empty row location from our cExcelUtils object:

```
lngNewRowNum = m_oXL.FindEmptyRow(m_xlWksht)
```

Then we use the m_xlWksht variable that contains the database worksheet and populate each column in the row with data from our class properties:

```
With m_xlWksht
  .Cells(lngNewRowNum, 1).Value = Me.ID
  .Cells(lngNewRowNum, 2).Value = Me.State
  .Cells(lngNewRowNum, 3).Value = Me.PhoneNumber
  .Cells(lngNewRowNum, 4).Value = Me.HeardOfProduct
  .Cells(lngNewRowNum, 5).Value = Me.WantsProduct
  .Cells(lngNewRowNum, 6).Value = Me.Followup
End With
```

Finally, we check that we have not received any errors, set the success flag to True, and then exit the function:

```
If Err.Number = 0 Then
  blnReturn = True
End If

Exit_Function:
  Save = blnReturn
  Exit Function
```

That's it for the cCustSurvey class. We've just built a class to hold our input values from the UserForm. It will find the next ID value for any new records and it will save the data to the worksheet we pass into the class in the next free row.

Coding the UserForm

We just created a class to handle our data and modified our Excel Utility class to help the cCustSurvey class. Let's put cCustSurvey to work by coding it into our UserForm.

Open the Customer Survey form (UserForm1). Open the code view by clicking the View Code button on the Project Explorer toolbar, as shown in Figure 4-7.

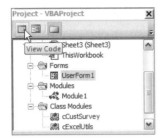

Figure 4-7. *The View Code button displays the code window for UserForm1 (selected).*

Add the following module-level variables in the UserForm code window:

```
Private m_oCustSurvey As cCustSurvey
Private m_blnSaved As Boolean
```

The m_oCustSurvey variable will do most of the work for us, and the m_blnSaved variable will store the return value from the m_oCustSurvey object's Save method.

Now let's put our initialization and cleanup code in place. Add the following code to the UserForm's UserForm_Initialize and UserForm_Terminate events:

```
Private Sub UserForm_Initialize()
  Set m_oCustSurvey = New cCustSurvey
  Set m_oCustSurvey.DBWorkSheet = Sheets("Sheet1")
  m_oCustSurvey.GetNextID
  lblID.Caption = m_oCustSurvey.ID
  m_blnSaved = False
  ClearForm
End Sub


Private Sub UserForm_Terminate()
  Set m_oCustSurvey = Nothing
End Sub
```

When the form is initialized, we're instantiating our cCustSurvey object. Then we're setting the DBWorksheet property. This is a very important step. This value must be stored right away so the class can determine the next valid ID and so it knows where to store the data it collects. Then we get the next available ID number and display it in a label. We then initialize our save success flag to False, and call a function to clear the form.

The ClearForm procedure does nothing more than blank out the text input fields and set the check boxes values to False (or not checked).

```
Private Sub ClearForm()
  Me.txtPhone.Value = ""
  Me.txtState.Value = ""
  Me.chkHeard.Value = False
  Me.chkInterested.Value = False
  Me.chkFollowup.Value = False
End Sub
```

Our form has three command buttons: one to save the data entered (Save), one to clear the form and add a new record (New), and one to cancel the data entry operation and close the form without saving the data (Cancel).

The Save button should perform a few functions for us:

- Sending the data to the cCustSurvey class

- Validating the data and returning a message if the data is not valid

- Saving the data if valid and returning a message if the save is successful

- Cleaning up the form after the save and resetting the saved flag

Here is the code for the Save button:

```
Private Sub cmdSave_Click()
  With m_oCustSurvey
    .State = txtState.Text
    .PhoneNumber = txtPhone.Text
    .HeardOfProduct = chkHeard.Value
    .WantsProduct = chkInterested.Value
    .Followup = chkFollowup.Value
  End With

  If Not m_oCustSurvey.ValidateData Then
    MsgBox "State and Phone Number required", vbOKOnly, "Cannot Save"
    Exit Sub
  Else
    m_blnSaved = m_oCustSurvey.Save
  End If

  DoAfterSave m_blnSaved
End Sub
```

The first section of the code is sending the values to the class. In the real world, our class would perform some input validations (such as validating that we entered a phone number using the correct format).

```
  With m_oCustSurvey
    .State = txtState.Text
    .PhoneNumber = txtPhone.Text
    .HeardOfProduct = chkHeard.Value
    .WantsProduct = chkInterested.Value
    .Followup = chkFollowup.Value
  End With
```

The second section of the code is calling the m_oCustSurvey.ValidateData method and displaying a message if both text fields do not contain data. If the data is present, the m_oCustSurvey.Save method is called.

Finally, we're calling a function called DoAfterSave to perform our cleanup. We're passing in our success flag so that this method will be the one calling out any messages to the user.

```
Private Sub DoAfterSave(success As Boolean)
  If success Then
    ClearForm
    lblID.Caption = m_oCustSurvey.GetNextID
    MsgBox "Record Saved"
  Else
    MsgBox "Could not save record"
  End If

  m_blnSaved = False 'resetting flag
End Sub
```

Our cleanup code clears the form, gets the next available ID number from the database, and sends the user a success (or failure) message.

The New command button has the job of clearing the form and getting a new ID from the database. Before it does that, it must check the text fields to see if they have any data entered. The code for the New command button follows:

```
Private Sub cmdNew_Click()
'sets form up for a new record
Dim iAnswer As Integer
'check that current record is saved (if any)
  If Not m_blnSaved Then 'see if any text data is entered that is not saved
    If (Len(Me.txtPhone.Value & "") + Len(Me.txtState.Value & "")) <> 0 Then
      iAnswer = MsgBox("There is unsaved data. Do you want to continue?", _
                  vbYesNo, "Unsaved Data")
      If iAnswer = vbYes Then
        ClearForm
      End If
    Else
      ClearForm
    End If
  End If
End Sub
```

We're using the following line of code to determine whether we have data in one of our two text input fields:

```
If (Len(Me.txtPhone.Value & "") + Len(Me.txtState.Value & "")) <> 0 Then
```

Once again, we use the Len function to help us make this determination. If the length of both strings summed together is greater than 0, then at least one of the fields contains data. If the result is True, then we prompt the user as to whether they want to continue with the new record and throw out the existing data.

The Cancel command button has a very simple job: clearing the form and closing it. Here is the code for the Cancel button:

```
Private Sub cmdCancel_Click()
  ClearForm
  Unload UserForm1
End Sub
```

The last step is to create a procedure in a standard module to launch our Customer Survey form. In the VBE, add a new standard code module and create a new subroutine named ShowForm. Add the following line of code to the procedure.

```
Sub ShowForm()
  UserForm1.Show
End Sub
```

If you renamed your UserForm object, use that name in place of UserForm1. Let's run our form and enter some data. In Excel, run the ShowForm macro, as shown in Figure 4-8.

Figure 4-8. *Running the ShowForm macro*

The Customer Survey form displays. The ID displayed is 103, and as you can see in Figure 4-9, the last entry in the table is 102. Also note that row 5 is the next row available for data.

Let's check our code. Enter **NY** in the State text box, but leave the phone number field blank, and then click the Save button.

Figure 4-10 shows that our cCustSurvey's ValidateData method finds that neither piece of required data is present, and returns a message to our client code in the UserForm. Click OK and enter a phone number, and then check one or more of the check boxes. Click Save.

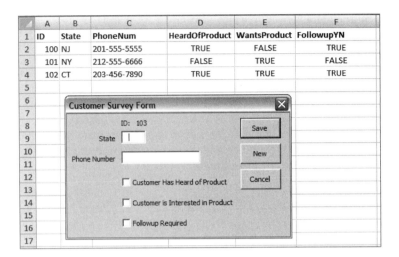

	A	B	C	D	E	F
1	ID	State	PhoneNum	HeardOfProduct	WantsProduct	FollowupYN
2	100	NJ	201-555-5555	TRUE	FALSE	TRUE
3	101	NY	212-555-6666	FALSE	TRUE	FALSE
4	102	CT	203-456-7890	TRUE	TRUE	TRUE

Figure 4-9. *The UserForm showing the next ID available*

	A	B	C	D	E	F	G
1	ID	State	PhoneNum	HeardOfProduct	WantsProduct	FollowupYN	
2	100	NJ	201-555-5555	TRUE	FALSE	TRUE	
3	101	NY	212-555-6666	FALSE	TRUE	FALSE	
4	102	CT	203-456-7890	TRUE	TRUE	TRUE	

Figure 4-10. *cCustSurvey class validation result*

The success message, shown in Figure 4-11, is displayed to the user, and row 5 now contains the data we entered on our UserForm. Notice that the ID label has been updated to show the ID for the next record.

	A	B	C	D	E	F	
1	ID	State	PhoneNum	HeardOfProduct	WantsProduct	FollowupYN	
2	100	NJ	201-555-5555	TRUE	FALSE	TRUE	
3	101	NY	212-555-6666	FALSE	TRUE	FALSE	
4	102	CT	203-456-7890	TRUE	TRUE	TRUE	
5	103	NY	555-555-1234	FALSE	TRUE	TRUE	
6							
7							
8							
9							
10							
11							
12							
13							
14							
15							
16							
17							

Figure 4-11. *Success message and new record displayed*

Let's test the New button before we move on to a more advanced UserForm. Clicking the New button with a blank or empty screen does nothing. If check boxes are checked but the text fields are empty, it will clear the screen without a prompt (this is because only the text fields are required). Enter a state and/or phone number and click the New button, and you'll receive a warning that the data has not been saved (as shown in Figure 4-12).

	A	B	C	D	E	F	G
1	ID	State	PhoneNum	HeardOfProduct	WantsProduct	FollowupYN	
2	100	NJ	201-555-5555	TRUE	FALSE	TRUE	
3	101	NY	212-555-6666	FALSE	TRUE	FALSE	
4	102	CT	203-456-7890	TRUE	TRUE	TRUE	
5	103	NY	555-555-1234	FALSE	TRUE	TRUE	
6							
7							
8							
9							
10							
11							
12							
13							
14							
15							
16							
17							

Figure 4-12. *Warning the user about unsaved data*

Clicking No returns the user to the form without making any changes. Clicking Yes will clear the form for new entry.

We made a useful addition to our cExcelUtils class. Let's export that file (overwriting the existing copy) so we can use that new functionality in other projects.

1. In the VBE Project Explorer, right-click any item in the project tree.

2. Choose Export File, as shown in Figure 4-13.

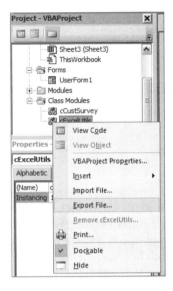

Figure 4-13. *Exporting a module*

3. Navigate to wherever you store your *.cls files, and save cExcelUtils.cls.

Creating Wizard-Style Data Entry UserForms

Wizard-style entry is a fairly common technique used to help users enter data in long or complex forms. Wizards allow you to break your data into related sections, allowing you to guide the user through an orderly data entry process.

From the sample files for this book, open the file named HRWizard.xlsm. This file consists of two worksheets. The employee database worksheet, named EmpData, is shown in Figure 4-14.

	A	B	C	D	E	F	G	H	I
1		Personal							
2	ID	Fname	MidInit	Lname	DOB	SSN	JobTitle	Dept	Email
3	929925	Jim	J	Dante	9/8/1967	555-55-5555	Manager	IT	jdante@MyCompany.com
4	125797	Anthony	P	Carson	10/29/1972	555-55-5556	Manager	Sales	acarson@MyCompany.com
5	365174	Cathy		Clark	11/13/1977	555-55-5557	Vice President	Operations	cclark@MyCompany.com
6	128295	Mark	N	Eastman	12/29/1984	555-55-5558	Developer	IT	meastman@MyCompany.com
7	879356	Carol	S	Morgan	7/15/1965	555-55-5559	Sales	Sales	cmorgan@MyCompany.com
8	765714	Eric	B	Anders	3/11/1966	555-55-5560	Sales	Sales	eanders@MyCompany.com
9	761049	Amy	C	Cannon	9/20/1983	555-55-5561	Project Manager	Operations	acannon@MyCompany.com
10	505322	Sherri		Early	9/21/1983	555-55-5562	Director	Operations	searly@MyCompany.com

Figure 4-14. *The HRWizard.xlsm EmpData database worksheet*

The second worksheet, ListMgr, contains various lists we'll be using when we create our wizard data entry form. Figure 4-15 shows the ListMgr worksheet.

	A	B	C	D
1	Dept	Locations	Network Lvl	ParkingSpot#
2	Customer Relations	CR1	1	A100
3	Graphics/Creative	CR2	2	A101
4	Human Resources	GC1	3	A102
5	Information Services	HR1	4	A103
6	Marketing	IS1	5	A104
7	Research	IS2		A105
8	Sales	IS3		A106
9		M1		A107
10		M2		A108
11		M3		A109
12		R1		A110
13		S1		B100
14		S2		B101
15		S3		B102
16				B103
17				B104

Figure 4-15. *The ListMgr worksheet contains list data for the wizard UserForm.*

For reference, any column on the EmpData worksheet that references a list has a blue color-coded column heading. Our EmpData worksheet data is divided into four sections: Personal, Address, Equipment, and Access, as shown in Figures 4-16 through 4-19.

	A	B	C	D	E	F	G	H	I
1		Personal							
2	ID	Fname	MidInit	Lname	DOB	SSN	JobTitle	Dept	Email
3	929925	Jim	J	Dante	9/8/1967	555-55-5555	Manager	IT	jdante@MyCompany.com
4	125797	Anthony	P	Carson	10/29/1972	555-55-5556	Manager	Sales	acarson@MyCompany.com
5	365174	Cathy		Clark	11/13/1977	555-55-5557	Vice President	Operations	cclark@MyCompany.com
6	128295	Mark	N	Eastman	12/29/1984	555-55-5558	Developer	IT	meastman@MyCompany.com
7	879356	Carol	S	Morgan	7/15/1965	555-55-5559	Sales	Sales	cmorgan@MyCompany.com
8	765714	Eric	B	Anders	3/11/1966	555-55-5560	Sales	Sales	eanders@MyCompany.com
9	761049	Amy	C	Cannon	9/20/1983	555-55-5561	Project Manager	Operations	acannon@MyCompany.com
10	505322	Sherri		Early	9/21/1983	555-55-5562	Director	Operations	searly@MyCompany.com

Figure 4-16. *Employee personal information*

	J	K	L	M	N	O	P
1	Addr						
2	StreetAddr	StreetAddr2	City	State	Zip	Phone	Cell
3	123 Main St.	Apt. 2	New York	NY	10001	212-555-1234	212-555-1253
4	9 W. 31st St.	Apt. 10-12	New York	NY	10011	212-555-1235	212-555-1254
5	10 MacArthur Dr.		Yonkers	NY	10701	212-555-1236	212-555-1255
6	4 Union St.		Newburgh	NY	12550	212-555-1237	212-555-1256
7	145 W. 23rd St.	Apt. 3005	New York	NY	10013	212-555-1238	212-555-1257
8	6 Jones Rd		Ossining	NY	10562	212-555-1239	212-555-1258
9	22 Rose Ct		Hartsdale	NY	10583	212-555-1240	212-555-1259
10	333 Delaware Ave.		Middletown	NY	10940	212-555-1241	212-555-1260

Figure 4-17. *Employee address information*

	Q	R	S	T
1	Equip			
2	PC type	Phone type	Loc	Fax YN
3	Laptop	Cell	IS1	N
4	Laptop	Cell	S1	N
5	Desktop	Desk	S2	Y
6	Desktop	Desk	IS2	N
7	Laptop	Cell	S3	N
8	Laptop	Cell	S3	N
9	Desktop	Desk	S2	N
10	Desktop	Desk	S2	Y

Figure 4-18. *Employee equipment information*

	U	V	W	X
1	Access			
2	Building	Network Lvl	Remote YN	ParkingSpot#
3	NYC	2	Y	A100
4	NYC	4	Y	B110
5	Upstate	4	Y	B100
6	NYC	3	Y	
7	Upstate	4	Y	
8	NYC	4	Y	
9	Upstate	5	N	
10	NYC	4	Y	C106

Figure 4-19. *Employee access information*

Our wizard UserForm will walk the user through entering this information for new employees. In turn, each piece of information will be forwarded to the appropriate department for processing.

Laying Out the Wizard Form

1. Open the VBE and add a new UserForm.

2. Set the form's height to 320 and its width to 332.

3. Rename the form to HRWizard.

4. Add a Label to the top of the form, set its caption property to **MyCompany - HR Wizard**, and set the font to a large size like 18 pt. This will be the main heading for our form.

5. Add a MultiPage control to the form.

6. Set its Height property to 216 and its Width property to 270.

7. Center it on the form, leaving room at the bottom.

Your form in Design view should look something like Figure 4-20.

Figure 4-20. *Initial layout for HRWizard UserForm*

Since we have four data collection sections, we need to add two additional pages to our MultiPage control.

1. Right-click either of the tabs at the top of the MultiPage control to display the shortcut menu.

2. Select New Page from the shortcut menu, as shown in Figure 4-21.

3. Repeat this one more time.

Figure 4-21. *Inserting a new page in the MultiPage control*

Your UserForm in Design view should look like Figure 4-22.

Figure 4-22. *UserForm after adding two new pages*

Adding Controls to the Form

The following sections will explain how to add the various controls to your form.

The Personal Information Page

Add controls to Page1 of the MultiPage control as listed in Table 4-3. These will correspond to the personal information column headings on the EmpData worksheet.

Table 4-3. *HRWizard UserForm Controls*

Item/Property	Value
Label	—
Caption:	First Name
TextBox	—
Name:	txtFname
Label	—
Caption:	Mid Init
TextBox	—
Name:	txtMidInit
Label	—
Caption:	Last Name
TextBox	—
Name:	txtLname
Label	—
Caption:	Date of Birth

Item/Property	Value
TextBox	—
Name:	txtDOB
Label	—
Caption:	SSN
TextBox	—
Name:	txtSSN
Label	—
Caption:	Department
ComboBox	—
Name:	cboDept
Label	—
Caption:	Job Title
TextBox	—
Name:	txtJobTitle
Label	—
Caption:	E-mail Address
TextBox	—
Name:	txtEmail

Resize the MultiPage control so there is room on the bottom of the UserForm for two command buttons (side by side) on the left side of the form and two command buttons (side by side) on the right side of the form. Table 4-4 lists the settings for these controls.

Table 4-4. *Command Button Settings*

Item/Property	Value
CommandButton	—
Name:	cmdPrevious
Caption:	<<<
CommandButton	—
Name:	cmdNext
Caption:	>>>
CommandButton	—
Name:	cmdSave
Caption:	Save
CommandButton	—
Name:	cmdCancel
Caption:	Cancel

The UserForm should now look something like Figure 4-23 in Design view.

Figure 4-23. *Personal information data entry page*

The Address Information Page

Add the controls listed in Table 4-5 to Page2 of the MultiPage control. These will correspond to the address information column headings on the EmpData worksheet.

Table 4-5. *Address Tab Control Settings*

Item/Property	Value
Label	—
Name:	lblEmpName
Caption:	lblEmpName
Label	—
Caption:	Street Address
TextBox	—
Name:	txtStreetAddr
Label	—
Caption:	Street Address 2
TextBox	—
Name:	txtStreetAddr2
Label	—
Caption:	City

Item/Property	Value
TextBox	—
Name:	txtCity
Label	—
Caption:	State
TextBox	—
Name:	txtState
Label	—
Caption:	ZIP Code
TextBox	—
Name:	txtZip
Label	—
Caption:	Phone Number
TextBox	—
Name:	txtPhone
Label	—
Caption:	Cell Phone
TextBox	—
Name:	txtCell

Page2 in Design view should look similar to Figure 4-24.

Figure 4-24. *Address information data entry on Page2*

The Equipment Information Page

Add the controls listed in Table 4-6 to Page3 of the MultiPage control. These will correspond to the equipment information column headings on the EmpData worksheet.

Table 4-6. *Equipment Tab Control Settings*

Item/Property	Value
Frame	—
Name:	fraPCType
Caption:	Computer Type
OptionButton	—
Name:	optDesktop
Caption:	Desktop
OptionButton	—
Name:	optLaptop
Caption:	Laptop
Frame	—
Name:	fraPhoneType
Caption:	Phone Type
OptionButton	—
Name:	optStandard
Caption:	Standard
OptionButton	—
Name:	optCell
Caption:	Cell Phone
Label	—
Caption:	Location
ComboBox	—
Name:	cboLocation
CheckBox	—
Name:	chkFaxYN
Caption:	Fax Machine Y/N

Page3 in Design view will look something like Figure 4-25.

Figure 4-25. *Equipment information data entry on Page3*

The Access Information Page

Add the controls listed in Table 4-7 to Page4 of the MultiPage control. These will correspond to the access information column headings on the EmpData worksheet.

Table 4-7. *Access Tab Control Settings*

Item/Property	Value
Label	—
Caption:	Network Access Level
ComboBox	—
Name:	cboNetworkLvl
Label	—
Caption:	Remote Access Y/N
ComboBox	—
Name:	cboRemoteAccess
Label	—
Caption:	Assigned Parking Spot
ComboBox	—
Name:	cboParkingSpot
Frame	—
Name:	fraBuilding
Caption:	Building

Continued

Table 4-7. *Continued*

Item/Property	Value
OptionButton	—
Name:	optNYC
Caption:	NYC
OptionButton	—
Name:	optNJ
Caption:	NJ

Page4 in Design view should look similar to Figure 4-26.

Figure 4-26. *Access level information data entry on Page4*

That's it for visual UI design. Next, we're going to design some classes to make this form work. At first glance, you might think having one class tied to the data record will suffice, but we are going to break up the functional areas when we define our classes, and we'll design a class or two to help us define our wizard steps. At the end of the process, we'll have a flexible wizard application that will give us the ability to change the order of the steps very easily and even make adding a step fairly simple.

HRWizard Classes

Since some of the employee information we are collecting will be passed on to other depart-ments for processing, we'll place the data from each screen in its own class. We're also going to need a class to monitor the steps in the wizard. We might also consider a class to help us populate those lists that use data from our ListMgr worksheet. Table 4-8 lists each class and describes some of its functionality.

Table 4-8. *HRWizard Application Class Modules*

Class	Description
cPerson	Holds all personal information for the new record
cAddress	Holds all address information for the new record
cEquipment	Holds all equipment information for the new record
cAccess	Holds all access information for the new record
cStep	Holds configuration values for each step of the wizard
cStepMgr	Controls the operation of the wizard and manages a collection of cStep objects
cListMgr	Controls the lists that will populate the combo boxes on the UserForm
cHRData	Transfers data to the database from the business objects; sends data from the database to the business objects

The HRWizard Business Objects

We'll begin by designing our business objects. These classes will store the data for each object (person, address, equipment, and access level) and will contain any business rules for each object.

Add a new class module to the project and name it cPerson. Add three more class modules, naming them cAddress, cEquipment, and cAccess. Our cPerson object will contain one each of cAddress, cEquipment, and cAccess objects. To keep them in sync, we'll add an ID property to each of our four business object classes.

In each class, add the following module-level declaration:

```
Private m_lngID As Long
```

Then add the Property Get and Let in each class:

```
Public Property Get ID() As Long
  ID = m_lngID
End Property

Public Property Let ID(newID As Long)
  m_lngID = newID
End Property
```

Save your work, and let's concentrate on our cPerson class. Each class essentially mirrors its input screen from our earlier UI design. Add the following module-level variable declarations to the cPerson class:

```
Private m_sFName As String
Private m_sMidInit As String
Private m_sLName As String
Private m_dtDOB As Date
Private m_sSSN As String
Private m_sJobTitle As String
Private m_sDepartment As String
Private m_sEmail As String
Private m_oAddress As cAddress
Private m_oEquipment As cEquipment
Private m_oAccess As cAccess
```

Notice that in addition to the data inputs from our screen design, we've included objects to hold the address, equipment, and access information.

The first thing we'll do here is initialize our cPerson class and set some default values. In the Class_Initialize event, add the following code:

```
Private Sub Class_Initialize()
  m_lngID = RandomNumber(100000, 999999)
  Set m_oAddress = New cAddress
  Set m_oEquipment = New cEquipment
  Set m_oAccess = New cAccess
  SetObjectIDs
End Sub
```

We're setting our private ID variable, m_lngID, to a random six-digit value, and initializing our private business object variables. We then call a private function that sets the ID values of all four of our business objects to the same value, SetObjectIDs. Add the following code to the cPerson class to generate the random number and synchronize the ID field:

```
Private Function RandomNumber(upper As Long, lower As Long) As Long
'generates a random number between upper & lower
  Randomize
  RandomNumber = Int((upper - lower + 1) * Rnd + lower)
End Function

Private Sub SetObjectIDs()
  m_oAddress.ID = m_lngID
  m_oEquipment.ID = m_lngID
  m_oAccess.ID = m_lngID
End Sub
```

We'll also add a call to this procedure in our ID Property Let function. This way, if we manually assign a value to the ID field, all the business objects will get the new value. The finished ID Property Let will look like this:

```
Public Property Let ID(newID As Long)
  m_lngID = newID
  SetObjectIDs 'keep all objects in sync with the same ID
End Property
```

The remainder of the cPerson class is very straightforward. Finish the cPerson class by adding the following code:

```
Property Get FName() As String
  FName = m_sFName
End Property

Property Let FName(newFName As String)
  m_sFName = newFName
End Property

Property Get MidInit() As String
  MidInit = m_sMidInit
End Property

Property Let MidInit(newMidInit As String)
  m_sMidInit = newMidInit
End Property

Property Get LName() As String
  LName = m_sLName
End Property

Property Let LName(newLName As String)
  m_sLName = newLName
End Property

Property Get DOB() As Date
  DOB = m_dtDOB
End Property

Property Let DOB(newDOB As Date)
  m_dtDOB = newDOB
End Property

Property Get SSN() As String
  SSN = m_sSSN
End Property

Property Let SSN(newSSN As String)
  m_sSSN = newSSN
End Property

Property Get JobTitle() As String
  JobTitle = m_sJobTitle
End Property
```

```
Property Let JobTitle(newJobTitle As String)
  m_sJobTitle = newJobTitle
End Property

Property Get Department() As String
  Department = m_sDepartment
End Property

Property Let Department(newDepartment As String)
  m_sDepartment = newDepartment
End Property

Property Get Email() As String
  Email = m_sEmail
End Property

Property Let Email(newEmail As String)
  m_sEmail = newEmail
End Property

Property Get Address() As cAddress
  Set Address = m_oAddress
End Property

Property Set Address(newAddress As cAddress)
  Set m_oAddress = newAddress
End Property

Property Get Equipment() As cEquipment
  Set Equipment = m_oEquipment
End Property

Property Set Equipment(newEquipment As cEquipment)
  Set m_oEquipment = newEquipment
End Property

Property Get Access() As cAccess
  Set Access = m_oAccess
End Property

Property Set Access(newAccess As cAccess)
  Set m_oAccess = newAccess
End Property
```

We've added the remaining Person data elements to our class, as well as three object properties using Property Get/Set statements. We may also want to add a property that returns the employee's full name. Add the read-only FullName property to cPerson:

```
Property Get FullName() As String
Dim sReturn As String
Dim blnMidInit As Boolean
  blnMidInit = Len(m_sMidInit & "") > 0

  If blnMidInit Then
    sReturn = m_sFName & " " & m_sMidInit & " " & m_sLName
  Else
    sReturn = m_sFName & " " & m_sLName
  End If

  FullName = sReturn
End Property
```

That's all we need for our cPerson class. Now we'll fill in our cAddress, cEquipment, and cAccess objects. Then we'll start putting our wizard application together. These classes are mapped directly to the screen elements from our HRWizard UserForm. The entirety of their code is shown in Listings 4-1 through 4-3.

Listing 4-1. *The cAddress Class*

```
Private m_lngID As Long
Private m_sStreetAddress As String
Private m_sStreeAddress2 As String
Private m_sCity As String
Private m_sState As String
Private m_sZipCode As String
Private m_sPhoneNumber As String
Private m_sCellPhone As String
'

Public Property Get ID() As Long
  ID = m_lngID
End Property

Public Property Let ID(newID As Long)
  m_lngID = newID
End Property

Public Property Get StreetAddress() As String
  StreetAddress = m_sStreetAddress
End Property

Public Property Let StreetAddress(newAddress As String)
  m_sStreetAddress = newAddress
End Property
```

```vb
Public Property Get StreetAddress2() As String
  StreetAddress2 = m_sStreeAddress2
End Property

Public Property Let StreetAddress2(newAddress2 As String)
  m_sStreeAddress2 = newAddress2
End Property

Public Property Get City() As String
  City = m_sCity
End Property

Public Property Let City(newCity As String)
  m_sCity = newCity
End Property

Public Property Get State() As String
  State = m_sState
End Property

Public Property Let State(newState As String)
  m_sState = newState
End Property

Public Property Get ZipCode() As String
  ZipCode = m_sZipCode
End Property

Public Property Let ZipCode(newZipCode As String)
  m_sZipCode = newZipCode
End Property

Public Property Get PhoneNumber() As String
  PhoneNumber = m_sPhoneNumber
End Property

Public Property Let PhoneNumber(newPhoneNumber As String)
  m_sPhoneNumber = newPhoneNumber
End Property

Public Property Get CellPhone() As String
  CellPhone = m_sCellPhone
End Property

Public Property Let CellPhone(newCellPhone As String)
  m_sCellPhone = newCellPhone
End Property
```

Listing 4-2. *The cEquipment Class*

```
Private m_lngID As Long
Private m_sPCType As String
Private m_sPhoneType As String
Private m_sLocation As String
Private m_sFaxYN As String
'


Public Property Get ID() As Long
  ID = m_lngID
End Property

Public Property Let ID(newID As Long)
  m_lngID = newID
End Property

Public Property Get PCType() As String
  PCType = m_sPCType
End Property

Public Property Let PCType(newPCType As String)
  m_sPCType = newPCType
End Property

Public Property Get PhoneType() As String
  PhoneType = m_sPhoneType
End Property

Public Property Let PhoneType(newPhoneType As String)
  m_sPhoneType = newPhoneType
End Property

Public Property Get Location() As String
  Location = m_sLocation
End Property

Public Property Let Location(newLocation As String)
  m_sLocation = newLocation
End Property

Public Property Get FaxYN() As String
  FaxYN = m_sFaxYN
End Property

Public Property Let FaxYN(newFaxYN As String)
  m_sFaxYN = newFaxYN
End Property
```

Listing 4-3. *The cAccess Class*

```
Private m_lngID As Long
Private m_sBuilding As String
Private m_iNetworkLevel As Integer
Private m_sRemoteYN As String
Private m_sParkingSpot As String
'

Public Property Get ID() As Long
  ID = m_lngID
End Property

Public Property Let ID(newID As Long)
  m_lngID = newID
End Property

Public Property Get Building() As String
  Building = m_sBuilding
End Property

Public Property Let Building(newBuilding As String)
  m_sBuilding = newBuilding
End Property

Public Property Get NetworkLevel() As Integer
  NetworkLevel = m_iNetworkLevel
End Property

Public Property Let NetworkLevel(newNetworkLevel As Integer)
  m_iNetworkLevel = newNetworkLevel
End Property

Public Property Get RemoteYN() As String
  RemoteYN = m_sRemoteYN
End Property

Public Property Let RemoteYN(newRemoteYN As String)
  m_sRemoteYN = newRemoteYN
End Property

Public Property Get ParkingSpot() As String
  ParkingSpot = m_sParkingSpot
End Property

Public Property Let ParkingSpot(newParkingSpot As String)
  m_sParkingSpot = newParkingSpot
End Property
```

Managing Lists

Some of the data inputs on our HRWizard UserForm are being displayed to the user via ComboBox controls. The HRWizard data file contains a worksheet named ListMgr that contains the data for each list. The data is stored in named ranges on the ListMgr worksheet.

Our cListManager class will contain functions that let us populate our combo boxes from these named ranges. We'll also add a method to bind a list to a VBA Collection object. This concept could easily be expanded to include lists gathered from any data source (like XML) or an ADO or DAO recordset.

Insert a new class module and name it cListManager. Add these two methods to the class:

```
Public Sub BindListToRange(ListRangeName As String, TheCombo As MSForms.ComboBox)
  TheCombo.RowSource = ListRangeName
End Sub


Public Sub BindListToCollection(TheCollection As Collection, ➥
                                TheCombo As MSForms.ComboBox)
Dim iNumItems As Integer
Dim i As Integer
  iNumItems = TheCollection.Count
  For i = 1 To iNumItems
    TheCombo.AddItem TheCollection(i)
  Next i
End Sub
```

The BindListToRange method takes a Range name string value and a ComboBox object, and sets the ComboBox's RowSource property to the named range. The BindListToCollection method simply loops through a collection and calls the ComboBox's AddItem method.

The Data Class

Our data class is named cHRData. This class is being designed specifically for our HRWizard application, and will be closely coupled with our cPerson object and our EmpData worksheet. Insert a new class module and name it cHRData. Add the following module-level variables, one property, and one method:

```
Private m_oWorksheet As Worksheet
Private m_lngNewRowNum As Long
Private m_oEmployee As cPerson
Private m_oXL As cExcelUtils
'


Public Property Get Worksheet() As Worksheet
  Set Worksheet = m_oWorksheet
End Property

Public Property Set Worksheet(newWorksheet As Worksheet)
  Set m_oWorksheet = newWorksheet
End Property
```

```
Public Function SaveEmployee(Employee As cPerson) As Boolean
Dim blnReturn As Boolean

  If m_oWorksheet Is Nothing Then
    GoTo Exit_Function
  End If

  m_lngNewRowNum = m_oXL.FindEmptyRow(m_oWorksheet)
  Set m_oEmployee = Employee

  SaveEmpData
  SaveAddressData
  SaveEquipmentData
  SaveAccessData

Exit_Function:
  SaveEmployee = blnReturn
  Exit Function
End Function
```

Add the following class initialization and cleanup code:

```
Private Sub Class_Initialize()
  Set m_oXL = New cExcelUtils
End Sub

Private Sub Class_Terminate()
  Set m_oXL = Nothing
End Sub
```

The Worksheet property lets us define where the data will be stored in our workbook. The SaveEmployee method does a few things for us when we pass in a cPerson object:

```
Public Function SaveEmployee(Employee As cPerson) As Boolean
```

It checks to see that the Worksheet property has been set so we know where to save our data:

```
  If m_oWorksheet Is Nothing Then
    GoTo Exit_Function
  End If
```

It finds the first empty row using the cExcelUtils object:

```
m_lngNewRowNum = m_oXL.FindEmptyRow(m_oWorksheet)
```

Then we assign the cPerson object we passed in to the method to a private module-level cPerson object that will be used in various save functions:

```
Set m_oEmployee = Employee
```

Lastly, it fires a few save functions, one for each data object:

```
SaveEmpData
SaveAddressData
SaveEquipmentData
SaveAccessData
```

The Save methods simply transfer the data values stored in the cPerson object (and its internal data objects) to a cell on the EmpData worksheet. Add the following Save methods to the cHRData class module:

```
Private Sub SaveEmpData()
  With m_oWorksheet
    .Cells(m_lngNewRowNum, 1).Value = m_oEmployee.ID
    .Cells(m_lngNewRowNum, 2).Value = m_oEmployee.FName
    .Cells(m_lngNewRowNum, 3).Value = m_oEmployee.MidInit
    .Cells(m_lngNewRowNum, 4).Value = m_oEmployee.LName
    .Cells(m_lngNewRowNum, 5).Value = m_oEmployee.DOB
    .Cells(m_lngNewRowNum, 6).Value = m_oEmployee.SSN
    .Cells(m_lngNewRowNum, 7).Value = m_oEmployee.JobTitle
    .Cells(m_lngNewRowNum, 8).Value = m_oEmployee.Department
    .Cells(m_lngNewRowNum, 9).Value = m_oEmployee.Email
  End With
End Sub

Private Sub SaveAddressData()
  With m_oWorksheet
    .Cells(m_lngNewRowNum, 10).Value = m_oEmployee.Address.StreetAddress
    .Cells(m_lngNewRowNum, 11).Value = m_oEmployee.Address.StreetAddress2
    .Cells(m_lngNewRowNum, 12).Value = m_oEmployee.Address.City
    .Cells(m_lngNewRowNum, 13).Value = m_oEmployee.Address.State
    .Cells(m_lngNewRowNum, 14).Value = m_oEmployee.Address.ZipCode
    .Cells(m_lngNewRowNum, 15).Value = m_oEmployee.Address.PhoneNumber
    .Cells(m_lngNewRowNum, 16).Value = m_oEmployee.Address.CellPhone
  End With
End Sub

Private Sub SaveEquipmentData()
  With m_oWorksheet
    .Cells(m_lngNewRowNum, 17).Value = m_oEmployee.Equipment.PCType
    .Cells(m_lngNewRowNum, 18).Value = m_oEmployee.Equipment.PhoneType
    .Cells(m_lngNewRowNum, 19).Value = m_oEmployee.Equipment.Location
    .Cells(m_lngNewRowNum, 20).Value = m_oEmployee.Equipment.FaxYN
  End With
End Sub
```

```
Private Sub SaveAccessData()
  With m_oWorksheet
    .Cells(m_lngNewRowNum, 21).Value = m_oEmployee.Access.Building
    .Cells(m_lngNewRowNum, 22).Value = m_oEmployee.Access.NetworkLevel
    .Cells(m_lngNewRowNum, 23).Value = m_oEmployee.Access.RemoteYN
    .Cells(m_lngNewRowNum, 24).Value = m_oEmployee.Access.ParkingSpot
  End With
End Sub
```

Notice the syntax used to retrieve the cPerson object's internal Address, Equipment, and Access object data:

```
m_oEmployee.Address.StreetAddress
m_oEmployee.Equipment.PCType
m_oEmployee.Access.Building
```

Using an object within an object gives you the flexibility of categorizing information within your objects. Anyone familiar with object-relational database technologies, such as InterSystems Cache (www.intersystems.com), may recognize this type of syntax.

■**Note** Object-oriented databases use objects rather than tables to represent data. If you're interested in object-oriented programming techniques and haven't checked out this technology, I highly recommend you do. InterSystems offers a free single-user download on its web site. Also, the online resource Wikipedia has a good article on the subject at http://en.wikipedia.org/wiki/Object_database.

Managing the Wizard

We'll build two classes to help us manage our wizard application. The first is a very simple class that will hold configuration data for each step. Then we'll create a class that will hold a collection of these "wizard step" objects. This class will manage the operation of the wizard process for us.

Insert a new class module and name it cStep. Add the following code:

```
Private m_iOrder As Integer
Private m_iPage As Integer
Private m_sCaption As String

Public Property Get Order() As Integer
  Order = m_iOrder
End Property

Public Property Let Order(newOrder As Integer)
  m_iOrder = newOrder
End Property
```

```
Public Property Get Page() As Integer
  Page = m_iPage
End Property

Public Property Let Page(newPage As Integer)
  m_iPage = newPage
End Property

Public Property Get Caption() As String
  Caption = m_sCaption
End Property

Public Property Let Caption(newCaption As String)
  m_sCaption = newCaption
End Property
```

The HRWizard.xlms workbook contains a worksheet named UFormConfig. This worksheet holds information about each step in the wizard. This is where we can change the order of the steps or insert a new step. This class will hold that information for us. How will it do that when it (apparently) only holds information on one step?

Table 4-9 lists the cStep class's properties and describes them.

Table 4-9. *cStep Properties*

Property	Description
Order	Holds the step's place in the wizard process's order
Page	Holds the page number corresponding to a page in the MultiPage control
Caption	The text to display on the currently active Page control

We are now going to design a class to manage the steps in the wizard. In that class, we'll create a collection of cStep objects that we'll use to keep track of where we are in the process and how many steps we have.

Insert a new class module and name it cStepManager. Add the following module-level variable declarations:

```
Dim m_oStep As cStep
Dim m_iNumSettings As Integer
Dim m_iNumSteps As Integer
Dim m_iCurrentPage As Integer
Dim m_iPreviousPage As Integer
Dim m_iNextPage As Integer
Dim WithEvents m_oPreviousButton As MSForms.CommandButton
Dim WithEvents m_oNextButton As MSForms.CommandButton
Dim m_oWorksheet As Worksheet
```

We have a cStep object, m_oStep, that we'll be using to populate a collection of steps for the wizard, followed by a few Integer variables. These tell us how many steps we have and how many properties each step has, and they track the current, next, and previous steps based on where in the wizard the user might be.

We then have a couple variables that are set to the MSForms.CommandButton object type. These are declared WithEvents. We are going to let our cStepManager class maintain the state of these buttons. The WithEvents declaration lets us trap their Click event and act on it inside of our class. We will use the Click event to determine whether the button should be enabled based on where the user is in the wizard process.

Add the following properties to cStepManager:

```
Public Property Get NumberOfSettings() As Integer
  NumberOfSettings = m_iNumSettings
End Property

Public Property Let NumberOfSettings(newNum As Integer)
  m_iNumSettings = newNum
End Property

'Worksheet Property: Gets/Sets the sheet containing the step information
Public Property Get Worksheet() As Worksheet
  Set Worksheet = m_oWorksheet
End Property

Public Property Set Worksheet(newWorksheet As Worksheet)
  Set m_oWorksheet = newWorksheet
End Property

Public Property Get CurrentPage() As Integer
  CurrentPage = m_iCurrentPage
End Property

Public Property Let CurrentPage(newPage As Integer)
  m_iCurrentPage = newPage
End Property

Public Property Get PreviousPage() As Integer
    PreviousPage = m_iCurrentPage - 1
End Property

Public Property Get NextPage() As Integer
    NextPage = m_iCurrentPage + 1
End Property

Public Property Set PreviousButton(newPreviousBtn As MSForms.CommandButton)
  Set m_oPreviousButton = newPreviousBtn
End Property
```

```
Public Property Set NextButton(newNextBtn As MSForms.CommandButton)
  Set m_oNextButton = newNextBtn
End Property
```

Table 4-10 lists the cStepManager class's properties and describes them.

Table 4-10. *cStepManager Properties*

Property	Description
NumberOfSettings	Contains the number of columns in our step configuration worksheet, UFormConfig
Worksheet	Tells the class where to find the information for each step of the wizard
CurrentPage	Stores the value of the current step in the wizard
PreviousPage	Calculated based on the CurrentPage property; returns the value of the preceding step in the wizard
NextPage	Calculated based on the CurrentPage property; returns the value of the next step in the wizard
PreviousButton	Stores a pointer to the button on the UserForm that will navigate to the preceding step in the wizard
NextButton	Stores a pointer to the button on the UserForm that will navigate to the next step in the wizard

We need to add one more property to our class. This read-only property will contain the collection of cStep objects that hold the information on each step of the wizard.

The PageSettings property will store this collection for us. It returns a Collection object that we will use in the client code behind our HRWizard UserForm.

The code for the PageSettings property looks like this:

```
Public Property Get PageSettings() As Collection
Dim colReturn As Collection
Dim numrows As Integer
Dim row As Integer
Dim col As Integer
Dim sKey As String
  Set colReturn = New Collection

  numrows = m_oWorksheet.Cells(Rows.Count, 1).End(xlUp).row
  For row = 2 To numrows
    Set m_oStep = New cStep
    For col = 1 To m_iNumSettings
    Select Case col
    Case 1
      m_oStep.Order = m_oWorksheet.Cells(row, col).Value
      sKey = CStr(m_oStep.Order)
    Case 2
      m_oStep.Page = m_oWorksheet.Cells(row, col).Value
```

```
    Case 3
      m_oStep.Caption = m_oWorksheet.Cells(row, col).Value
    End Select
    Next col
    colReturn.Add m_oStep, sKey
  Next row

  m_iNumSteps = colReturn.Count
  Set PageSettings = colReturn
End Property
```

The first thing we're doing is getting the number of rows in the used area on the work-sheet:

```
numrows = m_oWorksheet.Cells(Rows.Count, 1).End(xlUp).Row
```

■Note Although Excel's `Worksheet` object has a `Rows.Count` method, we cannot use that here (`m_oWorksheet.Rows.Count`). That would return the total number of rows in the worksheet, which would not only give us an incorrect value, but would also overflow our `Integer` variable.

Next we're using the number-of-used-rows value just returned in a loop that will populate the collection of `cStep` objects. Let's look at that code:

```
  For row = 2 To numrows
    Set m_oStep = New cStep
    For col = 1 To m_iNumSettings
    Select Case col
    Case 1
      m_oStep.Order = m_oWorksheet.Cells(row, col).Value
      sKey = CStr(m_oStep.Order)
    Case 2
      m_oStep.Page = m_oWorksheet.Cells(row, col).Value
    Case 3
      m_oStep.Caption = m_oWorksheet.Cells(row, col).Value
    End Select
    Next col
    colReturn.Add m_oStep, sKey
  Next row
```

The first thing we do is instantiate a new `cStep` object. Then we move into an inner loop to walk through the columns on the configuration worksheet, and assign them to the corresponding property in the internal `cStep` object. The `m_iNumSettings` value will have already been set via the `NumberOfSettings` property before this code is run.

Finally, we add the `cStep` object to our internal collection, `colReturn`, passing in the `Order` value as the key in the collection.

Note It is important to note the first line of code inside the outer loop, Set m_oStep = New cStep. If this is omitted, you will end up with four identical cStep objects in your collection (all containing the data from the last configuration item read from the worksheet). This is because the m_oStep object reference is still active, so every call to it modifies any existing instances. By using the New keyword, you create a new, separate instance of the object.

The last thing we're doing is setting the internal m_iNumSteps variable that is used to track our Previous and Next CommandButton availability, and finally we're returning the collection:

```
m_iNumSteps = colReturn.Count
Set PageSettings = colReturn
```

Now we will turn our attention to our PreviousButton and NextButton properties. You'll recall that our internal variables for these properties were declared WithEvents. When you declare an object WithEvents, you have access to that object's event code via the VB code window's Object box, as shown in Figure 4-27.

Figure 4-27. *The Object box lists objects declared WithEvents.*

Select m_oNextButton and m_oPreviousButton from the Object box to insert their event-handler stubs into the class module. Add the following code to each:

```
Private Sub m_oNextButton_Click()
    m_oNextButton.Enabled = Me.NextPage <> m_iNumSteps + 1
    m_oPreviousButton.Enabled = Me.PreviousPage <> 0
End Sub

Private Sub m_oPreviousButton_Click()
    m_oPreviousButton.Enabled = Me.PreviousPage <> 0
    m_oNextButton.Enabled = Me.NextPage <> m_iNumSteps + 1
End Sub
```

This code controls whether each button is enabled based on the value of the NextPage or PreviousPage properties of our cStepManager class. We'll add one more method to initialize the buttons when the class is first created in client code:

```
Public Sub HandleControls()
    m_oPreviousButton.Enabled = Me.PreviousPage <> 0
    m_oNextButton.Enabled = Me.NextPage <> m_iNumSteps + 1
End Sub
```

We've created a fair amount of code here, all stored in objects across many class modules. By compartmentalizing our functionality, we've made our job of maintaining this code very easy. If we need to bind lists to data sources we may not be currently handling, it is trivial to add a new method to the cListManger class. If we need to add a screen to our process, we design a new page on the MultiPage control, create a new class to store that screen's information, and add a row to our configuration table.

Your Class Modules folder in the Project Explorer should look like Figure 4-28 after all the classes have been added and coded.

Figure 4-28. *HRWizard class module list*

Coding the HRWizard UserForm

Now that we've done all the hard work, let's plug our objects into our HRWizard UserForm and put those objects to work.

Open the code window for the HRWizard UserForm. Add the following module-level variable declarations:

```
Dim m_oEmployee As cPerson
Dim m_oLM As cListManager
Dim m_oWizard As cStepManager
Dim m_colSteps As Collection
```

Although we created nine separate class modules to run our application, many are used internally by the classes listed in our declaration section. We'll be using the cPerson class to collect the data for a new employee; the cListManager to populate our various combo boxes on the HRWizard UserForm; and the cStepManager to determine which screen to show when and in what order, and to control the availability of the navigation command buttons. Finally, we are using a standard VBA Collection object. This will be used to store the cStepManager object's PageSettings collection.

Initializing the Application

In our HRWizard UserForm's Initialize event, we will initialize our custom objects and add code to set up the wizard, lists, and display form.

Add the following code to the UserForm_Initialize event:

```
Private Sub UserForm_Initialize()
  Set m_oEmployee = New cPerson
  Set m_oLM = New cListManager
  Set m_oWizard = New cStepManager

  InitWizard
  InitLists
  InitForm
End Sub
```

Now we'll create the three `Init` functions. These will set up our wizard, list manager, and UserForm objects.

Initializing the Wizard

Add a new subroutine to the UserForm code window and name it `InitWizard`. Add the following code:

```
Private Sub InitWizard()
  With m_oWizard
    Set .Worksheet = Sheets("UFormConfig")
    .NumberOfSettings = 3
    Set m_colSteps = .PageSettings
    Set .PreviousButton = Me.cmdPrevious
    Set .NextButton = Me.cmdNext
    .CurrentPage = MultiPage1.Value + 1
  End With
End Sub
```

This simple procedure does the following:

- Tells the `cStepManager` object where to find the configuration data

  ```
  Set .Worksheet = Sheets("UFormConfig")
  ```

- Tells the `cStepManager` object how many columns to retrieve data from

  ```
  .NumberOfSettings = 3
  ```

- Puts the page settings into a collection

  ```
  Set m_colSteps = .PageSettings
  ```

- Sets the navigation buttons

  ```
  Set .PreviousButton = Me.cmdPrevious
  Set .NextButton = Me.cmdNext
  ```

- Sets the current page

  ```
  .CurrentPage = MultiPage1.Value + 1
  ```

We are using the MultiPage control's Value property plus 1 to set the CurrentPage property because the MultiPage control's Page collection is zero-based. (Normally, collections are one-based, and I'm not sure why this collection is different, but that's the way it is.)

The cStepManager object must be set up before we initialize the form because the form will use the PageSettings collection to set itself up.

Initializing the Combo Boxes

The next step is to bind our combo boxes to their respective lists. The lists are stored on the ListMgr worksheet.

Add a new subroutine and name it InitLists. Add the following code:

```
Private Sub InitLists()
  With m_oLM
    .BindListToRange "Departments", Me.cboDept
    .BindListToRange "Locations", Me.cboLocation
    .BindListToRange "NetworkLvl", Me.cboNetworkLvl
    .BindListToRange "ParkingSpot", Me.cboParkingSpot
    .BindListToRange "YN", Me.cboRemoteAccess
  End With
End Sub
```

Again, this is very simple code that calls the cListManager object's BindListToRange method for each list in the application.

Initializing the Form

Our final step in setting up the application is to initialize the UserForm itself. Create a new subroutine named InitForm. Add the following code:

```
Private Sub InitForm()
Dim iFirstPage As Integer
Dim i As Integer
Dim iPageCount As Integer

  iFirstPage = m_colSteps("1").Order - 1
  Me.MultiPage1.Value = iFirstPage
  Me.MultiPage1.Pages((m_colSteps("1").Page) - 1).Caption = m_colSteps("1").Caption
  m_oWizard.HandleControls
  iPageCount = MultiPage1.Pages.Count
  For i = 1 To iPageCount - 1
    MultiPage1.Pages(i).Visible = False
  Next
End Sub
```

Here we are setting our MultiPage control's Value property to the PageSetting collection's (m_colSteps) item (whose key value is 1), and setting its caption:

```
iFirstPage = m_colSteps("1").Order - 1
Me.MultiPage1.Value = iFirstPage
Me.MultiPage1.Pages((m_colSteps("1").Page) - 1).Caption = m_colSteps("1").Caption
```

Remember that we passed in the value of the Order property as the key. This makes it very easy for us to determine which page to move to. When setting a MultiPage control's Value property, you are activating the page with a corresponding value. In this case, the value is 1.

Then we are calling the m_oWizard object's HandleControls method to initialize the navigation buttons to their correct settings:

```
m_oWizard.HandleControls
```

Next, we hide all the pages except the first page:

```
iPageCount = MultiPage1.Pages.Count
For i = 1 To iPageCount - 1
  MultiPage1.Pages(i).Visible = False
Next
```

Remember that the MultiPage control's Page collection is zero-based, so by starting our loop counter at 1, we keep that page visible.

At this point, you should be able to run the form.

1. In the VBE, double-click the form in the Project Explorer window.

2. Click the Run button on the Standard toolbar or press the F5 function key, as shown in Figure 4-29.

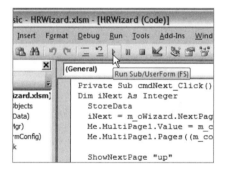

Figure 4-29. *The Run Sub/UserForm toolbar button*

Notice in Figure 4-30 that the caption appears in the tab handle and the Previous command button is disabled.

Figure 4-30. *Initialized HRWizard UserForm*

A look at the Department combo box in Figure 4-31 shows us our list manager did indeed bind the combo box to the Departments named range.

Figure 4-31. *Department combo box bound to named range*

3. Stop running the form by clicking the X button.

Adding Navigation to the Form

Our navigation buttons have the task of moving us from step to step in our wizard application. But they also need the ability to put the data from each screen into its place in the UserForm's cPerson object.

Add the following code to the cmdNext_Click event:

```
Private Sub cmdNext_Click()
Dim iNext As Integer
  StoreData
  iNext = m_oWizard.NextPage
  Me.MultiPage1.Value = m_colSteps(CStr(iNext)).Order - 1
  Me.MultiPage1.Pages((m_colSteps(CStr(iNext)).Page) - 1).Caption = ➥
                                      m_colSteps(CStr(iNext)).Caption
  ShowNextPage "up"
End Sub
```

The first thing we need to do before we move to the next step in the wizard is retain the values entered on the current form. The StoreData method determines which step the user is on and calls the correct store method based on that location, as shown in Listing 4-4.

Listing 4-4. *The StoreData Method Calls the Correct Method for Each Step in the Wizard.*

```
Private Sub StoreData()
  Select Case m_oWizard.CurrentPage
  Case 1
    StorePerson
  Case 2
    StoreAddress
  Case 3
    StoreEquipment
  Case 4
    StoreAccess
  End Select
End Sub
```

The code for the store method follows:

```
Private Sub StorePerson()
  With m_oEmployee
    .FName = Me.txtFname.Value
    .MidInit = Me.txtMidInit.Value
    .LName = Me.txtLname.Value
    If Len(Me.txtDOB.Value & "") > 0 Then
      .DOB = Me.txtDOB.Value
    End If
```

```vb
         .SSN = Me.txtSSN.Value
         .Department = Me.cboDept.Text
         .JobTitle = Me.txtJobTitle.Value
         .Email = Me.txtEmail.Value
      End With
End Sub

Private Sub StoreAddress()
   With m_oEmployee.Address
      .StreetAddress = Me.txtStreedAddr.Value
      .StreetAddress2 = Me.txtStreetAddr2.Value
      .City = Me.txtCity.Value
      .State = Me.txtState.Value
      .ZipCode = Me.txtZip.Value
      .PhoneNumber = Me.txtPhone.Value
      .CellPhone = Me.txtCell.Value
   End With
End Sub

Private Sub StoreEquipment()
Dim opt As MSForms.OptionButton
   With m_oEmployee.Equipment
      For Each opt In Me.fraPCType.Controls
         If opt.Value = True Then
            .PCType = opt.Caption
            Exit For
         End If
      Next

      For Each opt In Me.fraPhoneType.Controls
         If opt.Value = True Then
            .PhoneType = opt.Caption
            Exit For
         End If
      Next

      .Location = Me.cboLocation.Text

      If Me.chkFaxYN = True Then
         .FaxYN = "Y"
      Else
         .FaxYN = "N"
      End If
   End With
End Sub
```

```
Private Sub StoreAccess()
Dim opt As MSForms.OptionButton

  With m_oEmployee.Access
    If Len(Me.cboNetworkLvl.Text & "") > 0 Then
      .NetworkLevel = CInt(Me.cboNetworkLvl.Text)
    End If
    .ParkingSpot = Me.cboParkingSpot.Text
    .RemoteYN = Me.cboRemoteAccess.Text
    For Each opt In Me.fraBuilding.Controls
      If opt.Value = True Then
        .Building = opt.Caption
        Exit For
      End If
    Next
  End With
End Sub
```

This code simply takes the data from the screen and holds it in the corresponding object within cPerson.

Next, we determine what the next page should be (remember that the MultiPage Pages collection is zero-based, so we're subtracting 1 from our Order property to get the value of the next page).

```
iNext = m_oWizard.NextPage
Me.MultiPage1.Value = m_colSteps(CStr(iNext)).Order - 1
Me.MultiPage1.Pages((m_colSteps(CStr(iNext)).Page) - 1).Caption = ➡
                                        m_colSteps(CStr(iNext)).Caption
```

Then we call the ShowNextPage method, telling it which way we want to move:

```
ShowNextPage "up"
```

The ShowNextPage method looks like this:

```
Private Sub ShowNextPage(Direction As String)
Dim iCurrPage As Integer
Dim iUpDown As Integer
  iCurrPage = MultiPage1.Value
  If LCase(Direction) = "up" Then
    iUpDown = 1
  Else
    iUpDown = -1
  End If
  MultiPage1.Pages(iCurrPage + iUpDown).Visible = True
  MultiPage1.Pages(iCurrPage).Visible = False
End Sub
```

This method simply looks at the value of our CurrentPage property and adds or subtracts 1 based upon the Direction argument that is passed into the method.

The cmdPrevious button's `Click` event looks very similar:

```
Private Sub cmdPrevious_Click()
Dim iPrevious As Integer
  StoreData
  iPrevious = m_oWizard.PreviousPage
  Me.MultiPage1.Value = m_colSteps(CStr(iPrevious)).Order - 1
  Me.MultiPage1.Pages((m_colSteps(CStr(iPrevious)).Page) - 1).Caption = ➥
                                       m_colSteps(CStr(iPrevious)).Caption
  ShowNextPage "down"
End Sub
```

The only difference is that we are passing the keyword `down` to the `ShowNextPage` method so that we move the user in the proper direction.

Let's add one last event handler to assist us with our navigation. Whenever we change pages on a MultiPage control, the control's `Change` event fires. We'll use that event to grab the value of the current page and store it in our `m_oWizard` object's `CurrentPage` property.

Add the following code to the `MultiPage1` control's `Change` event:

```
Private Sub MultiPage1_Change()
  m_oWizard.CurrentPage = MultiPage1.Value + 1
End Sub
```

Now that we have our navigation working, let's give it a try:

1. With the UserForm open in Design view, click the Run button on the Standard toolbar or press the F5 key.

2. Once the form is open, click the Next Button to move to the second step in our wizard, as defined on our configuration worksheet. This should be the Address screen. Notice that both navigation buttons are now enabled, as shown in Figure 4-32.

3. Click the Previous button to navigate back to the Personal screen, and the Previous button will no longer be active.

4. Click the Next button until you are at the last screen as defined on our configuration worksheet. This should be the Network Access screen. The Next button will no longer be enabled, as shown in Figure 4-33.

5. Stop the form by clicking the X button.

Figure 4-32. *Both navigation buttons are enabled.*

Figure 4-33. *The Next button is disabled on the last screen in the wizard.*

Saving the Employee Record

We've done a lot of work so far, and we've got some pretty neat functionality provided to our
UserForm from our custom objects. The only thing missing is saving the data to the EmpData
worksheet.

Normally, we might create a subroutine, name it something like SaveData(), and call it from our cmdSave_Click event—but our cHRData class already has a SaveEmployee method. We can call that directly from cmdSave_Click with no need to create a save function on our form.

Insert the following code in the cmdSave_Click event:

```
Private Sub cmdSave_Click()
Dim oHRData As cHRData

  Set oHRData.Worksheet = Sheets("EmpData")
  oHRData.SaveEmployee m_oEmployee

  Set oHRData = Nothing
End Sub
```

After setting the Worksheet property so that our cHRData object knows where to save the data, we call the SaveEmployee method, passing in our m_oEmployee object, which contains all the data to save.

Cleaning Up

We've almost got a complete application finished. Let's finish off by adding code to our Cancel button and putting some cleanup code in our form's Terminate event.

Add the following line of code to the cmdCancel button's Click event:

```
Private Sub cmdCancel_Click()
  Unload Me
End Sub
```

This single line of code simply unloads the form without saving any values.

Now we'll clean up the objects used by our HRWizard UserForm. Add the following to the UserForm_Terminate event handler:

```
Private Sub UserForm_Terminate()
  Set m_oEmployee = Nothing
  Set m_oLM = Nothing
  Set m_oWizard = Nothing
End Sub
```

Now let's add a simple function to our project to open the Wizard form. In the VBE, add a standard module. Add the following method to the standard module:

```
Sub StartWizard()
  HRWizard.Show
End Sub
```

This single line of code will display the UserForm when it is run.

Testing the HRWizard Application

It's time to take our wizard for a test ride. Let's enter some data into each screen of the wizard and save it to the EmpData worksheet.

From the Excel workbook, run the StartWizard subroutine from the Macro dialog box, as shown in Figure 4-34.

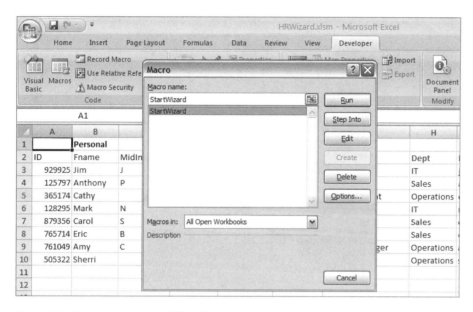

Figure 4-34. *Running the StartWizard macro*

Figures 4-35 to 4-39 show some sample input values and the saved data on the EmpData worksheet.

Figure 4-35. *Personal information added*

Figure 4-36. *Address information added*

Figure 4-37. *Equipment information added*

Figure 4-38. *Access level information added*

8	765714	Eric	B	Anders	3/11/1966	555-55-5560	Sales
9	761049	Amy	C	Cannon	9/20/1983	555-55-5561	Project Manager
10	505322	Sherri		Early	9/21/1983	555-55-5562	Director
11	334650	James	P	Page	4/5/1946	555-55-5563	Developer

Figure 4-39. *New employee data added to table*

Summary

This chapter has explored UserForms in Excel 2007. UserForms allow developers to provide a clean, easy-to-navigate data entry or retrieval experience to users. When users are entering data into a large or unwieldy spreadsheet, we can provide a logical user experience by creating applications with UserForms.

Form design is quick and easy using the controls provided in the UserForm Toolbox. Although both of the samples in this chapter used only one UserForm each, you can place as many as you need in your applications.

We used a somewhat nonstandard technique for adding functionality to our UserForms by wrapping our code in custom objects in class modules.

The code behind our form is much cleaner than if we had coded directly behind the form. How many module-level variables did we declare in our form's code-behind? Only four. How many might we have used if we had coded our functionality right on the form? Certainly more than four.

Even if using classes gave us nothing more than better-organized code, I'd say it would be worth the effort. And yes, it's a bit more effort than just dropping code in any standard module and trying to manage it. But we actually get more than organization. By wrapping our functionality in classes, we have the opportunity to give more thought to our code, and in some cases develop classes we can use in other projects.

■ ■ ■

Charting in Excel 2007

Excel 2007 provides us with an easy-to-use chart-creation tool that quickly lets us create and modify or enhance the charts we build. Microsoft has rebuilt the UI to include tools that make chart type selection quick and easy. There are tools to allow us to quickly change, remove, or add chart elements like titles, legends, data labels, and more. And charts now look even better through the use of ClearType fonts that improve readability.

Getting Started

As with many of the previous features we've explored, we'll manually create a few different charts and record macros to take a look at some of the chart object properties and methods. Then we'll write our own code to create charts for our users.

1. In the Download section for this book on the Apress web site, find the file named Chart01.xlsx and open the workbook.

2. Since we know we'll be inserting code into this workbook, let's save it in the macro-enabled format, as Chart01.xlsm.

3. Activate the Monthly Total Sales Amount worksheet.

The Chart01.xlsm file shown in Figure 5-1 contains three worksheets containing Northwind sales data, including sales by category, sales amounts by product, and total sales for products in the beverage product line.

4. On the Developer ribbon, choose Record Macro from the Code section.

5. Name the Macro MakeBeverageSalesChart, as shown in Figure 5-2.

6. Click OK to run the Macro Recorder.

7. Select the data in cells A1:E7, as in Figure 5-3.

	A	B	C	D	E	F	G	H
1		Beer	Chai	Coffee	Green Tea	Grand Total		
2	Jan	$1,400.00	$1,270.00	$1,322.00	$500.00	$4,492.00		
3	Feb	$1,000.00	$1,350.00	$1,200.00	$650.00	$4,200.00		
4	Mar	$2,500.00	$1,450.00	$2,875.00	$822.25	$7,647.25		
5	Apr	$5,418.00	$1,225.00	$2,500.00	$1,000.00	$10,143.00		
6	May	$6,000.00	$1,300.00	$2,750.00	$950.00	$11,000.00		
7	Jun	$8,000.00	$1,099.00	$2,233.00	$800.00	$12,132.00		
8	Grand Total	$24,318.00	$7,694.00	$12,880.00	$4,722.25	$49,614.25		
9								
10								
11								
12								
13								
14								
15								
16								
17								
18								
19								
20								
21								
22								
23								

◄ ◄ ► ► **Monthly Total Sales Amount** ╱ Sales By Category ╱ Sales Amount By Product ╲

Figure 5-1. *Northwind sales data on the Monthly Total Sales Amount worksheet*

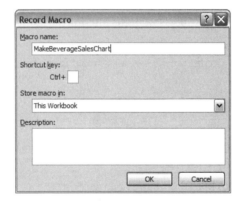

Figure 5-2. *Recording the MakeBeverageSalesChart macro*

	A	B	C	D	E	F	G
1		Beer	Chai	Coffee	Green Tea	Grand Total	
2	Jan	$1,400.00	$1,270.00	$1,322.00	$500.00	$4,492.00	
3	Feb	$1,000.00	$1,350.00	$1,200.00	$650.00	$4,200.00	
4	Mar	$2,500.00	$1,450.00	$2,875.00	$822.25	$7,647.25	
5	Apr	$5,418.00	$1,225.00	$2,500.00	$1,000.00	$10,143.00	
6	May	$6,000.00	$1,300.00	$2,750.00	$950.00	$11,000.00	
7	Jun	$8,000.00	$1,099.00	$2,233.00	$800.00	$12,132.00	
8	Grand Total	$24,318.00	$7,694.00	$12,880.00	$4,722.25	$49,614.25	
9							
10							

Figure 5-3. *Data selected for charting*

■**Note** You'll notice that we did not select the row or column containing the total sales amounts. Excel will include them in the chart, which will throw our vertical (value) axis amounts off.

8. On the Insert Ribbon, go to the Charts section, and click the Column chart type drop-down list to display the many column chart types available to you.

9. In the 3-D Column section, choose the first (leftmost) item, the 3-D Clustered Column chart type, as shown in Figure 5-4.

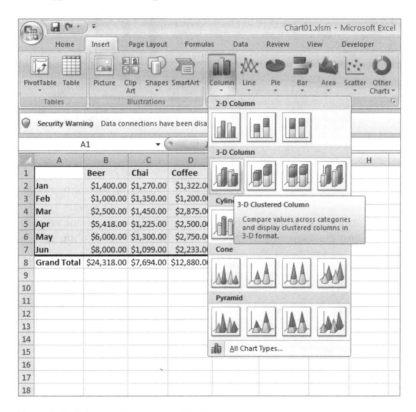

Figure 5-4. *Column chart type selection menu*

10. Stop the Macro Recorder.

The new chart is inserted in the worksheet. Notice in Figure 5-5 that Excel has highlighted the data ranges associated with each chart element (legend, values, and horizontal axis label ranges).

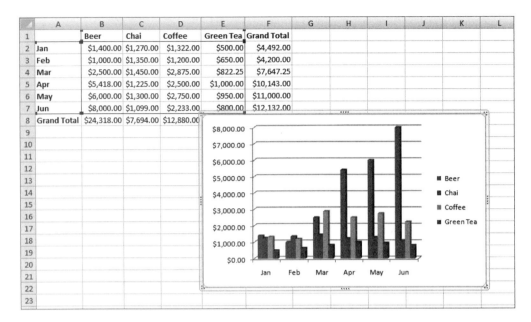

Figure 5-5. *The Beverage sales chart*

In addition to inserting the chart, Excel also added a context ribbon. Context ribbons provide commands relative to the currently selected object. In this case it's a chart, but it could be an inserted image or any other object that can be acted upon. Context ribbons are noted by a title bar above the ribbon area. Figure 5-6 shows the Chart Tools context ribbon. It contains three of its own ribbons: Design, Layout, and Format.

Figure 5-6. *The Chart Tools context ribbon*

Excel's default charting behavior is to display the data values by column (by product in this example). The vertical and horizontal axes may not show the data with the orientation you expected. Assuming that is the case here, let's record a macro so we can see the command Excel applies to switch the chart's data orientation from column to row.

1. On the Developer ribbon, click Record Macro.

2. Name the macro ChartByRow.

3. Select the chart by clicking anywhere inside of it.

4. Select the Design ribbon from Chart Tools.

5. From the Data section of the Design ribbon, select the Switch Row/Column command (Figure 5-7).

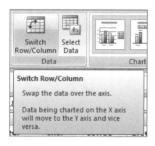

Figure 5-7. *The Switch Row/Column command on the Data tab*

6. Stop the Macro Recorder.

The chart should now look like Figure 5-8.

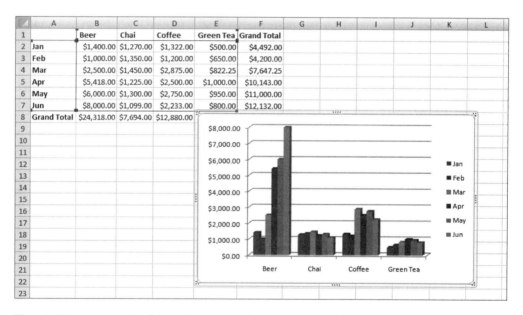

Figure 5-8. *Beverage sales chart with rows and columns switched*

The original chart in Figure 5-5 showed us the sales grouped by month, and was helpful in showing which product lines had strong sales in a given month. By choosing the Switch Row/Column command, we can quickly view the monthly sales trend for each product. Is it a coincidence that beer sales went up as summer approached?

Looking at the Code

Let's take a look at the code we've generated so far. The MakeBeverageSalesChart macro created a 3-D bar chart for us using a data range we selected. The ChartByRow macro switched the data orientation of the chart from the default, column, to row.

```
Sub MakeBeverageSalesChart()
'
' MakeBeverageSalesChart Macro
'


'
    Range("A1:E7").Select
    ActiveSheet.Shapes.AddChart.Select
    ActiveChart.SetSourceData Source:=Range( _
        "'Monthly Total Sales Amount'!$A$1:$E$7")
    ActiveChart.ChartType = xl3DColumnClustered
End Sub
```

The first line of code selects the data range for the chart. The next line adds a chart and activates it via its `Select` method. Charts are members of the `Shape` class, and the `AddChart` method returns a `Shape` object.

```
ActiveSheet.Shapes.AddChart.Select
```

The `AddChart` method has a few optional arguments (listed in Table 5-1) and no required arguments.

Table 5-1. *AddChart Method Arguments*

Name	Data Type	Description
Type	xlChartType	Type of chart (bar, line, pie, etc.)
Left	Variant	Distance from the left edge of the chart to the left edge of Column A
Top	Variant	Distance from the top edge of the chart to the top edge of the worksheet
Width	Variant	Width of the chart
Height	Variant	Height of the chart

The `Type` property is of data type `xlChartType`. This enumeration includes all of the chart types Excel ships with, as shown in Table 5-2.

Table 5-2. *The xlChartType Enumerations*

Name	Description	Value
xl3DArea	3D area	-4098
xl3DAreaStacked	3D stacked area	78
xl3DAreaStacked100	100% stacked area	79
xl3DBarClustered	3D clustered bar	60

Name	Description	Value
xl3DBarStacked	3D stacked bar	61
xl3DBarStacked100	3D 100% stacked bar	62
xl3DColumn	3D column	-4100
xl3DColumnClustered	3D clustered column	54
xl3DColumnStacked	3D stacked column	55
xl3DColumnStacked100	3D 100% stacked column	56
xl3DLine	3D line	-4101
xl3DPie	3D pie	-4102
xl3DPieExploded	Exploded 3D pie	70
xlArea	Area	1
xlAreaStacked	Stacked area	76
xlAreaStacked100	100% stacked area	77
xlBarClustered	Clustered bar	57
xlBarOfPie	Bar of pie	71
xlBarStacked	Stacked bar	58
xlBarStacked100	100% stacked bar	59
xlBubble	Bubble	15
xlBubble3DEffect	Bubble with 3D effects	87
xlColumnClustered	Clustered column	51
xlColumnStacked	Stacked column	52
xlColumnStacked100	100% stacked column	53
xlConeBarClustered	Clustered cone bar	102
xlConeBarStacked	Stacked cone bar	103
xlConeBarStacked100	100% stacked cone bar	104
xlConeCol	3D cone column	105
xlConeColClustered	Clustered cone column	99
xlConeColStacked	Stacked cone column	100
xlConeColStacked100	100% stacked cone column	101
xlCylinderBarClustered	Clustered cylinder bar	95
xlCylinderBarStacked	Stacked cylinder bar	96
xlCylinderBarStacked100	100% stacked cylinder bar	97
xlCylinderCol	3D cylinder column	98
xlCylinderColClustered	Clustered cone column	92
xlCylinderColStacked	Stacked cone column	93
xlCylinderColStacked100	100% stacked cylinder column	94
xlDoughnut	Doughnut	-4120
xlDoughnutExploded	Exploded doughnut	80

Continued

Table 5-2. *Continued*

Name	Description	Value
xlLine	Line	4
xlLineMarkers	Line with markers	65
xlLineMarkersStacked	Stacked line with markers	66
xlLineMarkersStacked100	100% stacked line with markers	67
xlLineStacked	Stacked line	63
xlLineStacked100	100% stacked line	64
xlPie	Pie	5
xlPieExploded	Exploded pie	69
xlPieOfPie	Pie of pie	68
xlPyramidBarClustered	Clustered pyramid bar	109
xlPyramidBarStacked	Stacked pyramid bar	110
xlPyramidBarStacked100	100% stacked pyramid bar	111
xlPyramidCol	3D pyramid column	112
xlPyramidColClustered	Clustered pyramid column	106
xlPyramidColStacked	Stacked pyramid column	107
xlPyramidColStacked100	100% stacked pyramid column	108
xlRadar	Radar	-4151
xlRadarFilled	Filled radar	82
xlRadarMarkers	Radar with data markers	81
xlStockHLC	High-low-close	88
xlStockOHLC	Open-high-low-close	89
xlStockVHLC	Volume-high-low-close	90
xlStockVOHLC	Volume-open-high-low-close	91
xlSurface	3D surface	83
xlSurfaceTopView	Surface (top view)	85
xlSurfaceTopViewWireframe	Surface (top view wireframe)	86
xlSurfaceWireframe	3D surface (wireframe)	84
xlXYScatter	Scatter	-4169
xlXYScatterLines	Scatter with lines	74
xlXYScatterLinesNoMarkers	Scatter with lines and no data markers	75
xlXYScatterSmooth	Scatter with smoothed lines	72
xlXYScatterSmoothNoMarkers	Scatter with smoothed lines and no data markers	73

The next line of code assigns the selected range of data to the chart's Source property:

```
ActiveChart.SetSourceData Source:=Range( ➥
        "'Monthly Total Sales Amount'!$A$1:$E$7")
```

The last line of the MakeBeverageSalesChart macro sets the type of chart directly using the `ChartType` property of the `ActiveChart` object:

```
ActiveChart.ChartType = xl3DColumnClustered
```

The `ChartType` property is the same property from the optional arguments of the `AddChart` method we saw in the second line of this macro. I've always been a proponent of using less code when possible. You could shorten the `MakeBeverageSalesChart` subroutine by leaving the direct assignment of the `ChartType` property out and setting the `ChartType` when calling the `AddChart` method.

The modified version of this code looks like Listing 5-1.

Listing 5-1. *Modified MakeBeverageSalesChart Macro*

```
Sub MakeBeverageSalesChart()
'
' MakeBeverageSalesChart Macro
'

'
    Range("A1:E7").Select
    ActiveSheet.Shapes.AddChart(xl3DColumnClustered).Select
    ActiveChart.SetSourceData Source:=Range( ➥
        "'Monthly Total Sales Amount'!$A$1:$E$7")
End Sub
```

Now let's look at the code we created to switch the chart data orientation from column to row in the ChartByRow macro:

```
Sub ChartByRow()
'
' ChartByRow Macro
'

'
    ActiveSheet.ChartObjects("Chart 1").Activate
    ActiveChart.PlotBy = xlRows
End Sub
```

You'll recall the first thing we did was select our chart. The first line of this code calls the `ChartObjects.Activate` method to activate the chart named Chart 1 (the default name given to our chart). A `ChartObject` represents a chart embedded on a worksheet. The `ChartObjects` object contains a collection of all the `ChartObject` objects on a chart sheet, dialog sheet, or worksheet. (I realize the word *object* was used an awful lot in that last sentence, but let me remind you that I did not name these objects!)

Like any other `Collection` object, `ChartObjects` in our ChartByRow macro refers to Chart 1 by name, but it also could have referred to it by its index in the collection, as follows:

```
ActiveSheet.ChartObjects(1).Activate
```

The next line of code is where the work is being done:

```
ActiveChart.PlotBy = xlRows
```

The `ActiveChart.PlotBy` property sets or returns a value of the `XlRowCol` enumeration. Table 5-3 lists the values of the `XlRowCol` enumerated items.

Table 5-3. *XlRowCol Enumeration*

Name	Value
xlRows	1
xlColumns	2

Summarizing with Pie Charts

In `Chart01.xlsm`, select the Sales By Category worksheet. Here you'll see a list of product categories with sales quantities by month, as in Figure 5-9.

	A	B	C	D
1	Category	Month	Quantity	
2	Baked Goods & Mixes	Jan	30	
3	Baked Goods & Mixes	Feb	20	
4	Baked Goods & Mixes	Mar	10	
5	Baked Goods & Mixes	Apr	45	
6	Beverages	Jan	135	
7	Beverages	Mar	925	
8	Beverages	Apr	387	
9	Beverages	Jun	5	
10	Candy	Feb	10	
11	Candy	Mar	100	
12	Candy	Apr	10	
13	Candy	Jun	80	
14	Canned Fruit & Vegetables	Jun	40	
15	Canned Meat	Apr	80	
16	Canned Meat	May	40	
17	Condiments	Mar	10	
18	Condiments	Apr	50	
19	Condiments	Jun	30	
20	Dairy Products	Apr	90	
21	Dried Fruit & Nuts	Jan	60	

Figure 5-9. *The Sales By Category worksheet*

This data provides us with a great format to display each category in a pie chart to see how overall sales looked by month for each product line. Before you begin charting data like this, it's a good idea to make sure the data is sorted correctly to make your selections for charting easier.

1. Put the cursor anywhere in the data table on the Sales By Category worksheet.

2. On the Data ribbon, choose the Sort command, as shown in Figure 5-10.

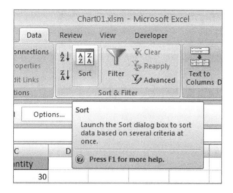

Figure 5-10. *The Sort command on the Data ribbon*

The Sort dialog box appears, as shown in Figure 5-11.

Figure 5-11. *The Sort dialog box*

In this case, Excel made a guess that we want to sort by the Month column (and we are going to override this).We want to sort by Category first, and then by Month.

■**Note** As I was testing this code, I had various results in what Excel decided would be the "Sort by" column. These results ranged from Month, as shown in Figure 5-11, to Category, to a blank value. Your results may vary.

---

3. Choose Category from the "Sort by" list under the Column listing, as shown in Figure 5-12.

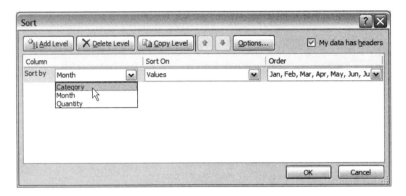

Figure 5-12. *Choosing Category as the first sort field*

4. Choose A-Z from the Order drop-down list, as shown in Figure 5-13.

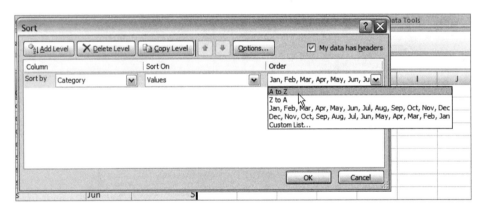

Figure 5-13. *Choosing the sort order for Category*

5. Click the Add Level button on the Sort dialog box to add a new blank sort item to the sort list, as shown in Figure 5-14.

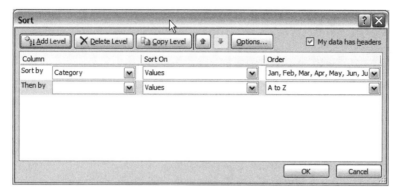

Figure 5-14. *New item added to the sort list*

6. In the "Then by" drop-down list, select Month, as shown is Figure 5-15.

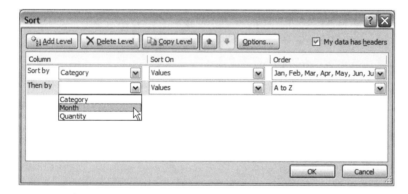

Figure 5-15. *Adding Month to the sort list*

7. Select Custom List from the Order drop-down, as in Figure 5-16. If we choose either alpha sort option, the months will sort alphabetically by name rather than ascending or descending order by month.

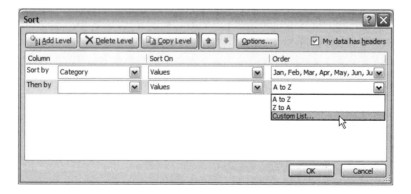

Figure 5-16. *Choosing Custom List*

8. The Custom Lists dialog box will appear. Choose the item labeled Jan, Feb, Mar, and so on, as shown in Figure 5-17.

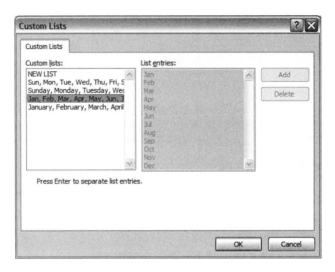

Figure 5-17. *Custom Lists dialog box*

9. Click OK to return to the Sort dialog box.

10. Click OK to close the Sort dialog box and sort the data.

The data should now look like that in Figure 5-9.

Creating the Pie Chart

In this example, we are going to create a pie chart based on the data for one product category. The chart will show the monthly sales for the category. Then we'll explore options to reuse the code and automate the creation of pie charts for each product line.

1. Select the Sales By Category worksheet.

2. Create a new macro and name it MakePieChart.

3. Select the data range that contains the data for the Baked Goods & Mixes category (A2:C5), as shown in Figure 5-18.

	A	B	C	D
1	Category	Month	Quantity	
2	Baked Goods & Mixes	Jan	30	
3	Baked Goods & Mixes	Feb	20	
4	Baked Goods & Mixes	Mar	10	
5	Baked Goods & Mixes	Apr	45	

Figure 5-18. *Selection for pie chart*

4. On the Insert ribbon, select Pie from the Charts section, as shown in Figure 5-19.

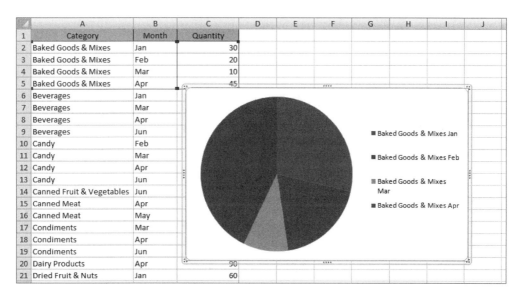

Figure 5-19. *Selecting a 2D pie chart from the ribbon*

The pie chart is displayed, but as Figure 5-20 shows, it is not exactly what we might have expected. Excel combined the first two columns of data and created the legend from them. The data itself is fine. With a couple of quick adjustments, we will modify the legend to show the month name only, and we'll add a title to the chart showing the product category.

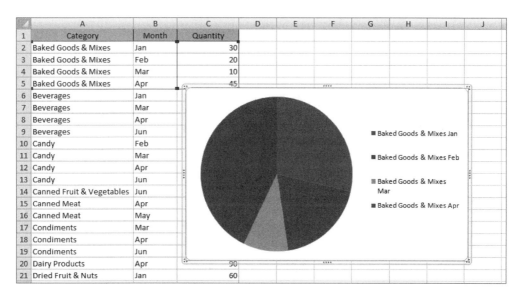

Figure 5-20. *The new pie chart as created*

5. With the Macro Recorder still running, select the pie chart if it's not already selected.

6. Go to Chart Tools ➤ Design ribbon, and choose the Select Data command, as shown in Figure 5-21.

Figure 5-21. *The Select Data command*

7. The Select Data Source dialog box will appear, as shown in Figure 5-22.

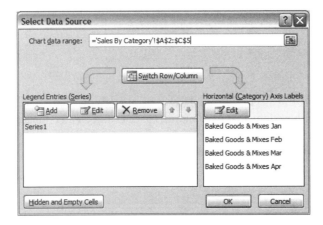

Figure 5-22. *The Select Data Source dialog box*

The Select Data Source dialog box contains functions to set the data range for the chart, to switch row/column orientation, to assign a range that contains the data values for the chart series, and to assign a range that contains the legend information.

We see in Figure 5-22 that the Chart data range, ='Sales By Category'!$A$2:$C$5, is correct, and we do not want to switch the row/column orientation. We need to correct the legend information display, and we want to use the category information to add a title to the chart.

8. In the Legend Entries (Series) section, at the bottom left of the Select Data Source dialog box, select Series 1 from the list.

9. Click the Edit button to display the Edit Series dialog box (shown in Figure 5-23).

Figure 5-23. *The Edit Series dialog box*

10. To add the title, in the Series name text box, type =**'Sales By Category'!$A$2** (or use the range selector to navigate to cell A2 and let Excel insert the range reference for you). Figure 5-24 shows the Edit Series dialog box with this value entered.

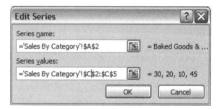

Figure 5-24. *Series name range reference added to the Edit Series dialog box*

11. Click OK to store the range reference.

12. In the Horizontal (Category) Axis Labels section, at the bottom right of the Select Data Source dialog box, click the Edit button to show the Axis Labels dialog box, as shown in Figure 5-25 (no selection is necessary).

Figure 5-25. *The Axis Labels dialog box*

13. In the "Axis label range" text box, type in =**'Sales By Category'!$B$2:$B$5** to tell Excel to show only the month names in the legend (or use the range selector to select cells B2:B5 and let Excel insert the range reference for you).

14. Click OK to store the range reference.

The Select Data Source dialog box should look like Figure 5-26.

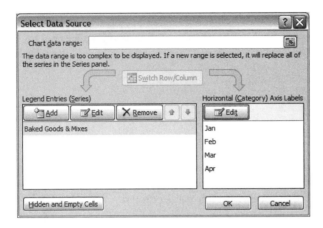

Figure 5-26. *The Select Data Source dialog after edits*

15. Click OK to close the Select Data Source dialog box and save the changes to the chart.

16. Stop the Macro Recorder.

Figure 5-27 shows the updated chart with the category as the chart title and the month names for the legend.

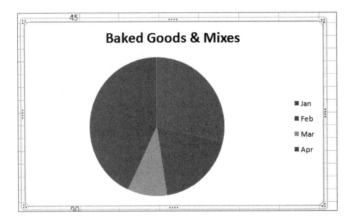

Figure 5-27. *The updated pie chart*

A Look at the Code

Now let's take a look at the code behind the process we just walked through. As you might expect, the first few lines look very similar to the MakeBeverageSalesChart macro, right up to the point where we set the chart type:

```
Sub MakePieChart()
'
' MakePieChart Macro
'

'
    Range("A2:C5").Select
    ActiveSheet.Shapes.AddChart.Select
    ActiveChart.SetSourceData Source:=Range("'Sales By Category'!$A$2:$C$5")
    ActiveChart.ChartType = xlPie
    ActiveChart.SeriesCollection(1).Name = "='Sales By Category'!$A$2"
    ActiveChart.SeriesCollection(1).XValues = "='Sales By Category'!$B$2:$B$5"
End Sub
```

The two lines of code following `ActiveChart.ChartType = xlPie`, where we set the chart type, define the name or title of the chart and the legend values (in this case the range B2:B5).

Let's look at the line of code that sets the name of the data series in our pie chart:

```
ActiveChart.SeriesCollection(1).Name = "='Sales By Category'!$A$2"
```

The `SeriesCollection(index)` object collection contains the data series for the chart. The index represents the order in which the series was added to the chart. In the case of our pie chart, there is only one series. Here we are setting the name to the first value in the Category column of our data range.

The last line of code changes the legend to simply show the month value without appending the category to each legend item.

```
ActiveChart.SeriesCollection(1).XValues = "='Sales By Category'!$B$2:$B$5"
```

More Pie for Everyone

So we've created a pie chart and modified some of its properties to make the data displayed more meaningful. We've got quite a few categories on our Sales By Category worksheet. Can we use what we've learned and the code we've created to generate charts for the remaining categories? Of course!

Excel does not always place charts in the most appropriate place on a worksheet, so before we begin, let's be sure to move the Baked Goods & Mixes chart to the right of the data range on the Sales By Category worksheet by dragging and dropping it, as shown in Figure 5-28.

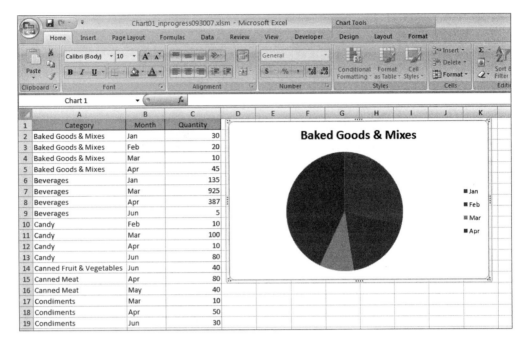

Figure 5-28. *Chart moved next to data range*

Next we'd like to chart the Beverages product category in a manner similar to the Baked Goods & Mixes pie chart. The simplest way to start is to copy the code from the MakePieChart macro we just recorded and modify it to use the data range A6:C9, which contains the Beverage category sales information.

1. If it's not already open, open the VBE by going to the Developer ribbon and selecting Code ➤ Visual Basic, or by pressing Alt+F11.

2. If it's not already open, open Standard Module1.

3. Copy the MakePieChart macro.

4. Paste the copy below MakePieChart and rename it MakePieChart2.

5. Modify all range references to refer to the data range containing the Beverage category sales information, as shown in Listing 5-2.

Listing 5-2. *MakePieChart2 Subroutine Modified to Chart the Beverage Category*

```
Sub MakePieChart2()
    Range("A6:C9").Select
    ActiveSheet.Shapes.AddChart.Select
    ActiveChart.SetSourceData Source:=Range("'Sales By Category'!$A$6:$C$9")
    ActiveChart.ChartType = xlPie
    ActiveChart.SeriesCollection(1).Name = "='Sales By Category'!$A$6"
    ActiveChart.SeriesCollection(1).XValues = "='Sales By Category'!$B$6:$B$9"
End Sub
```

As in our original example, we are selecting a range of data (A6:C9), and then adding a chart and setting the source data range to the selected range. Then we set the chart type to Pie (`xlPie`) and set the name and legend values.

6. Run the MakePieChart2 macro.

As shown in Figure 5-29, Excel still insists on placing the pie chart on top of our data range. In fact, if we had not moved the Baked Goods & Mixes pie chart, the new chart would be sitting on top of it (and it still is partially covering our existing chart)!

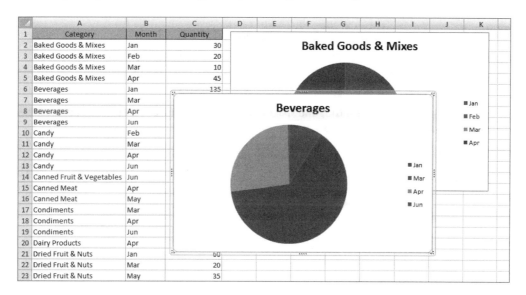

Figure 5-29. *Excel places any new chart on our data range.*

Not to worry. You'll recall that when we created our first chart using the Macro Recorder, Excel used the `AddChart` method to insert the chart. We looked at the optional arguments for that method in Table 5-1. These optional arguments include the type of chart and its top, left, width, and height settings (in pixels). We can use these optional arguments to place the new chart immediately below the existing chart, and align it with it as well.

1. Delete the Beverages pie chart from the Sales By Category worksheet.

   a. Select the chart by clicking it on its borders.

   b. Press the Delete key on your keyboard.

2. On Standard Module1, create a new subroutine and name it `PlaceChart`.

3. Add the following variable declarations to the `PlaceChart` subroutine:

```
Dim arrChartInfo(3) As Variant
Dim spacer As Integer
```

The `arrChartInfo(3)` variable will hold an array that contains information about the existing chart (Chart 1), such as its name and top, left, and height values. We'll use the `spacer` variable to place some empty space between our charts.

4. Add the following code after the variable declarations:

```
With ActiveSheet.ChartObjects(1)
  arrChartInfo(0) = .Name
  arrChartInfo(1) = .Top
  arrChartInfo(2) = .Left
  arrChartInfo(3) = .Height
End With


spacer = 25
```

Within the With...End With block, we are setting the array elements equal to the Name, Top, Left, and Height properties of the ChartObjects(1) item, which is of course the existing (and only) chart on the worksheet at the moment. We could also have referred to the chart by name, as in ActiveSheet.ChartObjects("Chart 1").

For this example, we're setting the spacer variable to a value of 25, but you can use any value that suits your purpose.

5. Press Enter twice to insert blank lines in the code after spacer = 25.

6. Copy the code from the MakePieChart2 macro and paste it after the blank lines.

The completed PlaceChart subroutine should look like Listing 5-3.

Listing 5-3. *The Completed PlaceChart Subroutine*

```
Sub PlaceChart()
Dim arrChartInfo(3) As Variant
Dim spacer As Integer

  With ActiveSheet.ChartObjects(1)
    arrChartInfo(0) = .Name
    arrChartInfo(1) = .Top
    arrChartInfo(2) = .Left
    arrChartInfo(3) = .Height
  End With

  spacer = 25
  '
  ' The following code is from MakePieChart2 Macro
  '
    Range("A6:C9").Select
    ActiveSheet.Shapes.AddChart(, arrChartInfo(2), ➡
                      (arrChartInfo(1) + arrChartInfo(3) + spacer)) ➡
                      .Select
    ActiveChart.SetSourceData Source:=Range("'Sales By Category'!$A$6:$C$9")
```

```
ActiveChart.ChartType = xlPie
ActiveChart.SeriesCollection(1).Name = "='Sales By Category'!$A$6"
ActiveChart.SeriesCollection(1).XValues = "='Sales By Category'!$B$6:$B$9"
```

End Sub

7. Return to the Sales By Category worksheet and run the PlaceChart procedure.

Figure 5-30 shows the result of our placement efforts.

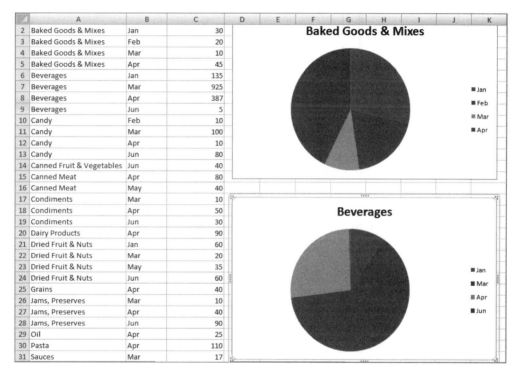

Figure 5-30. *Beverages chart aligned with Baked Goods & Mixes chart*

Fantastic! We modified the original MakePieChart code by changing the range references and referring to the location of the original chart to determine where to put the new chart. But let's make this code a bit more dynamic. Our users aren't going to give us ranges of data to chart, they most likely will want to create them on the fly as needed.

In our next example, we are going to give the user the ability to select a range of data to be charted. In addition, we'll make the placement of the chart more dynamic as well. In our last example, we knew we wanted to refer to the first chart on the worksheet. Now that we've got more than one chart on the worksheet, we'll need to grab the location of the last chart inserted and place our new chart below that.

Dynamically Placing a Chart

In the VBE, on Standard Module1, create a new subroutine called PlaceChartDynamic. Copy the code from the PlaceChart procedure and paste it into PlaceChartDynamic.

Before we begin our exercise, we're going to move the opening lines of code into their own function. This subroutine begins by getting location information about the chart we want to use as a placement reference, but is not directly involved in creating a chart. It's always a good idea from a maintenance perspective to keep our functional operations separate, so we are going to create a function that returns the location of a chart in an array.

Storing Chart Location in an Array

1. On Standard Module1, create a new function named GetChartInfo().

2. Add the following argument to the function:

   ```
   Private Function GetChartInfo(MyChart As ChartObject) As Variant
   ```

   The argument MyChart will pass a ChartObject into our function. From this object, we'll return the location information in GetChartInfo.

3. Add a variable: Dim varReturn As Variant. This will hold the return value for our function.

4. Move the code shown in bold in the following code block from the PlaceChartDynamic subroutine into GetChartInfo, under the variable declaration we just added.

The GetChartInfo code should look like this:

```
Private Function GetChartInfo(MyChart As ChartObject) As Variant
Dim varReturn As Variant
Dim arrChartInfo(3) As Variant
  With MyChart
    arrChartInfo(0) = .Name
    arrChartInfo(1) = .Top
    arrChartInfo(2) = .Left
    arrChartInfo(3) = .Height
  End With
End Function
```

5. Add the following code to assign the array to the return variable, and finally to assign varReturn as the return value of the function:

   ```
   varReturn = arrChartInfo

   GetChartInfo = varReturn
   ```

The completed function should look like that in Listing 5-4.

Listing 5-4. *The GetChartInfo Subroutine*

```
Private Function GetChartInfo(MyChart As ChartObject) As Variant
Dim varReturn As Variant
Dim arrChartInfo(3) As Variant
  With MyChart
    arrChartInfo(0) = .Name
    arrChartInfo(1) = .Top
    arrChartInfo(2) = .Left
    arrChartInfo(3) = .Height
  End With
  varReturn = arrChartInfo

  GetChartInfo = varReturn
End Function
```

Completing the PlaceChartDynamic Procedure

The PlaceChartDynamic subroutine currently looks like Listing 5-5, and is ready for a few modifications, including using the GetChartInfo method we just created.

Listing 5-5. *The PlaceChartDynamic Routine Is Ready for Modifications*

```
Sub PlaceChartDynamic()
Dim spacer As Integer

  spacer = 25

    Range("A6:C9").Select
    ActiveSheet.Shapes.AddChart(, arrChartInfo(2), ➥
                            (arrChartInfo(1) + arrChartInfo(3) + spacer)) ➥
                            .Select
    ActiveChart.SetSourceData Source:=Range("'Sales By Category'!$A$6:$C$9")
    ActiveChart.ChartType = xlPie
    ActiveChart.SeriesCollection(1).Name = "='Sales By Category'!$A$6"
    ActiveChart.SeriesCollection(1).XValues = "='Sales By Category'!$B$6:$B$9"
End Sub
```

Add the following variable declarations to PlaceChartDynamic:

```
Dim varChartInfo As Variant
Dim iChartIndex As Integer
```

The varChartInfo variable will hold the array returned from the GetChartInfo function and will be used to place our new chart. iChartIndex will hold the index value of the last chart added to the worksheet.

Let's take a look at the remaining code in the `PlaceChartDynamic` procedure to get an idea of the changes we'll make to make this routine much more flexible.

We see numerous hard-coded range references. Our new code will have to

- Find the last chart added and use its coordinates to insert the new chart below it

- Define the data range for the chart

- Define the cell that contains the name of the product category to display in the chart title

- Define the range containing the month values for the chart legend

Let's attack these one at time. First, let's get the chart location information from the `GetChartInfo` function.

Getting the Coordinates from the Existing Chart

Add the following lines of code:

```
iChartIndex = ActiveSheet.ChartObjects.Count
varChart = GetChartInfo(ActiveSheet.ChartObjects(iChartIndex)
```

The `ChartObjects.Count` property will return the value of the last chart added. Then we use that index to get the chart information.

As I noted at the end of the last example, we are going to let the user define the range to chart by selecting the data for a particular product category.

Defining the Data Range and Legend Information

Before we modify the remaining code and its range references, let's add a few variables to hold the range references from the user-defined selection.

1. Add the following variables:

   ```
   Dim sDataRange As String
   Dim sTitleRange As String
   Dim sLegendRange As String
   ```

2. Since the user will select the data for us, we can remove the following line of code:

   ```
   Range("A6:C9").Select
   ```

3. Put your cursor in the blank line created by removing the code in step 2, and add the following code:

   ```
   sDataRange = Selection.Address
   sTitleRange = Selection.Cells(1, 1).Address
   sLegendRange = Selection.Cells(1, 2).Address & ":" ➥
                  & Selection.Cells(1, 2).Offset(Selection.Rows.Count - 1).Address
   ```

The `Selection` object (which is of the generic `Object` type) holds a `Range` object in this case. Using the `Range`'s `Address` and `Cells` properties, we can determine the address of the entire range of the selection, the cell containing the title text (always the first cell in the data range), and the range of cells containing the legend information (always column B for each row in the selected range).

4. Moving to the next line of code, we are going to replace all references to the arrChartInfo array that we are no longer using with a reference to the return value of the GetChartInfo function, varChartInfo.

```
ActiveSheet.Shapes.AddChart(, arrChartInfo(2), ➡
                        (arrChartInfo(1) + arrChartInfo(3) + spacer)) ➡
                        .Select
```

When finished, the line of code that adds and places the new chart will look like this:

```
ActiveSheet.Shapes.AddChart(, varChartInfo(2), ➡
                        (varChartInfo(1) + varChartInfo(3) + spacer)) ➡
                        .Select
```

Setting the Data Range and Legend Information

Now we'll modify the line of code that sets the chart's data range.

1. Put your cursor on this line of code:

```
ActiveChart.SetSourceData Source:=Range("'Sales By Category'!$A$6:$C$9")
```

2. Modify it to read as follows:

```
ActiveChart.SetSourceData Source:=Range("'Sales By Category'!" & sDataRange)
```

3. Leave the next line of code as is:

```
ActiveChart.ChartType = xlPie
```

4. Now we'll set the title range. Put your cursor on this line of code:

```
ActiveChart.SeriesCollection(1).Name = "='Sales By Category'!$A$6"
```

5. Modify it to read as follows:

```
ActiveChart.SeriesCollection(1).Name = "='Sales By Category'!" & sTitleRange
```

6. All that's left is to set the legend text data range. Put your cursor on the last line of code:

```
ActiveChart.SeriesCollection(1).Name = "='Sales By Category'!" & sTitleRange
```

7. Modify it to read as follows:

```
ActiveChart.SeriesCollection(1).XValues = "='Sales By Category'!" ➡
                                            & sLegendRange
```

The completed subroutine should now look like Listing 5-6.

Listing 5-6. *The Completed PlaceChartDynamic Subroutine*

```
Sub PlaceChartDynamic()
Dim spacer As Integer
Dim varChartInfo As Variant
Dim iChartIndex As Integer
Dim sDataRange As String
Dim sTitleRange As String
Dim sLegendRange As String

    iChartIndex = ActiveSheet.ChartObjects.Count
    varChartInfo = GetChartInfo(ActiveSheet.ChartObjects(iChartIndex))

    spacer = 25


    sDataRange = Selection.Address
    sTitleRange = Selection.Cells(1, 1).Address
    sLegendRange = Selection.Cells(1, 2).Address & ":" ➠
                & Selection.Cells(1, 2).Offset(Selection.Rows.Count - 1).Address

    ActiveSheet.Shapes.AddChart(, varChartInfo(2), _
                            (varChartInfo(1) + varChartInfo(3) + spacer)) ➠
                            .Select
    ActiveChart.SetSourceData Source:=Range("'Sales By Category'!" & sDataRange)
    ActiveChart.ChartType = xlPie
    ActiveChart.SeriesCollection(1).Name = "='Sales By Category'!" & sTitleRange
    ActiveChart.SeriesCollection(1).XValues = "='Sales By Category'!" ➠
                                                        & sLegendRange
End Sub
```

Testing the Code

Now that we've got our code rewritten to be much more flexible, let's select a data range and create a formatted chart placed below the last chart on the Sales By Category worksheet.

1. Select the data for the Candy product line (cells A10:C13), as shown in Figure 5-31.

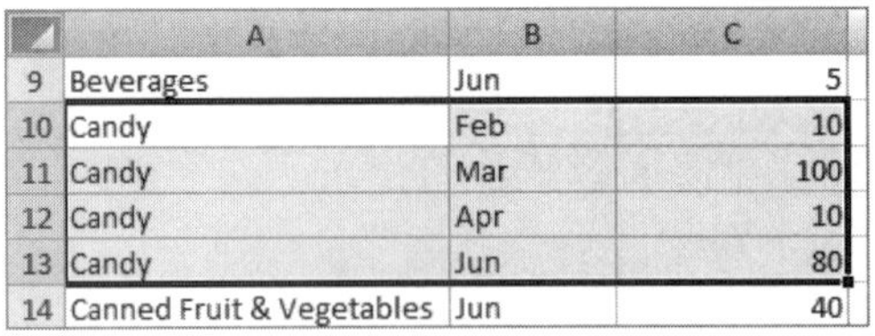

	A	B	C
9	Beverages	Jun	5
10	Candy	Feb	10
11	Candy	Mar	100
12	Candy	Apr	10
13	Candy	Jun	80
14	Canned Fruit & Vegetables	Jun	40

Figure 5-31. *Data selected for dynamic charting*

2. Run PlaceChartDynamic by going to the Developer ribbon and choosing Code ➤ Macros.

3. The new chart is inserted below the Beverages chart and is aligned to its left side, as shown in Figure 5-32.

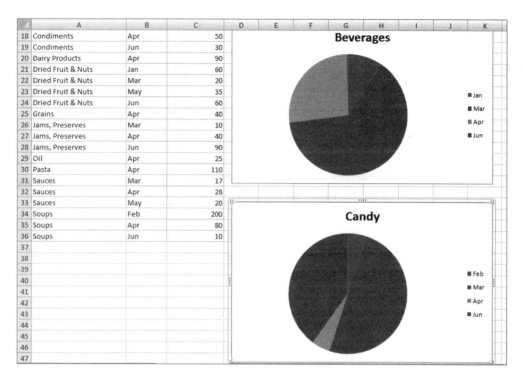

	A	B	C
18	Condiments	Apr	50
19	Condiments	Jun	30
20	Dairy Products	Apr	90
21	Dried Fruit & Nuts	Jan	60
22	Dried Fruit & Nuts	Mar	20
23	Dried Fruit & Nuts	May	35
24	Dried Fruit & Nuts	Jun	60
25	Grains	Apr	40
26	Jams, Preserves	Mar	10
27	Jams, Preserves	Apr	40
28	Jams, Preserves	Jun	90
29	Oil	Apr	25
30	Pasta	Apr	110
31	Sauces	Mar	17
32	Sauces	Apr	28
33	Sauces	May	20
34	Soups	Feb	200
35	Soups	Apr	80
36	Soups	Jun	10
37			
38			
39			
40			
41			
42			
43			
44			
45			
46			
47			

Figure 5-32. *The Candy chart is properly formatted and inserted below the Beverages chart.*

Summary

In this chapter, we've been exploring charting in Excel. We began by recording a macro while manually creating a bar chart. We examined the AddChart method, which adds a new chart to a worksheet, and we saw the SetSourceData method, which assigns a range of data to the chart. We saw in Table 5-2 the many types of charts Excel makes available to us. We also looked at the PlotBy property, which allows us to switch a chart's data orientation from row to column and vice versa.

We then looked at pie charts, and as we did, we also learned a bit about sorting data in Excel. Next, we learned how to use some of the AddChart method's arguments to place a chart at a given location on a worksheet. And finally, we expanded on that idea to create dynamic code that lets the user select a data range to chart, and we built routines to create a chart from that data, placing it below the last chart on the worksheet.

Charts are a great way to make large sets of data more understandable for analysis by compressing the data into a visual image. In the next chapter, we'll look at another one of Excel's excellent analysis tools: PivotTables.

■ ■ ■

CHAPTER 6

PivotTables

PivotTables are a neat feature of Excel 2007 that allows users to summarize and analyze data. By adding or removing data elements from an onscreen selection tool, your users can easily reshape their data for analysis or reporting.

A PivotTable report provides an interactive method to quickly and easily summarize large amounts of data (without the need to export the data to an external database system like Microsoft Access or an external reporting tool).

Here are some examples of when you might want to use a PivotTable to display your data:

- To query large amounts of data and create different views

- To aggregate and subtotal data, and/or create custom calculations and formulas

- To expand and collapse levels of data

- To move rows to columns or columns to rows to see different summaries of the source data (hence the term *pivot*)

PivotTables enable you to take huge amounts of data and present a concise, easy-to-read view of that data.

Putting Data into a PivotTable Report

In the Download section for this book on the Apress web site, find the file named PivotTable01.xlsx and open it.

Remember our fictitious band "VBA" from Chapter 1? Well, they've been out touring and their manager wants to see what's selling and what's not, and where items are selling best. PivotTable01.xlsx contains sales data from the first quarter of their tour, as shown in Figure 6-1.

	A	B	C	D	E	F
1	**Date**	**Product**	**City**	**State**	**Qty**	**Amount**
2	1/19/07	CD	New York	NY	72	720
3	1/19/07	T-Shirt	New York	NY	13	195
4	1/19/07	Tank Top	New York	NY	3	36
5	1/20/07	CD	Trenton	NJ	61	610
6	1/20/07	T-Shirt	Trenton	NJ	41	615
7	1/20/07	Tank Top	Trenton	NJ	10	120
8	1/26/07	CD	Philadelphia	PA	55	550
9	1/26/07	T-Shirt	Philadelphia	PA	67	1005
10	1/26/07	Tank Top	Philadelphia	PA	11	132
11	1/27/07	CD	Reading	PA	29	290
12	1/27/07	T-Shirt	Reading	PA	78	1170
13	1/27/07	Tank Top	Reading	PA	0	0
14	2/2/07	CD	Cherry Hill	NJ	63	630
15	2/2/07	T-Shirt	Cherry Hill	NJ	5	60
16	2/2/07	Tank Top	Cherry Hill	NJ	31	372
17	2/3/07	CD	New York	NY	34	340
18	2/3/07	T-Shirt	New York	NY	78	1170
19	2/3/07	Tank Top	New York	NY	25	300

Figure 6-1. *Tour sales data*

A good way for the manager to look at this data is via an Excel 2007 PivotTable report. We're going to record a macro while we create a PivotTable. Then we'll take a look at some of the properties and methods available to us.

1. Start the Macro Recorder (Developer ribbon ➤ Record Macro).

2. Name the new macro MakePivotTable.

3. Put the cursor anywhere inside the sales data.

4. Choose Insert Ribbon ➤ Tables ➤ PivotTable. The Create PivotTable dialog box will be displayed, as shown in Figure 6-2.

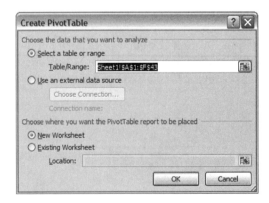

Figure 6-2. *Create PivotTable dialog box*

The Create PivotTable dialog box contains two sections. The first section is where you can choose a data source. This can be a table or range within an Excel workbook or data from an external source. External data is accessed through a connection file, such as an Office Data Connection (ODC) file (.odc) or a Universal Data Connection (UDC) file (.udcx).

The second section lets you dictate where you would like the PivotTable report to be placed.

5. For now, just accept the defaults and click OK. A blank PivotTable report will be inserted on Sheet4, as shown in Figure 6-3.

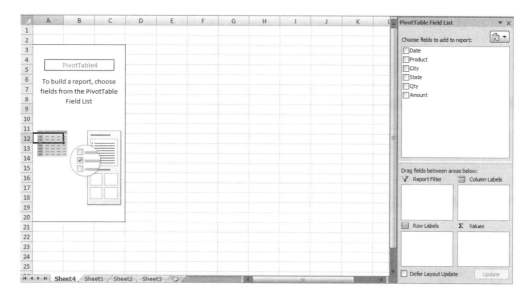

Figure 6-3. *Excel 2007 PivotTable report default view*

The new PivotTable report has a revamped interface that allows for easy manipulation of pivot data. All fields in the table are listed in the PivotTable Field List pane, which you can see on the right side of Figure 6-3. Check boxes are provided for users to choose the fields they want to include in the report. Text fields will by default place themselves in the Row Labels list and numeric fields will default to the Values list.

An easier way to create a report is to drag the field from the selection section at the top of the PivotTable Field List pane to the correct list below (shown in Figure 6-4).

Figure 6-4. *Dragging the State field to the Row Labels section*

Once you drop the field, the PivotTable updates to show the text or data (when available), as shown in Figure 6-5.

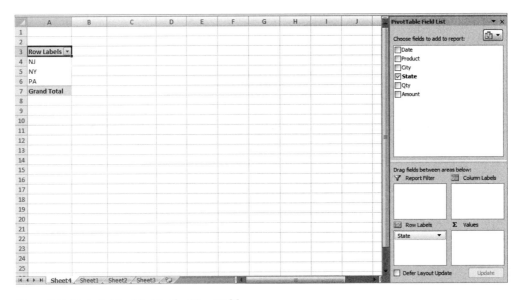

Figure 6-5. *State field added to the PivotTable*

6. Drag the Product field to the Column Labels list.

7. Drag the Qty field to the Values list. The PivotTable Field List pane should look like Figure 6-6.

Figure 6-6. *PivotTable Field List with all fields added*

The PivotTable report will look like Figure 6-7.

	A	B	C	D	E
1					
2					
3	Sum of Qty	Column Labels ▼			
4	Row Labels ▼	CD	Tank Top	T-Shirt	Grand Total
5	NJ	124	41	46	211
6	NY	345	255	447	1047
7	PA	180	27	234	441
8	Grand Total	649	323	727	1699
9					
10					
11					
12					

Figure 6-7. *The completed PivotTable report*

We see a sales summary by product line by state. But what if we also need to see sales by city within each state?

8. Drag the City field to the Row Labels list and place it under the State field.

The finished report should now look like Figure 6-8.

	A	B	C	D	E	
1						
2						
3	Sum of Qty	Column Labels ▾				
4	Row Labels ▾	CD	Tank Top	T-Shirt	Grand Total	
5	⊟ NJ	124	41	46	211	
6	Cherry Hill	63	31	5	99	
7	Trenton	61	10	41	112	
8	⊟ NY	345	255	447	1047	
9	Albany	9	41	78	128	
10	Buffalo	99	52	81	232	
11	New York	143	116	194	453	
12	Syracuse	85	5	16	106	
13	Trenton	9	41	78	128	
14	⊟ PA	180	27	234	441	
15	Philadelphia	151	27	156	334	
16	Reading	29	0	78	107	
17	Grand Total	649	323	727	1699	
18						
19						
20						
21						

Figure 6-8. *City added to PivotTable report*

9. Stop the Macro Recorder by clicking the Stop Recording command on the Developer ribbon.

If you have had any experience with previous versions of Excel PivotTable reports, you probably immediately noticed a change in the UI of the blank PivotTable.

The PivotTable Field List pane in Excel 2007 now does the work of all three components shown in Figure 6-9. The user experience is much cleaner this way, and makes using PivotTables much easier for users.

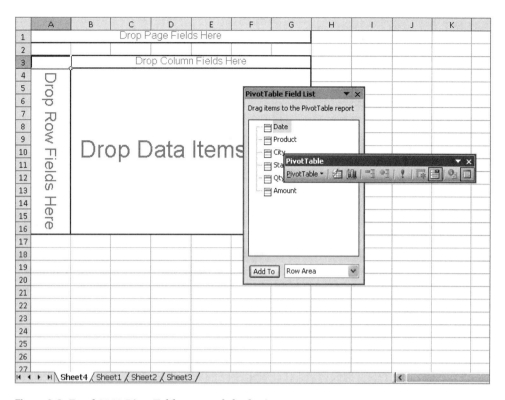

Figure 6-9. *Excel 2003 PivotTable report default view*

The Macro Code

Listing 6-1 shows the code the Macro Recorder generated for us.

Listing 6-1. *MakePivotTable Macro Code*

```
Sub MakePivotTable()
'
' MakePivotTable Macro
'

'
Sheets.Add
ActiveWorkbook.PivotCaches.Create(SourceType:=xlDatabase, SourceData:= ➥
    "Sheet1!R1C1:R43C6", Version:=xlPivotTableVersion12).CreatePivotTable ➥
    TableDestination:="Sheet4!R3C1", TableName:="PivotTable1", DefaultVersion ➥
    :=xlPivotTableVersion12
Sheets("Sheet4").Select
Cells(3, 1).Select
```

```
With ActiveSheet.PivotTables("PivotTable1").PivotFields("State")
    .Orientation = xlRowField
    .Position = 1
End With
With ActiveSheet.PivotTables("PivotTable1").PivotFields("Product")
    .Orientation = xlColumnField
    .Position = 1
End With
ActiveSheet.PivotTables("PivotTable1").AddDataField ActiveSheet.PivotTables(➥
    "PivotTable1").PivotFields("Qty"), "Sum of Qty", xlSum
With ActiveSheet.PivotTables("PivotTable1").PivotFields("City")
    .Orientation = xlRowField
    .Position = 2
End With
End Sub
```

The first thing the code does is add a new worksheet to the workbook. Then it creates the PivotTable using the source data range we provided in the Create PivotTable dialog box. Then it places the PivotTable on the new sheet (in this case Sheet4) and gives it a default name.

```
Sheets.Add
ActiveWorkbook.PivotCaches.Create(SourceType:=xlDatabase, SourceData:= ➥
    "Sheet1!R1C1:R43C6", Version:=xlPivotTableVersion12).CreatePivotTable ➥
    TableDestination:="Sheet4!R3C1", TableName:="PivotTable1", DefaultVersion ➥
    :=xlPivotTableVersion12
```

The PivotCaches.Create method takes three arguments, of which only one (SourceType) is required. The SourceData argument is required when SourceType does not equal xlExternal. Table 6-1 lists the PivotCaches.Create method's arguments and describes them.

Table 6-1. *PivotCaches.Create Method Arguments*

Name	Required (Y/N)	Data Type	Description
SourceType	Y	xlPivotTableSourceType	Choices are xlConsolidation, xlDatabase, or xlExternal
SourceData	N	Variant	The data for the new PivotTable cache
Version	N	Variant	Version of the PivotTable

The PivotCaches.Create method returns a PivotCache object. The Macro Recorder very cleverly calls the CreatePivotTable method based on the return from the Create method in one long (but readable) line of code:

```
ActiveWorkbook.PivotCaches.Create(SourceType:=xlDatabase, SourceData:= ➥
    "Sheet1!R1C1:R43C6", Version:=xlPivotTableVersion12).CreatePivotTable ➥
    TableDestination:="Sheet4!R3C1", TableName:="PivotTable1", DefaultVersion ➥
    :=xlPivotTableVersion12
```

The CreatePivotTable method defines where the table will be placed, its name, and its default version. Table 6-2 lists the CreatePivotTable method's arguments.

Table 6-2. *CreatePivotTable Method Arguments*

Name	Required (Y/N)	Data Type	Description
TableDestination	Y	Variant	The cell in the top-left corner of the PivotTable's destination range.
TableName	N	Variant	The name of the PivotTable report.
ReadData	N	Variant	Set to True to create a PivotTable cache that contains all of the records from the data source (can be very large). Set to False to enable setting some fields as server-based page fields before the data is read.
DefaultVersion	N	Variant	The default version of the PivotTable report.

The code then selects the new sheet and the starting range location for the PivotTable.

```
Sheets("Sheet4").Select
Cells(3, 1).Select
```

We added two text fields (State and Products) to the PivotTable Field List pane and one data field containing the item quantities (Qty):

```
With ActiveSheet.PivotTables("PivotTable1").PivotFields("State")
    .Orientation = xlRowField
    .Position = 1
End With
With ActiveSheet.PivotTables("PivotTable1").PivotFields("Product")
    .Orientation = xlColumnField
    .Position = 1
End With
ActiveSheet.PivotTables("PivotTable1").AddDataField ActiveSheet.PivotTables( ➥
    "PivotTable1").PivotFields("Qty"), "Sum of Qty", xlSum
```

This is where the code is telling the PivotTable how to display the data assigned to each PivotField object. The Orientation property is set to a value of the xlPivotFieldOrientation enumeration type, as shown in Table 6-3.

Table 6-3. *xlPivotFieldOrientation Enumerations*

Name	Value	Description
xlRowField	1	Row
xlColumnField	2	Column
xlPageField	3	Page
xlDataField	4	Data
xlHidden	0	Hidden

The Position property notes where in the row or column hierarchy the field belongs, and therefore how the data will be grouped on the PivotTable. After we added the City field to the Row Labels list in the PivotTable Field List pane, the next bit of code was added:

```
With ActiveSheet.PivotTables("PivotTable1").PivotFields("City")
    .Orientation = xlRowField
    .Position = 2
End With
```

Notice that its Orientation property is set to xlRowField, denoting row data, and its position is 2. So in the table's rows, we have State in position 1 and City in position 2. If you refer back to Figure 6-8, you can see the data hierarchy displayed.

Let's save this workbook as a macro-enabled workbook. Click the Office button and choose Save As ➤ Excel Macro-Enabled Workbook, leaving the name the same (except for the extension), as shown in Figure 6-10.

Figure 6-10. *Saving the file as macro-enabled*

Unfortunately, if we rerun the MakePivotTable macro again, we'll get an error, as shown in Figure 6-11.

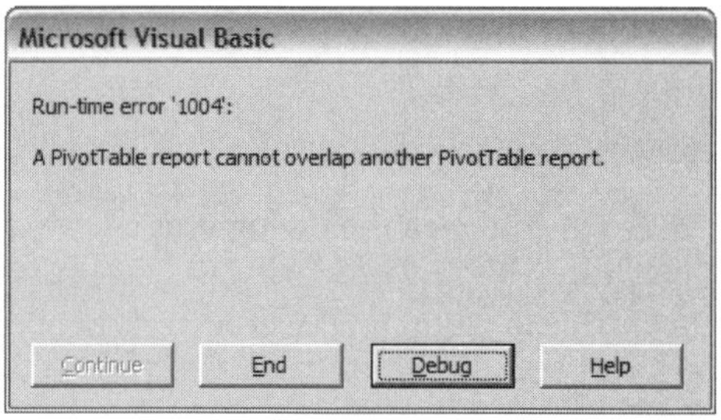

Figure 6-11. *Running MakePivotTable a second time generates an error.*

■Note The runtime error 1004 shown in Figure 6-11 was generated in Windows XP. Windows Vista users will still see runtime error 1004, but its description will read "Application-defined or object-defined error."

We can't drop another PivotTable on top of an existing PivotTable. Let's make a few changes to our code to allow us to create our PivotTables dynamically based upon data that is currently being viewed by the user.

There are two issues that stand out in our existing code:

- We have to add a new worksheet for an additional PivotTable for the data because we can't use the existing sheet (or we have to find a new location on the existing worksheet).

- What if the source data range expands (or shrinks) the next time we get this data?

In the VBE, add a new subroutine and name it MakeDynamicPivotTable. Copy the code from the MakePivotTable procedure, and then make the following modifications. Add the following variable declarations at the top of the MakeDynamicPivotTable procedure:

```
Dim ws As Worksheet
Dim rngRangeToPivot As Range
Dim sPivotLoc As String
```

The first variable, ws, will be used to store the new worksheet that we'll be adding. The next variable, rngRangeToPivot, will get the data source range for us regardless of number of rows. The last variable, sPivotLoc, will hold a string value denoting the range to place the new PivotTable.

The first thing we'll do is get the location of the data range that we'll be putting into our PivotTable. We'll do this first because once we add a new sheet, the data viewed by the user will no longer be active.

Add the following line of code to assign the current data region (the region where the cursor is currently placed):

```
Set rngRangeToPivot = ActiveCell.CurrentRegion
```

The `ActiveCell.Current` region property will retrieve the range of the contiguous set of cells surrounding the cursor location.

Now let's add a new worksheet and define the PivotTable location on the new worksheet:

```
Set ws = Sheets.Add
sPivotLoc = ws.Name & "!R3C1"
```

We're adding a new worksheet and assigning that worksheet to the `ws` variable. Then we're looking at that worksheet to determine its name and concatenating it to the cell location where the PivotTable will be place on the new worksheet. We're using Excel's default location of row 3/column 1, but you can place the PivotTable anywhere you like on your worksheet.

Finally, add the two commands shown in Listing 6-2 to make the `PivotCaches.Create` method and the `PivotCache.CreatePivotTable` table commands act on our new dynamic variables.

Listing 6-2. *Dynamic PivotTable Creation Code*

```
ActiveWorkbook.PivotCaches.Create(SourceType:=xlDatabase, SourceData:= ➥
    rngRangeToPivot, Version:=xlPivotTableVersion12).CreatePivotTable ➥
    TableDestination:=sPivotLoc, TableName:="PivotTable1", DefaultVersion ➥
    :=xlPivotTableVersion12
```

```
ws.Select
```

Compare this to the original version of these lines of code in Listing 6-3.

Listing 6-3. *Static Macro Recorder–Generated PivotTable Creation Code*

```
ActiveWorkbook.PivotCaches.Create(SourceType:=xlDatabase, SourceData:= ➥
    "Sheet1!R1C1:R43C6", Version:=xlPivotTableVersion12).CreatePivotTable ➥
    TableDestination:="Sheet4!R3C1", TableName:="PivotTable1", DefaultVersion ➥
    :=xlPivotTableVersion12
  Sheets("Sheet4").Select
```

In the original code, the macro recorder set `SourceData:="Sheet1!R1C1:R43C6"`. We changed that to refer to the `rngRangeToPivot` variable, `SourceData=rngRangeToPivot`. Regardless of how many rows are in the data range, the data source for our PivotTable will reflect the correct data.

The next line to compare is our call to the `PivotCache` object's `CreatePivotTable` method. The original code set the `TableDestination` to a location in a hard-coded reference to a worksheet: `CreatePivotTable TableDestination:="Sheet4!R3C1"`. We replaced that with a call to our dynamic variable `sPivotLoc`, which refers to the name of the new worksheet we added, whatever that might be: `CreatePivotTable TableDestination:=sPivotLoc`.

The last difference is that the original code selects the hard-coded worksheet, Sheets("Sheet4").Select, while our new dynamic code simply refers to the ws variable and selects the worksheet it contains using the Worksheet object's Select method, ws.Select.

Listing 6-4 shows the completed MakeDynamicPivotTable subroutine.

Listing 6-4. *Complete MakeDynamicPivotTable Subroutine*

```
Sub MakeDynamicPivotTable()
Dim ws As Worksheet
Dim rngRangeToPivot As Range
Dim sPivotLoc As String 'where to place the PivotTable on the new sheet

    Set rngRangeToPivot = ActiveCell.CurrentRegion
    Set ws = Sheets.Add
    sPivotLoc = ws.Name & "!R3C1"

    ActiveWorkbook.PivotCaches.Create(SourceType:=xlDatabase, SourceData:= ➥
        rngRangeToPivot, Version:=xlPivotTableVersion12).CreatePivotTable ➥
        TableDestination:=sPivotLoc, TableName:="PivotTable1", DefaultVersion ➥
        :=xlPivotTableVersion12
    ws.Select
    Cells(3, 1).Select
    With ActiveSheet.PivotTables("PivotTable1").PivotFields("State")
        .Orientation = xlRowField
        .Position = 1
    End With
    With ActiveSheet.PivotTables("PivotTable1").PivotFields("City")
        .Orientation = xlRowField
        .Position = 2
    End With
    With ActiveSheet.PivotTables("PivotTable1").PivotFields("Product")
        .Orientation = xlColumnField
        .Position = 1
    End With
    ActiveSheet.PivotTables("PivotTable1").AddDataField ActiveSheet.PivotTables ➥
        ("PivotTable1").PivotFields("Qty"), "Sum of Qty", xlSum End Sub
```

Refreshing Data in an Existing PivotTable Report

How do we handle keeping our data fresh in a PivotTable? When rows are modified, added, or deleted, how do we pass that on to our PivotTable reports?

If our data had come from an external source like an Access or SQL Server database, refreshing the data would be as simple as running the following command with the PivotTable activated:

```
ActiveSheet.PivotTables("PivotTable1").PivotCache.Refresh
```

How do we handle updating our PivotTable data when the data does not sit in a DBMS? If the data on Sheet1 in our example is modified, how do we refresh the PivotTable?

When we created our macro to build the PivotTable, we assigned a dedicated range of data to the PivotTable using the `ActiveCell.CurrentRegion` property. The Refresh command cannot recalculate the `CurrentRegion` property we used because it knows nothing about it. So when we apply the `Refresh` command, whether through Excel's UI or via VBA code, it only refreshes the data range we initially supplied. Any values that have changed within that range (or any deleted rows) would be updated, but any additions to the data would not be applied to the PivotTable.

To update the PivotTable report we created, we will write a subroutine that determines the original data range of the PivotTable and uses that to recalculate the current data range. It will then apply that data range to the PivotTable's `SourceData` property, and then refresh the PivotTable.

In the VBE, create a new subroutine and name it `RefreshPivotTableFromWorksheet`. Add the following code:

```
Sub RefreshPivotTableFromWorksheet()
Dim sData As String
Dim iWhere As Integer
Dim rngData As Range

    sData = ActiveSheet.PivotTables("PivotTable1").SourceData
    iWhere = InStr(1, sData, "!")
    sData = Left(sData, iWhere)

    Set rngData = ➥
        ActiveWorkbook.Sheets(Left(sData, iWhere - 1)).Cells(1, 1).CurrentRegion

    ActiveSheet.PivotTables("PivotTable1").SourceData = ➥
                                    sData & rngData.Address(, , xlR1C1)
End Sub
```

Let's take a look at what this code is doing. We have three variables declared. sData will hold the value of the current range for the PivotTable's source data. We want to find the bang character (!) so we can retrieve the name of the worksheet the data came from. We'll store that in the iWhere variable. And finally, we have a variable of type Range, rngData, that will be assigned the CurrentRegion of cell A1 on the data worksheet. With this information, we have the tools to refresh our pivot data any time detail data is added on the data worksheet.

The first step is to get the current data source for the PivotTable:

```
sData = ActiveSheet.PivotTables("PivotTable1").SourceData
```

Next we'll find the ! character:

```
iWhere = InStr(1, sData, "!")
```

Now we want the worksheet name including the !:

```
sData = Left(sData, iWhere)
```

We modify sData because we only needed it to determine the worksheet name. The original data source range is going to be replaced, so we discard it at this time.

Now we'll assign the CurrentRegion property of cell A1 of the worksheet stored in sData to the rngData variable:

```
Set rngData = ➡
    ActiveWorkbook.Sheets(Left(sData, iWhere - 1)).Cells(1, 1).CurrentRegion
```

Once we have the CurrentRegion, we can replace the current SourceData value of the PivotTable object with it:

```
ActiveSheet.PivotTables("PivotTable1").SourceData = ➡
                            sData & rngData.Address(, , xlR1C1)
```

We're passing in the xlR1C1 enum for the ReferenceStyle argument. This is the string format the SourceData property is looking for.

Now that we've set the SourceData for the PivotTable to the new CurrentRegion of the data worksheet, all that's left to do is call the Refresh command:

```
ActiveSheet.PivotTables("PivotTable1").PivotCache.Refresh
```

Let's give it a test. On Sheet1, add the following data to the grid for the city of Rochester, NY, as shown in Figure 6-12.

	A	B	C	D	E	F	
1	Date	Product	City	State	Qty	Amount	
35	3/10/07	CD	Buffalo	NY	27	270	
36	3/10/07	T-Shirt	Buffalo	NY	61	915	
37	3/10/07	Tank Top	Buffalo	NY	40	480	
38	3/17/07	CD	Trenton	NY	9	90	
39	3/17/07	T-Shirt	Trenton	NY	78	1170	
40	3/17/07	Tank Top	Trenton	NY	41	492	
41	3/31/07	CD	New York	NY	27	270	
42	3/31/07	T-Shirt	New York	NY	61	915	
43	3/31/07	Tank Top	New York	NY	85	1020	
44	4/7/07	CD	Rochester	NY	9	90	
45	4/7/07	T-Shirt	Rochester	NY	78	1170	
46	4/7/07	Tank Top	Rochester	NY	41	492	
47							
48							
49							

Figure 6-12. *New rows added to PivotTable source data*

Open Sheet4 (or the sheet your PivotTable is on, if different). Click any cell inside the PivotTable. When the PivotTable is selected, a couple of new ribbons are displayed, as shown in Figure 6-13.

Figure 6-13. *The PivotTable Tools ribbon (Options ribbon shown)*

On the PivotTable Tools ribbon, select Options ➤ Data ➤ Refresh. Click OK on the Windows Vista security warning. Nothing happens—the Rochester data does not display.

On the Developer ribbon, run the RefreshPivotTableFromWorksheet subroutine. Now the new city appears in the data summary, as shown in Figure 6-14.

1					
2					
3	**Sum of Qty**	Column Labels			
4	**Row Labels**	CD	Tank Top	T-Shirt	Grand Total
5	⊟ **NJ**	124	41	46	211
6	Cherry Hill	63	31	5	99
7	Trenton	61	10	41	112
8	⊟ **NY**	354	296	525	1175
9	Albany	9	41	78	128
10	Buffalo	99	52	81	232
11	New York	143	116	194	453
12	Syracuse	85	5	16	106
13	Trenton	9	41	78	128
14	Rochester	9	41	78	128
15	⊟ **PA**	180	27	234	441
16	Philadelphia	151	27	156	334
17	Reading	29	0	78	107
18	**Grand Total**	658	364	805	1827
19					
20					
21					
22					

Figure 6-14. *Rochester data displayed after RefreshPivotTableFromWorksheet is run*

Applying Formatting to a PivotTable Report

You will probably find that some of the default formatting Excel applies to your PivotTable reports needs some modification—things such as the general number format, the table formatting without lines, the default naming of calculated fields to "Sum of *field name*," and its handling of null or blank entries.

In the Download section for this book on the Apress web site, find the file named PivotTable02_Formatting.xlsm, and open it.

Blank Data Records

To see the effect of blank records on a PivotTable report, let's make Sheet1 active and remove the data for Reading, PA's tank top sales. The Quantity and Sales Total values are 0, but we want to make them blank as though no data were added (as shown in Figure 6-15).

8	1/26/07	CD	Philadelphia	PA	55	550
9	1/26/07	T-Shirt	Philadelphia	PA	67	1005
10	1/26/07	Tank Top	Philadelphia	PA	11	132
11	1/27/07	CD	Reading	PA	29	290
12	1/27/07	T-Shirt	Reading	PA	78	1170
13	1/27/07	Tank Top	Reading	PA		
14	2/2/07	CD	Cherry Hill	NJ	63	630
15	2/2/07	T-Shirt	Cherry Hill	NJ	5	60
16	2/2/07	Tank Top	Cherry Hill	NJ	31	372

Figure 6-15. *Blank data for Reading, PA tank top sales*

1. Activate the worksheet containing the PivotTable report.

2. Refresh the data (either through the UI or the `RefreshPivotTableFromWorksheet` proce-dure). Figure 6-16 shows Excel 2007's default behavior when we have blank values in a PivotTable.

	A	B	C	D	E
1					
2					
3	Sum of Qty	Column Labels			
4	Row Labels	CD	Tank Top	T-Shirt	Grand Total
5	NJ	124	41	46	211
6	Cherry Hill	63	31	5	99
7	Trenton	61	10	41	112
8	NY	354	296	525	1175
9	Albany	9	41	78	128
10	Buffalo	99	52	81	232
11	New York	143	116	194	453
12	Syracuse	85	5	16	106
13	Trenton	9	41	78	128
14	Rochester	9	41	78	128
15	PA	180	27	234	441
16	Philadelphia	151	27	156	334
17	Reading	29		78	107
18	Grand Total	658	364	805	1827

Figure 6-16. *Blank values display as blank on PivotTable report*

3. Drag the Sum of Qty label back up to the field selection list in the PivotTable Field List.

There is a little quirk that exists in the UI that you might encounter when coding PivotTables that bears a quick mention here. When Excel finds blank or null data in a range of data used in a PivotTable, and that field is used in the summary section, it defaults the summary field to "Count of *field name*" even though "Sum of *field name*" may be a more appropriate selection.

4. Drag the Qty field back down to the Values list.

Figure 6-17 shows Excel displaying "Count of *field name*" when we want to sum.

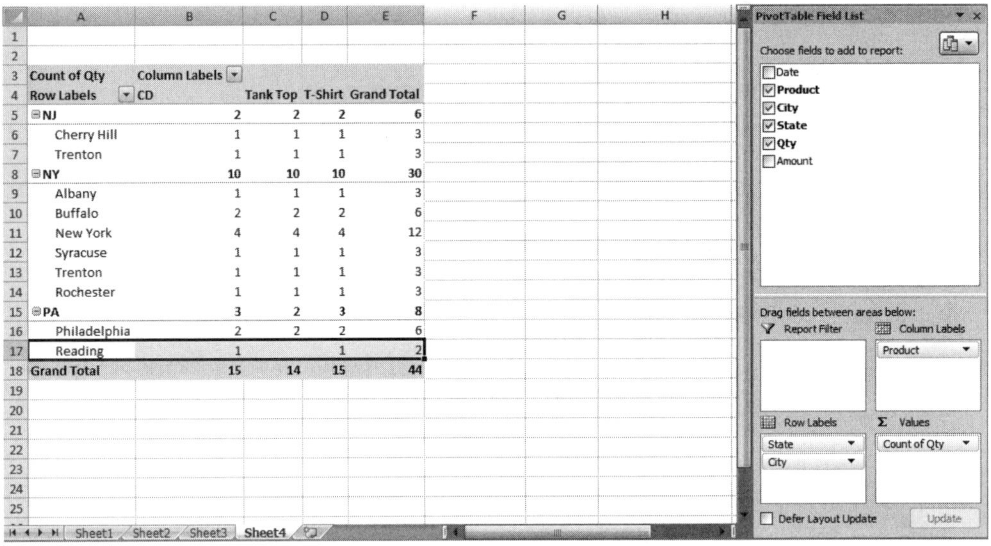

Figure 6-17. *Count of Qty is the default due to the blank data record.*

5. To prevent blank data from displaying, we can use the `NullString` property of the `PivotTable` object. In the VBE, add the following subroutine to the project:

```
Sub ZeroForBlanks()
    ActiveSheet.PivotTables("PivotTable1").NullString = "0"
End Sub
```

6. From the Macros dialog box, run the subroutine. Figure 6-18 shows the result of running the ZeroForBlanks macro.

7. To fix Excel's inaccurate guess that we wanted to count the number of Qty records in the summary section of our PivotTable, we can use the `Function` property of the `PivotField` object. Add the following subprocedure to the standard code module:

```
Sub ChangeSummaryFunction()
    With ActiveSheet.PivotTables("PivotTable1").PivotFields("Count of Qty")
        .Caption = "Sum of Qty"
        .Function = xlSum
    End With
End Sub
```

Once this code runs, the PivotTable will look like it did in Figure 6-16.

	A	B	C	D	E	
1						
2						
3	**Count of Qty**	Column Labels ▾				
4	**Row Labels** ▾	CD	Tank Top	T-Shirt	Grand Total	
5	⊟ **NJ**	2	2	2	6	
6	Cherry Hill	1	1	1	3	
7	Trenton	1	1	1	3	
8	⊟ **NY**	10	10	10	30	
9	Albany	1	1	1	3	
10	Buffalo	2	2	2	6	
11	New York	4	4	4	12	
12	Syracuse	1	1	1	3	
13	Trenton	1	1	1	3	
14	Rochester	1	1	1	3	
15	⊟ **PA**	3	2	3	8	
16	Philadelphia	2	2	2	6	
17	Reading	1	0	1	2	
18	**Grand Total**	15	14	15	44	
19						
20						
21						

Figure 6-18. *Zeros displayed instead of blanks*

Table 6-4 lists the possible choices for the Function property.

Table 6-4. *XlConsolidationFunction Enumeration*

Name	Value	Description
xlAverage	-4106	Averages all numeric values
xlCount	-4112	Counts all cells including numeric, text, and errors; equal to the worksheet function =COUNTA()
xlCountNums	-4113	Counts numeric values only; equal to the worksheet function =COUNT()
xlMax	-4136	Shows the largest value
xlMin	-4139	Shows the smallest value
xlProduct	-4149	Multiplies all the cells together
xlStDev	-4155	Standard deviation based on a sample
xlStDevP	-4156	Standard deviation based on the whole population
xlSum	-4157	Returns the total of all numeric data
xlUnknown	1000	No subtotal function specified
xlVar	-4164	Variation based on a sample
xlVarP	-4165	Variation based on the whole population

Changing the Number Format

The default number format in a new PivotTable is Excel's general number format. Most of us like to see commas or currency symbols, which make the data more readable. To change the number format, you use the `PivotField.NumberFormat` property. The `NumberFormat` property sets or returns the string value that represents the format code for the numeric value. The format code is the same string value given by the Format Codes option in the Format Cells dialog box shown in Figure 6-19.

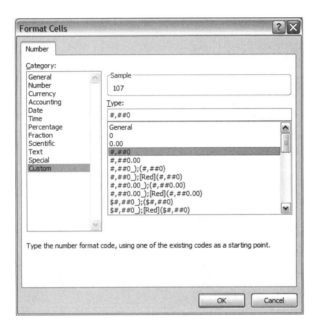

Figure 6-19. *The Format Cells dialog box*

Add the following routine to a standard module:

```
Sub FormatNumbersComma()
    With ActiveSheet.PivotTables("PivotTable1").PivotFields("Sum of Qty")
        .NumberFormat = "#,##0"
    End With
End Sub
```

Run the `FormatNumbersComma` subroutine from the Macros dialog box. The result should look like Figure 6-20.

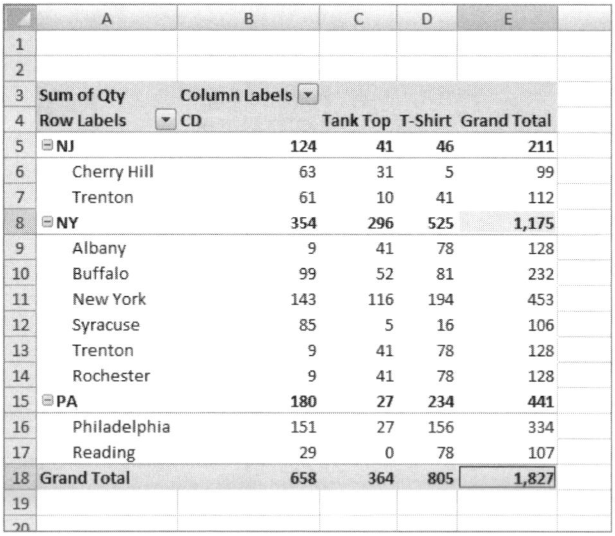

	A	B	C	D	E
1					
2					
3	Sum of Qty	Column Labels ▾			
4	Row Labels ▾	CD	Tank Top	T-Shirt	Grand Total
5	⊟NJ	124	41	46	211
6	Cherry Hill	63	31	5	99
7	Trenton	61	10	41	112
8	⊟NY	354	296	525	1,175
9	Albany	9	41	78	128
10	Buffalo	99	52	81	232
11	New York	143	116	194	453
12	Syracuse	85	5	16	106
13	Trenton	9	41	78	128
14	Rochester	9	41	78	128
15	⊟PA	180	27	234	441
16	Philadelphia	151	27	156	334
17	Reading	29	0	78	107
18	Grand Total	658	364	805	1,827
19					
20					

Figure 6-20. *Grand Total rows with commas added*

Changing Field Names

By default, Excel uses the name "Sum of *field name*" or "Count of *field name*" when you add summary value fields to a PivotTable. You can change the names to something with more visual appeal using VBA code.

Add the Amount field to the Values list in the PivotTable Field List. Change the Count value to Sum in the Value Field Settings dialog box (as shown in Figure 6-21) by clicking the Amount field in the Values list and choosing Value Field Settings from the right-click shortcut menu. Figure 6-22 shows the result of changing the field names.

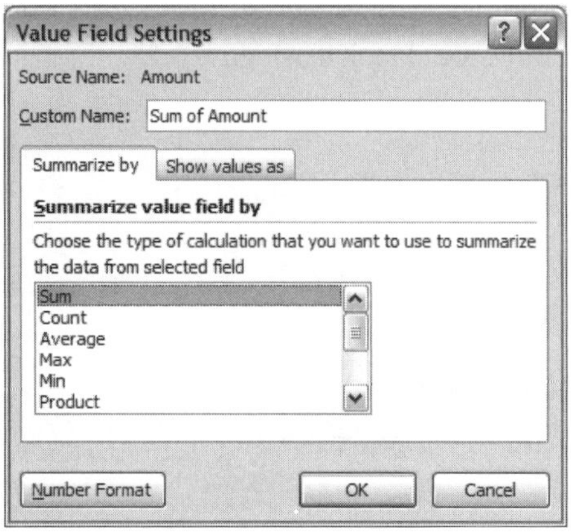

Figure 6-21. *Value Field Settings dialog box*

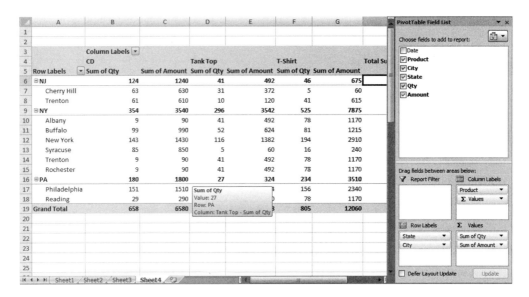

Figure 6-22. *PivotTable showing Sum of Qty and Sum of Amount fields*

Use the `PivotField.Caption` property to change the captions to something more easily readable.

Add the following subroutine to a standard code module:

```
Sub ChangeColHeading()
    ActiveSheet.PivotTables("PivotTable1").PivotFields("Sum of Qty").Caption = ➥
        "Item Qty"
    ActiveSheet.PivotTables("PivotTable1").PivotFields("Sum of Amount").Caption = ➥
        "Item Amount"
End Sub
```

Run the code from the Macros dialog box. The result should look like Figure 6-23.

	A	B	C	D	E	F	G	H
1								
2								
3		Column Labels ▼						
4		CD		Tank Top		T-Shirt		Total Item Qty Tota
5	Row Labels ▼	Item Qty	Item Amount	Item Qty	Item Amount	Item Qty	Item Amount	
6	⊟NJ	124	1240	41	492	46	675	211
7	Cherry Hill	63	630	31	372	5	60	99
8	Trenton	61	610	10	120			112
9	⊟NY	354	3540	296	3542			1175
10	Albany	9	90	41	492			128
11	Buffalo	99	990	52	624	81	1215	232
12	New York	143	1430	116	1382	194	2910	453
13	Syracuse	85	850	5	60	16	240	106
14	Trenton	9	90	41	492	78	1170	128
15	Rochester	9	90	41	492	78	1170	128
16	⊟PA	180	1800	27	324	234	3510	441
17	Philadelphia	151	1510	27	324	156	2340	334
18	Reading	29	290	0	0	78	1170	107
19	Grand Total	658	6580	364	4358	805	12060	1827
20								
21								
22								
23								
24								
25								

Item Qty
Value: 5
Row: NJ - Cherry Hill
Column: T-Shirt - Item Qty

Sheet1 Sheet2 Sheet3 **Sheet4**

Figure 6-23. *Summary field headings modified*

Adding Formatting to a PivotTable Report

The default PivotTable report Excel generates looks okay, but Excel 2007 does provide us with 75 different formatting options. To change the look of a PivotTable report using VBA code, use the PivotTable object's TableStyle2 property. This property is named TableStyle2 because there is already a TableStyle property (but it's not a member of the PivotTable object's properties—go figure).

Add a new subroutine to a standard code module and add the following code:

```
Sub ApplyTableStyle()
    ActiveSheet.PivotTables("PivotTable1").TableStyle2 = "PivotStyleLight1"
    'ActiveSheet.PivotTables("PivotTable1").TableStyle2 = "PivotStyleLight22"
    'ActiveSheet.PivotTables("PivotTable1").TableStyle2 = "PivotStyleMedium23"
End Sub
```

Before we run this code, let's remove the Item Qty field from the Values list in the PivotTable Field List to make the PivotTable smaller and the formatting easier to see.

Run the code from the Macros dialog box to apply the PivotStyleLight1 formatting to the PivotTable, as shown in Figure 6-24.

	A	B	C	D	E	F
1						
2						
3	Item Amount	Column Labels ▼				
4	Row Labels ▼	CD	Tank Top	T-Shirt	Grand Total	
5	⊟NJ	1240	492	675	2407	
6	Cherry Hill	630	372	60	1062	
7	Trenton	610	120	615	1345	
8	⊟NY	3540	3542	7875	14957	
9	Albany	90	492	1170	1752	
10	Buffalo	990	624	1215	2829	
11	New York	1430	1382	2910	5722	
12	Syracuse	850	60	240	1150	
13	Trenton	90	492	1170	1752	
14	Rochester	90	492	1170	1752	
15	⊟PA	1800	324	3510	5634	
16	Philadelphia	1510	324	2340	4174	
17	Reading	290	0	1170	1460	
18	Grand Total	6580	4358	12060	22998	
19						
20						
21						

Figure 6-24. *PivotStyleLight1 formatting applied*

Comment out the first line of code in the ApplyTableStyle procedure and uncomment the second line. Run the subroutine from the Macros dialog box to apply PivotStyleLight22 formatting, as shown in Figure 6-25.

	A	B	C	D	E	F
1						
2						
3	Item Amount	Column Labels ▼				
4	Row Labels ▼	CD	Tank Top	T-Shirt	Grand Total	
5	⊟NJ	1240	492	675	2407	
6	Cherry Hill	630	372	60	1062	
7	Trenton	610	120	615	1345	
8	⊟NY	3540	3542	7875	14957	
9	Albany	90	492	1170	1752	
10	Buffalo	990	624	1215	2829	
11	New York	1430	1382	2910	5722	
12	Syracuse	850	60	240	1150	
13	Trenton	90	492	1170	1752	
14	Rochester	90	492	1170	1752	
15	⊟PA	1800	324	3510	5634	
16	Philadelphia	1510	324	2340	4174	
17	Reading	290	0	1170	1460	
18	Grand Total	6580	4358	12060	22998	
19						
20						

Figure 6-25. *PivotStyleLight22 formatting applied*

Comment out the second line of code in the `ApplyTableStyle` procedure and uncomment the third line. Run the subroutine from the Macros dialog box to apply PivotStyleMedium23 formatting, as shown in Figure 6-26.

	A	B	C	D	E	F
1						
2						
3	Item Amount	Column Labels ▼				
4	Row Labels ▼	CD	Tank Top	T-Shirt	Grand Total	
5	⊟NJ	1240	492	675	2407	
6	Cherry Hill	630	372	60	1062	
7	Trenton	610	120	615	1345	
8	⊟NY	3540	3542	7875	14957	
9	Albany	90	492	1170	1752	
10	Buffalo	990	624	1215	2829	
11	New York	1430	1382	2910	5722	
12	Syracuse	850	60	240	1150	
13	Trenton	90	492	1170	1752	
14	Rochester	90	492	1170	1752	
15	⊟PA	1800	324	3510	5634	
16	Philadelphia	1510	324	2340	4174	
17	Reading	290	0	1170	1460	
18	Grand Total	6580	4358	12060	22998	
19						
20						
21						

Figure 6-26. *PivotStyleMedium23 formatting applied*

Summary

PivotTables in Excel 2007 provide users with a very easy-to-use interface with which they can analyze and summarize large amounts of data. In this chapter, we took a look at code generated by Excel's Macro Recorder to get a feel for the `PivotTable` and `PivotCache` objects' properties and methods. We then saw how we could modify that code to make it more flexible and dynamic.

Excel 2007 PivotTable reports are not linked to their data, but use the `PivotCache` object to store a pointer to the data. When the data on a worksheet changes, the PivotTable does not automatically update with those changes, especially if new data is appended. We created a method to let the user refresh the PivotTable if the worksheet data on which it was based was appended to.

Finally, we looked at some of the formatting options available to us using VBA code. We were able to fix some of Excel 2007's default formatting behaviors, such as its use of the general number format, generic summary field names, and its handling of blank rows. We also saw how applying styles can dress up a PivotTable report.

■ ■ ■

CHAPTER 7

Debugging and Error Handling

Debugging technique is an often overlooked part of a developer's set of skills. In this chapter, we are going to explore some debugging techniques that will save you time when troubleshooting your code, and make you a more efficient coder.

Error handling is another area in which we often find ourselves taking shortcuts. We will also look at error handling methods in this chapter, and we'll see how to deliver user-friendly messages to our users.

Debugging

Debugging is the process of stepping through code to find inconsistencies due to coding errors when output is not what you expected, or to find the cause of errors at runtime.

Here are some examples of output not displaying what's expected:

- When reading file names from an array, the file you expected does not open. Something causes your code to find the incorrect array element. How do you determine where that incorrect value came from?

- You're reading data from a database but there is nothing there, or the data is not the data you expected. Is your SQL correct? Is the database there?

- You're reading information from a collection but the collection is empty. Why is the collection empty?

To determine what's happening under the covers while our code is running, we need the ability to see inside the variables as they are populated with data. We need to be able to follow our code through any looping or branching structures, and we need a way to stop code at a predetermined point (or points), or based upon whether certain conditions are met.

The Debugger's Toolkit

The VBE gives us tools to do all of the above and more. The Debug menu, shown in Figure 7-1, contains the VBE's debugging command. The Debug toolbar (Figure 7-2) contains commonly used commands from the Debug menu.

Figure 7-1. *The Debug menu*

Figure 7-2. *The Debug toolbar*

Table 7-1 describes the commands on the Debug menu and shows the corresponding Debug toolbar button for that command when one is available. Table 7-2 describes the remaining commands on the Debug toolbar.

Table 7-1. *Descriptions of the Debug Menu and Toolbar Commands*

Debug Toolbar Button (If Applicable)	Command	Shortcut Key	Description
—	Compile VBA Project	—	Compiles the project. It does not create an executable or redistributable component, but it does check that the syntax is correct.
	Step Into	F8	Executes code one statement at a time. The next statement displayed is the next statement in the current procedure (break mode does not flow into the called procedure or function).
	Step Out	Ctrl+Shift+F8	Executes the remaining lines of a procedure or function from where the current execution point lies.
—	Run to Cursor	Ctrl+F8	Executes code from the current location to the statement at the cursor location. This is useful when there's a need to avoid stepping through large loops.

Debug Toolbar Button (If Applicable)	Command	Shortcut Key	Description
—	Add Watch	—	Displays the Add Watch dialog box, where you enter a *watch expression* (a user-defined expression that enables you to see the contents of a variable or the result of an expression). The expression can be any valid Visual Basic expression (e.g., `MyVariable = "New York"`).
—	Edit Watch	Ctrl+W	Displays the Edit Watch dialog box, in which you can edit or delete a watch expression.
66	Quick Watch	Shift+F9	Displays the Quick Watch dialog box with the current value of the selected expression.
🖑	Toggle Breakpoint	Shift+F9	Inserts or removes a breakpoint at the current line.
—	Clear All Breakpoints	Ctrl+Shift+F9	Removes all breakpoints in a project.
—	Set Next Statement	Ctrl+F9	Sets the execution point to the line of code you choose. You can set a different line of code to execute after the currently selected statement by selecting the line of code you want to execute and choosing the Set Next Statement command, or by dragging the Current Execution Line indicator to the line of code you want to execute.
—	Show Next Statement	—	Highlights the next statement to be executed.

There are a few additional commands available to us on the Debug toolbar. Some are common commands from the Debug menu and others are commonly used items from the View menu. They are described in Table 7-2.

Table 7-2. *Description of the Debug Toolbar Commands*

Debug Toolbar Button	Command	Shortcut Key	Description
🖉	Design Mode	—	Turns design mode for a UserForm off or on.
▶	Continue	F5	Runs the current procedure if the cursor is in a procedure. Runs a UserForm if the UserForm is active. Opens the Macro dialog box if neither the code window nor a UserForm is active.
⏸	Break	Ctrl+Break	Stops execution of a procedure and switches to break mode.
⏹	Reset	—	Stops execution of a procedure, clears module-level variables, and resets the project.

Continued

Table 7-2. *Continued*

Debug Toolbar Button	Command	Shortcut Key	Description
	Locals Window	—	Displays the Locals window. The Locals window displays all of the variables in the current procedure and their values.
	Immediate Window	Ctrl+G	Displays the Immediate window. The Immediate window allows you to type or paste code and press Enter to run it.
	Watch Window	—	Displays the Watch window. The Watch window is where you define expressions to be monitored (in the Watch window).
	Call Stack	Ctrl+L	Displays the Call Stack dialog box. The Call Stack dialog box lists procedures that have started but have not finished, in the order they were called.

So there we have the tools we'll use to search out errors in our code. Before we begin putting these to work and seeing what they can do for us, though, let's take a very quick look at one line of code that the VBE will add for you that can help eliminate some coding errors from the start: Option Explicit.

Option Explicit

The default installation of any Microsoft Office product and the VBE do not require variable declaration before use. VBA will create the variable automatically the first time it is used. If you include a call to Option Explicit at the top of your code modules, VBA will require that each variable be declared before use.

Tip Why go to the trouble? Option Explicit helps the compiler catch any variable names you may have mistyped. It also helps you avoid confusion when the scope of a variable may not be clear.

To turn Option Explicit on, do the following:

1. From any Excel workbook, open the VBE.

2. From any open workbook, choose the Visual Basic command from the Code tab of the Developer ribbon, or press Alt+F11.

3. In the VBE, choose Tools ➤ Options to display the Options dialog box, as shown in Figure 7-3.

4. If it's not already checked, in the Code Settings section in the top half of the Options dialog box, click the Require Variable Declaration check box. In Figure 7-3, the arrow cursor points to this item.

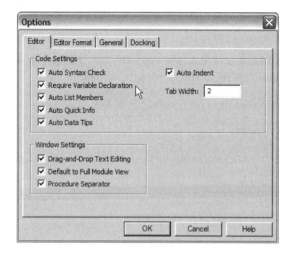

Figure 7-3. *The VBE's Options dialog box*

5. Click OK to save the changes and close the Options dialog box.

Once this is done, any time you create a new code module or open the code module attached to any worksheet, the Option Explicit command will already be inserted at the top of the module.

Quick Debugging

The VBE provides us with a couple of easy-to-use tools for simple debugging needs. There will be times where running code through the debugger may be more than you need. In those cases, here are the tools available to us:

Message boxes: These are used to display information about the code while it's running.

The Debug *object*: The Debug object hosts two methods that will ease our debugging efforts while code is running as well. These are Print and Assert.

Displaying Information with Message Boxes

Message boxes are useful tools for simple debugging. They allow us to display the values of variables inside our code while the code is running, and they interrupt the running of the code. Let's take a look at an example in which we are not getting an expected result and we'd like to see what's happening under the covers.

■**Note** No one is perfect! As I was writing the code for this example, I actually made the typo we are going to troubleshoot. When I ran the code to make sure it worked (my plan was to break the code for this example), I did not get the result I expected!

1. In the Download section for this book on the Apress web site, find the file named DebugExample01.xlsm and open it. This file contains sample sales data, but we'll ignore that for the time being.

2. Open the VBE by choosing the Visual Basic command from the Code tab of the Developer ribbon, or by pressing Alt+F11.

3. Open Standard Module1 by double-clicking its folder in the VBA Project window, as shown in Figure 7-4.

Figure 7-4. *Opening Standard Module1*

On Module1, you'll find a very useful function named BirthYear, as shown in Listing 7-1.

Listing 7-1. *The BirthYear Function*

```
Function BirthYear(Age As Integer, HadBDay As Boolean)
Dim iReturn As Integer
Dim iCurrYear As Integer

  iCurrYear = Year(Date)
  iReturn = iCurrYear = Age

  If Not HadBDay Then
    iReturn = iReturn - 1
  End If

  BirthYear = iReturn
End Function
```

This function takes two inputs—an Integer containing your age and a Boolean flag denoting whether you've had your birthday yet this year—and it returns your birth year. Let's run the code in the Immediate window.

1. Open the Immediate window from the VBE by choosing View ➤ Immediate Window or by pressing Ctrl+G.

2. Type in the following: **?BirthYear(30,True)**.

3. Press Enter to see the result.

■**Note** In the Immediate window, when you precede a command or variable name with the ? character, the result of the command (or contents of the variable) will be output to the Immediate window. Otherwise, the command will just run, unless there are errors.

We passed in 30 as the Age parameter (you didn't think I'd put my real age in there, did you?) and set the flag to True, indicating that the birthday had passed for this year. This code was run in the year 2007, so the result I would expect to see is 1977—but that's not what we see in Figure 7-5, is it?

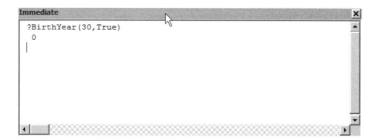

Figure 7-5. *Unexpected result in Immediate window*

Let's check our variables and make sure they're holding correct values by inserting a few message boxes. You can create message boxes by calling the MsgBox function. As shown in Figure 7-6, the MsgBox function takes a few arguments, but since we're not presenting these to a user at this time, we'll just pass in the first argument, the prompt or message.

```
MsgBox
    MsgBox(Prompt, [Buttons As VbMsgBoxStyle = vbOKOnly], [Title], [HelpFile], [Context]) As VbMsgBoxResult
```

Figure 7-6. *The MsgBox function's argument list*

1. In the BirthYear function, add the following code above the If...End If statement:

```
MsgBox "Current Year: " & CStr(iCurrYear)
MsgBox "Birth Year before If: " & CStr(iReturn)
```

2. Insert a blank line after the If...End If statement.

3. Add the following code:

```
MsgBox "Birth Year after If: " & CStr(iReturn)
```

Your code should now look like Listing 7-2.

Listing 7-2. *BirthYear Function with MsgBox Debugging*

```
Function BirthYear(Age As Integer, HadBDay As Boolean)
Dim iReturn As Integer
Dim iCurrYear As Integer

  iCurrYear = Year(Date)
  iReturn = iCurrYear = Age

  MsgBox "Current Year: " & CStr(iCurrYear)
  MsgBox "Birth Year before If: " & CStr(iReturn)
  If Not HadBDay Then
    iReturn = iReturn - 1
  End If
  MsgBox "Birth Year after If: " & CStr(iReturn)

  BirthYear = iReturn
End Function
```

We're checking to see that the Year function is returning the correct value, and we're checking our return value before and after the If...End If statement to see if the code fell into it and possibly changed there.

4. Run the code in the Immediate window, clicking OK at each message box.

Figures 7-7, 7-8, and 7-9 show us that our current year value looks good but the iReturn value has a problem. The problem must lie in our logic.

Figure 7-7. *Current Year is correct.*

Figure 7-8. *The iReturn variable is incorrect before the If...End If statement.*

Figure 7-9. *The iReturn variable did not fall into the If...End If statement, and it is still incorrect.*

Now we know we've got an issue at the point in the code where we set the iReturn variable value. Let's take a look at that line of code:

```
iReturn = iCurrYear = Age
```

It's fairly obvious at this point, but instead of subtracting the age from the year, this code is creating a conditional statement setting iReturn to True or False if the year *equals* Age.

5. Change the second = to a minus sign (-) so that the code reads as follows:

```
iReturn = iCurrYear - Age
```

6. In the Immediate window, run the code again (clicking OK on each message box, which should now hold the correct value for iReturn). The result should look like Figure 7-10.

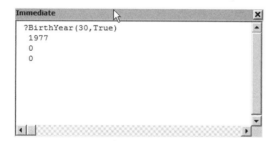

Figure 7-10. *The correct value is returned.*

Using the Debug Object

The Debug object contains two methods that we can use to debug our code: Print and Assert. The Print method directs output to the Immediate window, and the Assert method lets us set a condition that puts our code in break mode if the condition fails.

Debug.Print

Whereas the MsgBox function interrupts the execution of our code, the Debug.Print method allows the code to run through to finish, sending its output to the Immediate window. This is especially useful when debugging code in a loop.

1. As a very simple example, enter the code from Listing 7-3 on Standard Module1 in the DebugExample01.xlsm project.

Listing 7-3. *Simple Routine Using Debug.Print to Send Output to the Immediate Window*

```
Sub DebugLoop()
Dim i As Integer

   For i = 1 To 15
     Debug.Print "Debug loop: " & i
   Next i
End Sub
```

2. Run the code in the Immediate window, as shown in Figure 7-11, by typing the following command and pressing Enter:

```
debugloop
```

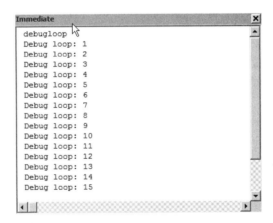

Figure 7-11. *Debugging a loop*

Imagine checking the value of the variable i with a message box. No fun there, and that's a small loop! Let's modify the BirthYear function to use Debug.Print instead of MsgBox so our code can run without interruption and still show us the variable values as the code runs.

1. On Standard Module1, replace each instance of MsgBox with Debug.Print. The code should look like Listing 7-4.

Listing 7-4. *BirthYear Function Using the Debug.Print Method*

```
Function BirthYear(Age As Integer, HadBDay As Boolean)
Dim iReturn As Integer
Dim iCurrYear As Integer

  iCurrYear = Year(Date)
  iReturn = iCurrYear - Age

  Debug.Print "Current Year: " & CStr(iCurrYear)
  Debug.Print "Birth Year before If: " & CStr(iReturn)
  If Not HadBDay Then
    iReturn = iReturn - 1
  End If
  Debug.Print "Birth Year after If: " & CStr(iReturn)

  BirthYear = iReturn
End Function
```

2. In the Immediate window, run BirthYear, passing in False to the HadBday argument, by typing the following:

```
?birthyear(30, False)
```

3. Press Enter to run the code. The output to the Immediate window is shown in Figure 7-12.

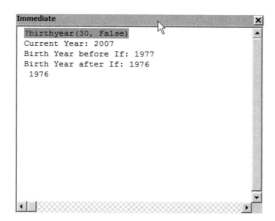

Figure 7-12. *Output of BirthYear function sent to Immediate window*

We see the three messages we were looking for, plus the bottom line shows us the return of the function. Here we see that our code did fall into the If...End If statement where it subtracted one from the result because the birthday did not yet occur this year.

■**Tip** Message boxes are easy to add, but don't forget to remove (or comment) them when your code goes into production. Otherwise, you'll have some very confused users.

Debug.Print statements, on the other hand, only appear in the Immediate window. Although it's wise to remove or comment them, your users won't see the output.

Debug.Assert

Assertions are another tool you can use to check for conditions within your code. Assertions are conditional statements that you create that will put your code in break mode if the conditions are not met. Listing 7-5 shows a sample method you can use as an example.

Listing 7-5. *Sample Subroutine Using Debug.Assert*

```
Sub TestAssert()
Dim iTest As Integer
   iTest = 10
   Debug.Assert iTest = 9
   Debug.Print "Test Value: " & iTest
End Sub
```

1. Copy the code in Listing 7-5 into Standard Module1 in the DebugExample01.xlsm file.

2. Open the Immediate window by choosing View ➤ Immediate Window or by pressing the Ctrl+G shortcut keys.

3. In the Immediate window, type **TestAssert**.

4. Press Enter.

Our assertion is testing to see if the iTest variable equals 9. Since we set that variable to 10 in the line of code preceding the assertion, it will return a value of False and put the code in break mode. Figure 7-13 shows the code in break mode as it stops on the assertion.

Of course, we forced this false condition, but if we need to know when a condition other than what we expect might happen when testing our code, assertions provide us with that option.

5. Press F5 to continue running the code to its end.

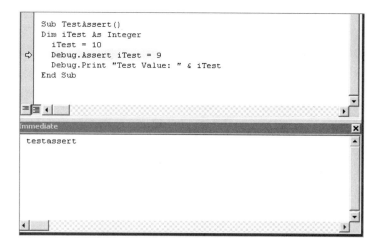

Figure 7-13. *A false condition in the Assert method puts the code in break mode.*

A Deeper Look

Let's take a look at some of the other tools we can use to make our debugging more efficient. In this section, we'll look at the following:

- Step-through options

- The Immediate window

- The Locals window

- The Watch window

- The call stack

Stepping Through Code

Assertions are great at stopping code if a condition is false, but we need a method to move back and forth through our code if we are to find out why our condition failed. The VBE has commands we can use to move through our code line by line, and to move directly to a line of code as well. Figure 7-14 shows the step section of the Debug menu.

Figure 7-14. *Step-through-code options from the Debug menu*

Earlier in this chapter, Table 7-1 gave a quick overview of these functions. Now we'll take a closer look at them.

In Standard Module1 in the DebugExample01.xlsm file, add the code from Listing 7-6.

Listing 7-6. *Sample Code for Debugging*

```
Function TestLoop() As Long
Dim i As Integer
Dim lngResult As Long

  lngResult = 1
  For i = 1 To 10
    lngResult = lngResult * i
    ExternalProcess lngResult
 Next i

TestLoop = lngResult
End Function

Sub ExternalProcess(TheValue As Long)
  If TheValue > 10000 Then
    TheValue = 0
  End If

End Sub
```

We're going to use this code to explore the various ways we can step through our code line by line, and we'll also see how to make use of additional tools like the Immediate window and the call stack.

The code in Listing 7-6 is a simulation of a construct we see often in our code. In the TestLoop function, we have a loop that runs a fixed number of times (in real-life situations, this may or may not be the case) and returns a value at the end of the process. Within that loop, we call a procedure to act on or process data or perform an action based on the value of variables in the loop. In this case, we have the appropriately named ExternalProcess subroutine.

Our TestLoop function is designed to multiply a value by the loop counter; the expected result of our process is the value 3628800. The ExternalFunction procedure is purposely coded to give an incorrect result. Let's run the code.

1. Open the VBE.

2. Show the Immediate window by choosing View ➤ Immediate Window or by pressing Ctrl+G.

3. In the Immediate Window, type **?testloop**.

The result is shown in Figure 7-15.

Figure 7-15. *The TestLoop function returns an incorrect value.*

Let's begin debugging by inserting a breakpoint in our code.

1. In the code window, find the TestLoop function.

2. Move the mouse pointer to the gray left margin next to the start of the For...Next loop, and click. A maroon break marker is inserted, as shown in Figure 7-16.

```
Function TestLoop() As Long
Dim i As Integer
Dim lngResult As Long

   lngResult = 1
   For i = 1 To 10
      lngResult = lngResult * i
      ExternalProcess lngResult
   Next i

TestLoop = lngResult
End Function
```

Figure 7-16. *Breakpoint inserted*

3. In the Immediate window, run the code again by typing TestLoop and pressing Enter.

4. The code runs as far as the beginning of the loop, and then stops, as shown in Figure 7-17.

Once you're in break mode, the break line text (the code at the breakpoint) and the execution line text (the currently executing line of code as you step through) are highlighted. The default highlight color is maroon for the break line text and yellow for the currently executing line of text. This color coding is user-definable on the Tools ➤ Options menu on the Editor Format tab, as shown in Figure 7-18.

At the first breakpoint, you will get a combination of the break and execution line colors.

```
Function TestLoop() As Long
Dim i As Integer
Dim lngResult As Long

   lngResult = 1
⊂ ▌For i = 1 To 10
      lngResult = lngResult * i
      ExternalProcess lngResult
   Next i

TestLoop = lngResult
End Function

Sub ExternalProcess(TheValue As Long)
   If TheValue > 10000 Then
      TheValue = 0
   End If

End Sub
```

mmediate
```
?testloop
 0
```

Figure 7-17. *VBE enters break mode when a breakpoint is reached.*

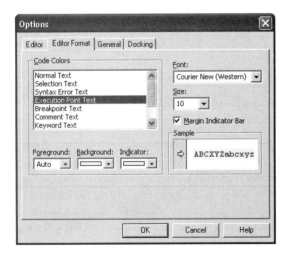

Figure 7-18. *Options dialog box showing VBE color options*

5. The Step Into command moves you through your code one line at a time. Press the F8 key (or choose Debug ➤ Step Into) to move to the first line of code inside the loop. The color coding should now be more easily seen, as in Figure 7-19.

```
Function TestLoop() As Long
Dim i As Integer
Dim lngResult As Long

  lngResult = 1
  For i = 1 To 10
    lngResult = lngResult * i
    ExternalProcess lngResult
  Next i

TestLoop = lngResult
End Function
```

Figure 7-19. *Better view of the break and execution lines of code*

6. Press the F8 key twice to move the execution line to the ExternalProcess routine.

7. Press F8 again to move the execution line into the ExternalProcess procedure.

As you can see, the Step Into command moves you through the code one line at time. When it encounters another procedure call, it moves you into that procedure. At the moment, our execution point is inside the ExternalProcess subroutine. To move out of this procedure without moving line by line, use the Step Out command by choosing Debug ➤ Step Out or by pressing Ctrl+Shift+F8. The Step Out command moves you out of the current procedure and to the next line of code in the procedure that called the current procedure.

8. Press Ctrl+Shift+F8 to move the execution point back into the TestLoop function at the end of the loop structure, as shown in Figure 7-20.

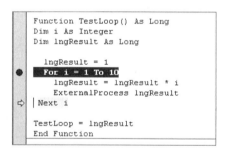

Figure 7-20. *Result of Step Out command*

9. Press F8 two times. The execution point should be back on the call to ExternalProcess, as shown in Figure 7-21.

If you don't have a need to step through this external procedure and want to skip over this call, you can use the Step Over command.

10. Choose Debug ➤ Step Over or press Shift+F8.

11. The execution point moves to the bottom of the loop without stepping through the procedure call, as shown in Figure 7-22.

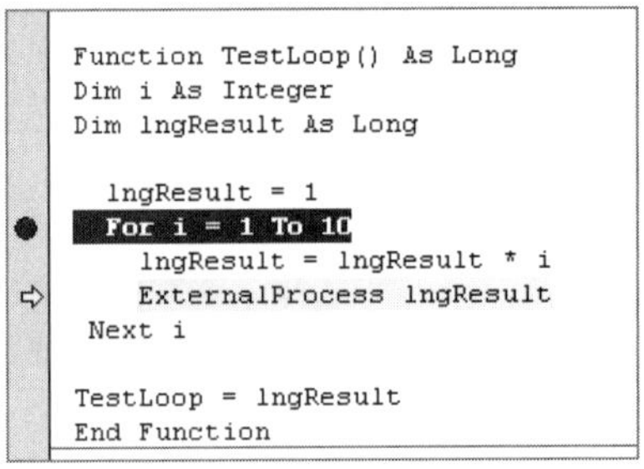

```
Function TestLoop() As Long
Dim i As Integer
Dim lngResult As Long

  lngResult = 1
  For i = 1 To 10
     lngResult = lngResult * i
     ExternalProcess lngResult
 Next i

 TestLoop = lngResult
 End Function
```

Figure 7-21. *Execution point on a procedure call*

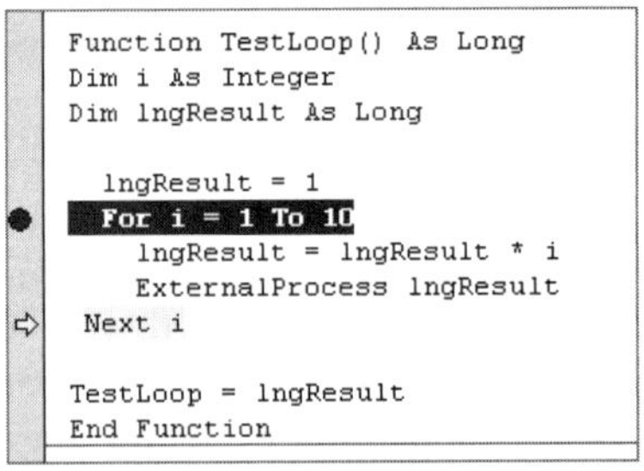

```
Function TestLoop() As Long
Dim i As Integer
Dim lngResult As Long

  lngResult = 1
  For i = 1 To 10
     lngResult = lngResult * i
     ExternalProcess lngResult
 Next i

 TestLoop = lngResult
 End Function
```

Figure 7-22. *The execution point moves directly to the next line of code when the Step Over command is used.*

What if you decide that you should have stepped into the procedure you just stepped over? (In a loop like this, you may need to test that procedure with the current counter variable in place.) The VBE gives us a command called Set Next Statement that makes this very easy to do.

To bring the execution point back to the call to ExternalProcess, do the following:

12. Put the cursor on the line of the next statement that you want executed (in this case, the call to ExternalProcess).

13. Choose Debug ➤ Set Next Statement or press Ctrl+F9.

The result is shown in Figure 7-23.

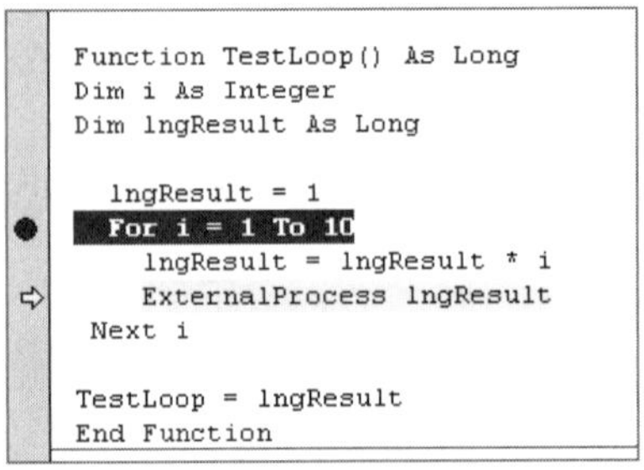

```
Function TestLoop() As Long
Dim i As Integer
Dim lngResult As Long

  lngResult = 1
  For i = 1 To 10
     lngResult = lngResult * i
     ExternalProcess lngResult
 Next i

 TestLoop = lngResult
 End Function
```

Figure 7-23. *The Set Next Statement command moves the execution point to the selected line of code.*

The Set Next Statement command can be used to move the execution point forward as well as backward. You can also use the mouse to drag the execution arrow (shown in the gray margin on the left side of the code window in Figure 7-23) to the location of the code you'd like to run.

■**Warning** The Set Next Statement command can be used to move the execution point backward or forward in the code. It will not reverse values in a loop. If you need to see counters or incremented values as they happen, remember to check them in their current context in a loop.

One last command you can use is the Run To Cursor command. The Run To Cursor command lets you place the cursor on a line of code, and when that line is reached, the code will resume break mode.

Let's bring the execution point to the cursor location as follows:

14. Put the cursor on the last line of code in the TestLoop function.

15. Choose Debug ➤ Run To Cursor or press Ctrl+F8.

The execution point moves to the last line of code, as shown in Figure 7-24.

```
Function TestLoop() As Long
Dim i As Integer
Dim lngResult As Long

    lngResult = 1
    For i = 1 To 10
        lngResult = lngResult * i
        ExternalProcess lngResult
    Next i

TestLoop = lngResult
End Function
```

Figure 7-24. *The Run To Cursor command moves the execution point to the cursor location.*

Checking Variables in Break Mode

Our execution point is on the last line of code before the function is finished. Don't move the execution point just yet. We have the ability in the VBE to view the values of variables in our procedures as they change in real time.

We can use any of the following to view variable values:

- The Immediate window

- The Locals window

- The code window

The Immediate Window

To check the value of a variable in the Immediate window, simply type the name of variable and its value will be displayed.

1. In the Immediate window, type **?i**.

2. Press Enter.

3. In the Immediate window, type **?lngResult**.

4. Press Enter.

Figure 7-25 shows that this returns the values 11 (since our loop reached its last iteration) and 0, respectively.

Figure 7-25. *Checking the value of variables in the Immediate window*

5. To run the code to the end from the current execution point, press F5.

■**Tip** Did you know that you can test loops from within the Immediate window? Just type them using the following syntax:

```
for i = 1 to 5:debug.print "Test " & i:next i
```

The result of running this is shown in Figure 7-26.

```
Immediate
    for i = 1 to 5:debug.print "Test " & i:next i
    Test 1
    Test 2
    Test 3
    Test 4
    Test 5
```

Figure 7-26. *Testing loops in the Immediate window*

The Locals Window

The Locals window lets you see all current variables and their values in break mode in one place. To see the Locals window at work, we are going to run an existing macro in the DebugExample01.xlsm file against the sales data on Sheet1.

We saw this data and code in our 1-MacroExample01.xlsm file in Chapter 1. In this example, the data has been slightly modified and will generate an error that we'll track down using the tools explained thus far.

1. In the Excel window, open Worksheet1 in the DebugExample01.xlsm file.

2. Open the Developer ribbon and click the Macros command to open the Macros dialog box.

3. Run the AddSalesTotal macro.

A type mismatch error occurs, as shown in Figure 7-27.

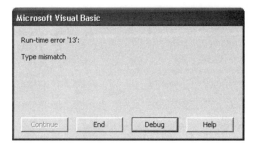

Figure 7-27. *Type mismatch error 13*

4. Click the Debug button to put the code in break mode.

5. Open the Locals window by choosing View ➤ Locals Window.

The Locals window will open, as shown in Figure 7-28.

Looking at the Locals window in Figure 7-28, we see the values for the GetSalesTotal function and for the variables currReturn, temp, and cell. We also see the values for the range we pass into the function, RangeToTotal.

GetSalesTotal and currReturn both have a value of 0, as they are not set until the end of the function. The variable temp, which is set during the loop that walks the range, has a value of 303 so far.

The cell variable is a bit different, as is the RangeToTotal variable. These variables are references to range objects. This means that they have more than just a value. They have properties—and lots of them!

6. Click the plus sign to the left of the cell variable.

7. Scroll down until you see the Value2 property.

Figure 7-28. *The Locals window displays values for all in-scope variables.*

The Value2 property stores the current cell's value. In this case, it's the string N/A. It looks like someone didn't have a value for DVD sales in the East region, and entered a string rather than leaving it blank or entering a 0. We've found our problem.

Before we fix the issue, let's take a look at a feature that's available from the Locals window as well as the View menu: the *call stack*. The call stack lists any procedures that are currently running, starting with the first procedure you ran. In this case, we ran the AddSalesTotal macro, which in turn called the GetSalesTotal function.

Click the ellipsis button (...) at the top-right corner of the Locals window to open the Call Stack window (you can also choose View ➤ Call Stack or press Ctrl+L). The Call Stack window for our currently running code is shown in Figure 7-29.

Figure 7-29. *The Call Stack window shows all functions called in the current process.*

You'll notice in Figure 7-29 that the most current procedure call is at the top of the stack. Once GetSalesTotal completes and execution returns to AddSalesTotal, it will be removed from the stack.

8. Close the Call Stack window.

With the code still in break mode, we're going to look at one last method of checking variable values. Then we'll fix our problem and run the code successfully.

The Code Window

The code window also has the ability to show us the values of variables. By simply holding your mouse pointer over any in-scope variable, you can see its value in a tool tip–style pop-up.

In the VBE code window, move the mouse pointer over any variable to see its value. Figure 7-30 shows the mouse hovering over the cell.Value variable, showing its value, N/A.

```
(General)                              GetSalesTotal

    Function GetSalesTotal(RangeToTotal As Range) As Currency
    Dim currReturn As Currency
    Dim cell As Range
    Dim temp As Currency

        For Each cell In RangeToTotal
            temp = temp + cell.Value
        Next cell           cell.Value = "N/A"

        currReturn = temp
        GetSalesTotal = currReturn
    End Function
```

Figure 7-30. *Checking variable values in the code window*

Stop the code from running by clicking the Reset button on the toolbar, as shown in Figure 7-31.

Figure 7-31. *The Reset button stops code execution.*

Let's fix the error and rerun the code. On Sheet1 in Excel, change the value of cell D4 to 0, or leave it blank and run the AddSalesTotal macro again. Figure 7-32 shows Sheet1 with the total added after successfully running AddSalesTotal.

◢	A	B	C	D	E	F
1	QTR 1 Sales					
2		North	South	East	West	
3	CDs	30	23	82	28	
4	DVDs	58	82		43	
5	Hats	36	67	28	74	
6	Shirts	47	35	74	41	
7						
8	Grand Total		$748.00			
9						
10						

Figure 7-32. *The worksheet after fixing the data*

The Watch Window

The Watch window is a tool that allows you to set conditions on which you can put your code into break mode. The Watch window, shown in Figure 7-33, has a few options as to how to handle watched values.

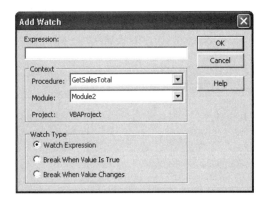

Figure 7-33. *The Watch window*

You enter an expression in the Expression text box, and then select the context of the expression from the Procedure and Module drop-down lists. Then you select a watch type. Watch types are described in Table 7-3.

Table 7-3. *Watch Types*

Watch Type	Description
Watch Expression	Code execution will not be stopped. In break mode, the values of watched expressions will be displayed in the Watch window.
Break When Value Is True	Code execution will enter break mode when the watched value is True.
Break When Value Changes	Code execution will enter break mode when the value of the watched expression changes.

In this example, we'll add a watch to the GetSalesTotal function and set it to break when the value is True.

1. Open the VBE and open Standard Module2.

2. Display the GetSalesTotal function.

3. Right-click any occurrence of the variable cell in the For Each...Next loop.

4. Select Add Watch from the shortcut menu, as shown in Figure 7-34.

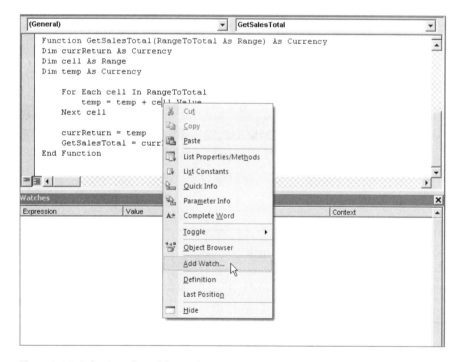

Figure 7-34. *Selecting the Add Watch command*

5. Enter the information shown in Figure 7-35 into the Add Watch dialog box.

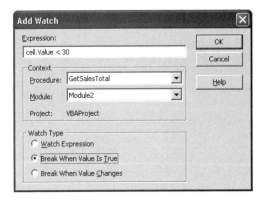

Figure 7-35. *Adding a watch expression*

■**Tip** If you put the insertion point anywhere on the variable you want to watch and add the watch, the variable name will automatically be inserted in the Expression box for you.

---

6. Click OK to close the Add Watch dialog box.

7. If not already open, open the Watch window in the VBE by clicking View ➤ Watch Window. Figure 7-36 shows the Watch window with our expression added.

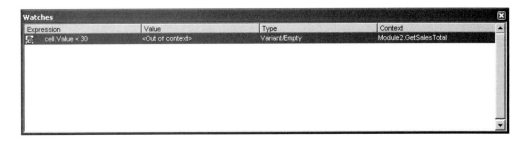

Figure 7-36. *Watch expression added to Watch window*

Notice that the value is currently out of context because the code is not yet running.

8. Run the AddSalesTotal macro from Worksheet1 in Excel. The code enters break mode in the For Each...Next loop, and the Watch window shows us that the value of our condition is True, as shown in Figure 7-37.

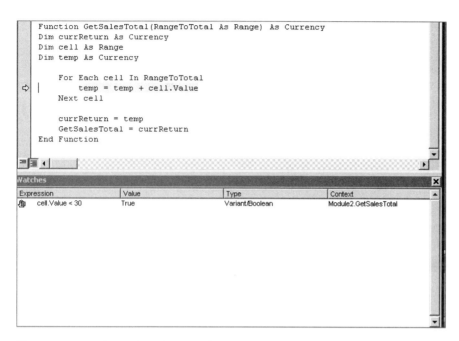

```
Function GetSalesTotal(RangeToTotal As Range) As Currency
Dim currReturn As Currency
Dim cell As Range
Dim temp As Currency

    For Each cell In RangeToTotal
        temp = temp + cell.Value
    Next cell

    currReturn = temp
    GetSalesTotal = currReturn
End Function
```

Expression	Value	Type	Context
cell.Value < 30	True	Variant/Boolean	Module2.GetSalesTotal

Figure 7-37. *Watch window showing the true condition with the code in break mode*

9. Press F5 to continue running the code. Any time the watch encounters a cell value of less than 30, the code will enter break mode.

10. Press F5 until the code runs to completion.

Now that we've seen how to debug and troubleshoot our code, let's take a look at how to prevent errors from occurring and how to graciously notify users of errors.

Error Handling

Effective error handling is one of the major keys in providing a friendly experience to your users. It's right up there with UI design in importance, and it can be the difference between a dream and a nightmare from the user's perspective.

The Microsoft Office suite of tools is still VBA-based. Therefore we are still limited to the On Error GoTo syntax for error handling. Be that as it may, we will look at some methods of handling errors, and then we'll see how to deliver user-friendly messages to our users.

Is the File There?

One common error occurs when we try to open a file that is not available. In Chapter 3, we opened files that contained various information ranging from CD lists to employee data. What if the file wasn't there or was misnamed?

In the Download section for this book on the Apress web site, find the file named
...XML_data.xlsm, and open the file. This is a blank workbook that includes code modules
from Chapter 3.

1. Open the VBE by clicking the Visual Basic command on the Code tab of the Developer
   ribbon, or by pressing Alt+F11.

2. Open Standard Module1.

3. Find the GetXMLData subroutine. It is shown in Listing 7-7.

Listing 7-7. *GetXMLData Procedure Before Modification*

```
Sub GetXMLData()
  ActiveWorkbook.XmlImport URL:= ➥
    "C:\Chapter 3\files\cds.xml", ImportMap:= ➥
    Nothing, Overwrite:=True, Destination:=Range("$A$1")
End Sub
```

■**Note** The path to the XML file will vary based on where you are storing the files that came with this book.

---

4. In the GetXMLData subroutine, change the name of the XML file we're opening to
   cd.xml. The subroutine should look like Listing 7-8 now.

Listing 7-8. *GetXMLData Procedure After Modification*

```
Sub GetXMLData()
  ActiveWorkbook.XmlImport URL:= ➥
    "C:\Chapter 3\files\cd.xml", ImportMap:= ➥
    Nothing, Overwrite:=True, Destination:=Range("$A$1")
End Sub
```

5. In Excel, make Worksheet1 the active sheet.

6. From the Macro dialog box, run the GetXMLData procedure. We get a very ugly error, as shown in Figure 7-38.

Figure 7-38. *A non-intuitive error message is presented to the user.*

7. Click the End button.

In cases like this, where it's an issue of resource availability, we don't need to code an actual error handler to assist the user. What we need to do is check for the existence of the file before we try to open it. If the file is not present, we'll tell the user in a friendlier and more understandable manner.

In the VBE, add a standard code module. Add the code from Listing 7-9.

Listing 7-9. *The FileExists Function*

```
Function FileExists(FilePathName As String) As Boolean
Dim blnReturn As Boolean
  blnReturn = Len(Dir(FilePathName)) > 0

  FileExists = blnReturn
End Function
```

On Standard Module1, modify the GetXMLData subroutine as in Listing 7-10.

Listing 7-10. *GetXMLData Subroutine with Modifications*

```
Sub GetXMLData()
Dim sFileName As String

  sFileName = "C:\Book\Chapters\Chapter 3\files\cd.xml"
  If FileExists(sFileName) Then
    ActiveWorkbook.XmlImport URL:= _
      sFileName, ImportMap:= _
      Nothing, Overwrite:=True, Destination:=Range("$A$1")
  Else
    MsgBox "Could not find the requested file", vbOKOnly, "File Not Found"
  End If
End Sub
```

Let's take a look at what we changed:

- We took the string containing the file name out of the XmlImport method call and assigned it to the variable sFileName.

- We then wrapped our XmlImport method call in an If statement. Based upon the existence of the file, we either import the data or present the user with the friendly message shown in Figure 7-39.

Figure 7-39. *Friendly error message: File Not Found*

The moral of this story in this case is that the best defense is a good offense. By considering in advance where our code might fail, we can avoid errors and provide users with feedback they can use.

Trapping Specific Errors

A rule of thumb when considering error handling is that error handling should not be an afterthought or something to add later. Trap your errors when you create your code.

■**Tip** Three good error handling rules to live by are (1) check for the error, (2) handle it, and (3) proceed accordingly.

Returning our attention to the DebugExample01.xlsm file, let's trap for the type mismatch error we got in our first go around with this file. We'll begin by resetting the file as follows:

1. On Sheet1, enter **N/A** in cell D4.

2. If there is a totals row present, delete it.

3. Save the file.

A type mismatch error is error number 13, and occurs when you try to place a value of one data type into an incompatible data type (in this example, a string into a numeric data type). See Figure 7-27 in our earlier example for an example of a type mismatch error. We are going to modify our code to trap for error 13 and display a friendly message to the user.

Open the VBE by clicking the Visual Basic command on the Code tab of the Developer ribbon, or by pressing Alt+F11. Open Standard Module2, and find the GetSalesTotal function.

In the GetSalesTotal function, we have a loop (Figure 7-40) that uses a temporary placeholder variable, temp, to hold the running total value of the cells in the range passed in. This variable is defined as a Currency data type. The Currency data type can hold an awfully large numeric value, but it cannot hold a string.

```
For Each cell In RangeToTotal
    temp = temp + cell.Value
Next cell
```

Figure 7-40. *The looping structure totals the cells in the temp variable.*

There are a couple of things we have to do to set up a procedure for error handling:

1. Turn error handling on (also known as *enabling* error handling).

2. Add line labels so our code knows where to go when an error condition is fired.

3. Handle the error.

4. Resume code execution at the appropriate location.

Let's modify the GetSalesTotal function and add an error handler.

1. Add a variable declaration after the declaration for temp:

```
Dim sErrMsg As String
```

The sErrMsg variable will hold the text of the message we'll show our users should an error occur. The variables should now look like those in Listing 7-11.

Listing 7-11. *Variable List for GetSalesTotal*

```
Dim currReturn As Currency
Dim cell As Range
Dim temp As Currency
Dim sErrMsg As String
```

2. Immediately below the variable declarations, add the following line of code to enable error handling:

```
On Error GoTo Err_Handle
```

Here is where we tell the compiler where in our code to go if an error is fired. Err_Handle is a line label that refers to a specific point in our code. We'll add it in just a moment.

3. Add two blank lines between the last two lines of code in the GetSalesTotal function, as follows:

```
currReturn = temp


GetSalesTotal = currReturn
```

4. Put your cursor in the second blank line and add the following line label:

```
Exit_Function:
```

5. Insert a blank line above the End Function line and type the following:

```
Exit Function
```

The code after the loop should now look like Listing 7-12.

Listing 7-12. *Exit_Function Line Label Added*

```
currReturn = temp

Exit_Function:
    GetSalesTotal = currReturn
    Exit Function
End Function
```

So far, with the exception of enabling error handling, our code works just like it did originally. Now let's write code to handle the type mismatch error.

6. Put the insertion point at the end of the Exit Function line of code and press Enter.

7. Type the following line label:

```
Err_Handle:
```

8. Press Enter.

When we enabled error handling by adding the On Error GoTo statement, we referred it to this label. You can name yours according to your own naming convention. Just be sure the label used at the top of the procedure is the same as that used to name the error handler section of code at the bottom of the procedure.

9. Add the following code at the insertion point:

```
If Err.Number = 13 Then
    sErrMsg = "A value in your data may not be numeric. Please check your
data"
Else
    sErrMsg = "An unexpected error " & Err.Number & " has occurred"
End If

MsgBox sErrMsg, vbOKOnly, "Error"
Resume Exit_Function
```

If an error occurs, the code redirects to the Err_Handle section. Here we placed conditional logic that looks for a specific error number. If we were aware of other error conditions, we could simply add them to the If...Else block or even use a Select Case statement.

Inside the If statement, we are assigning the appropriate error message to the sErrMsg variable based on what error occurred. Then we show the user the message. The last line of the error handler section tells the code where to resume once the error is dealt with. In this case, we're telling it to resume at the line label Exit_Function where we assign an output value to our function.

10. Save the code.

11. In Excel, run the AddSalesTotal Macro.

Our friendly message is displayed to the user informing her of the issue with the data, as shown in Figure 7-41.

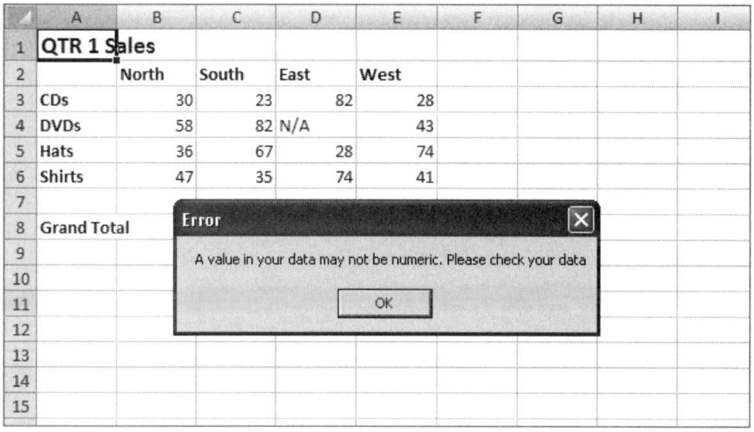

	A	B	C	D	E	F	G	H	I
1	QTR 1 Sales								
2		North	South	East	West				
3	CDs	30	23	82	28				
4	DVDs	58	82	N/A	43				
5	Hats	36	67	28	74				
6	Shirts	47	35	74	41				
7									
8	Grand Total	Error ✕							
9		A value in your data may not be numeric. Please check your data							
10									
11		OK							
12									
13									
14									
15									

Figure 7-41. *User-friendly error message*

12. Click OK to continue.

As shown in Figure 7-42, there is a small issue with the output from the GetSalesTotal function. It returned a value of 0.

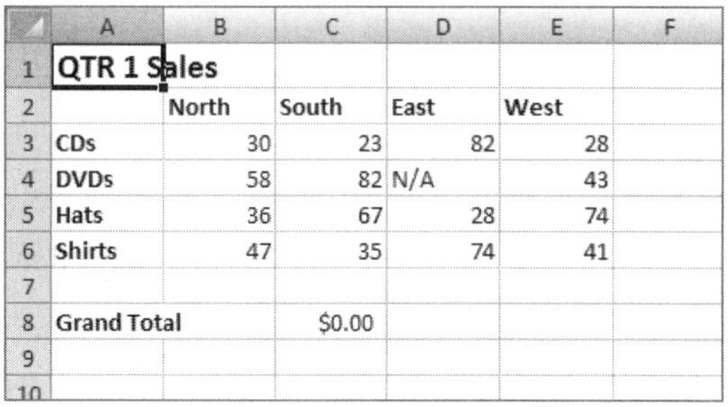

	A	B	C	D	E	F
1	QTR 1 Sales					
2		North	South	East	West	
3	CDs	30	23	82	28	
4	DVDs	58	82	N/A	43	
5	Hats	36	67	28	74	
6	Shirts	47	35	74	41	
7						
8	Grand Total		$0.00			
9						
10						

Figure 7-42. *Zero value returned from GetSalesTotal function*

Let's see what happened. Return to the VBE and look at the GetSalesTotal function (Listing 7-13).

Listing 7-13. *GetSalesTotal Function with Error Handling*

```
Function GetSalesTotal(RangeToTotal As Range) As Currency
Dim currReturn As Currency
Dim cell As Range
Dim temp As Currency
Dim sErrMsg As String
  On Error GoTo Err_Handle


    For Each cell In RangeToTotal
        temp = temp + cell.Value
    Next cell


    currReturn = temp

Exit_Function:
    GetSalesTotal = currReturn
    Exit Function
Err_Handle:
  If Err.Number = 13 Then
    sErrMsg = "A value in your data may not be numeric. Please check your data"
  Else
    sErrMsg = "An unexpected error " & Err.Number & " has occurred"
  End If

  MsgBox sErrMsg, vbOKOnly, "Error"
  Resume Exit_Function
End Function
```

Debugging the Error Handler

After our error message is displayed, we tell our code to resume at the Exit_Function line label. Since we know the code worked fine with all numeric values in our original example and our error message was displayed successfully upon trapping the error, lets add a breakpoint at the point where we resume execution, as shown in Figure 7-43.

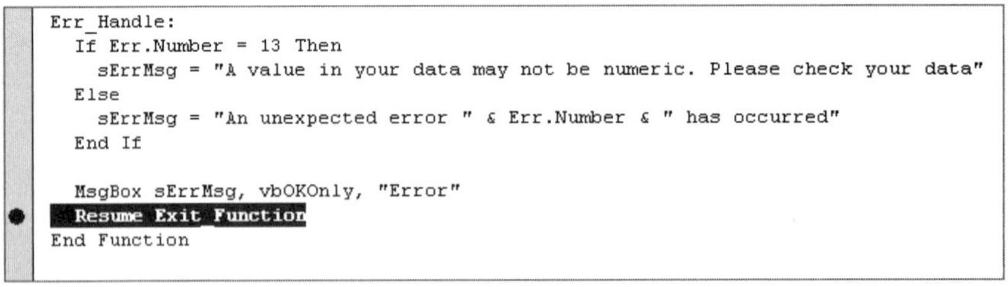

```
Err_Handle:
  If Err.Number = 13 Then
    sErrMsg = "A value in your data may not be numeric. Please check your data"
  Else
    sErrMsg = "An unexpected error " & Err.Number & " has occurred"
  End If

  MsgBox sErrMsg, vbOKOnly, "Error"
  Resume Exit_Function
End Function
```

Figure 7-43. *Breakpoint added in error handler*

1. Return to Excel.

2. Run the AddSalesTotal macro.

3. Click OK when the error message appears, and the code will go into break mode.

4. Press F8 once to step to the next line of code. The execution point will move into the Exit_Function section.

5. Hold your mouse pointer over the currReturn variable to check its value. As shown in Figure 7-44, it has a 0 value.

```
Function GetSalesTotal(RangeToTotal As Range) As Currency
Dim currReturn As Currency
Dim cell As Range
Dim temp As Currency
Dim sErrMsg As String
  On Error GoTo Err_Handle

    For Each cell In RangeToTotal
        temp = temp + cell.Value
    Next cell

    currReturn = temp

Exit_Function:
    GetSalesTotal = currReturn
    Exit Function        currReturn = 0
Err_Handle:
  If Err.Number = 13 Then
    sErrMsg = "A value in your data may not be numeric. Please check your data"
  Else
    sErrMsg = "An unexpected error " & Err.Number & " has occurred"
  End If

    MsgBox sErrMsg, vbOKOnly, "Error"
    Resume Exit Function
End Function
```

Figure 7-44. *Checking the value of currReturn*

6. Press F5 to let the code run to finish.

Since our loop never finished running, currReturn was never assigned a value. We have a couple of choices on how to handle this. We can show no total in case of an error, or we can show the total of the numeric values.

To show a total and get the loop to finish running, we need to modify the behavior of our Resume statement. The Resume statement has three forms, as shown in Table 7-4.

Table 7-4. *The Resume Statement*

Statement	Description
Resume	Resumes code execution with the statement that caused the error. If the error was not handled, it becomes fatal.
Resume Next	Resumes code execution with the statement following the statement that triggered the error.
Resume *Line*	Resumes code execution at a line label or number within the procedure containing the error handler.

Our type mismatch error occurs in our loop, and in order to populate currReturn with a value, we'll need to complete the loop.

1. Remove the breakpoint.

2. In the GetSalesTotal function error handler, change the Resume statement to read as follows:

    ```
    Resume Next
    ```

3. In Excel, run the AddSalesTotal macro again.

4. Click OK when the error message is displayed. The correct total for the numeric values will be displayed, as shown in Figure 7-45.

⊿	A	B	C	D	E	F
1	QTR 1 Sales					
2		North	South	East	West	
3	CDs	30	23	82	28	
4	DVDs	58	82	N/A	43	
5	Hats	36	67	28	74	
6	Shirts	47	35	74	41	
7						
8	Grand Total		$748.00			
9						
10						

Figure 7-45. *Result of using Resume Next to complete our loop*

Our On Error GoTo statement refers to a specific line label to handle errors. If you know that any errors you might encounter in a routine are not going to be fatal and can be skipped, you can use the On Error Resume Next statement.

Listing 7-14 shows a modified version of the GetSalesTotal function that uses On Error Resume Next.

Listing 7-14. *GetSalesTotal Function Using On Error Resume Next*

```
Function GetSalesTotal(RangeToTotal As Range) As Currency
Dim currReturn As Currency
Dim cell As Range
Dim temp As Currency
Dim sErrMsg As String
  On Error Resume Next

    For Each cell In RangeToTotal
        temp = temp + cell.Value
    Next cell

    currReturn = temp
```

```
Exit_Function:
    GetSalesTotal = currReturn
    Exit Function
End Function
```

On Error Resume Next essentially turns error trapping off. If there's a chance that another section of your code could throw an error, you can turn error trapping back on by adding an On Error GoTo statement inside your code. Figure 7-46 shows the GetSalesTotal function with error trapping turned off for the loop, but turned back on again for the return variable assignments.

```
Function GetSalesTotal(RangeToTotal As Range) As Currency
Dim currReturn As Currency
Dim cell As Range
Dim temp As Currency
Dim sErrMsg As String
  On Error Resume Next

    For Each cell In RangeToTotal
        temp = temp + cell.Value
    Next cell

    On Error GoTo Err_Handle
    currReturn = temp

Exit_Function:
    GetSalesTotal = currReturn
    Exit Function
Err_Handle:
  If Err.Number = 13 Then
    sErrMsg = "A value in your data may not be numeric. Please check your data"
  Else
    sErrMsg = "An unexpected error " & Err.Number & " has occurred"
  End If

  MsgBox sErrMsg, vbOKOnly, "Error"
  Resume Next
End Function
```

Figure 7-46. *Error trapping turned on by adding an On Error GoTo statement*

Now if an error should occur after the loop runs, we can trap it and handle it appropriately in the error handler.

Summary

The VBE in Excel 2007 provides us with many tools to debug our code. The better we get at using these tools, the faster we can correct our code, and the more our productivity will increase. In this chapter, we looked at the Debug menu and the Debug toolbar, and we explored their commands.

The ability to step through code and move the execution point forward and backward are invaluable assets when debugging code. The Immediate window provides us with an easy way to run code and to view the values of in-scope variables. In this chapter, we explored these aspects of the Immediate window, and even how to run a loop from it. The Locals window provides a great way to view all the variables and their values in one place. The Locals window also shows us objects and their properties as we step through our code in break mode.

We also learned about setting breakpoints to stop our code to help us pinpoint issues. We explored some concepts to apply before coding to help prevent errors, including the `Option Explicit` command, which forces us to declare all variables before using them.

In the next chapter, we'll look at ways Excel can interact with other Microsoft Office products like Word and PowerPoint.

CHAPTER 8

■■■

Office Integration

One of the really great things about VBA in Microsoft Office is that it allows programmatic access to each application from the others. This powerful functionality lets us automate many business processes, including data integration and document creation and management. It also allows us to create workflows within the Office suite of applications.

In this chapter, we will see how we can turn an Excel workbook into a summary report in Microsoft Word. We'll also take that same workbook and create a presentation in Microsoft PowerPoint. Both documents will include text and chart data from our Excel project.

The code we've been writing so far has accessed properties of Microsoft Excel 2007 using the Excel Document Object Model (DOM). We will now explore some of the common DOM objects for Word and PowerPoint as we delve into Office automation.

Creating a Report in Word

In Chapter 5, we explored charting in Excel 2007. We are going to turn one of our chart reports into a summary report using the Word 2007 DOM from the Excel 2007 VBE.

In this example, you'll learn how to do the following:

- Open an instance of Microsoft Word programmatically

- Create a new document within the instance of Word

- Add text

- Apply styles

- Insert chart objects from Excel

Let's start by opening an existing Excel project that contains numeric and chart data. We'll use the charts in our summary report in Word.

1. From the source files for this book, open the file `Chapter 8\Files\Chart08.xslm`.

The file contains sales data and pie charts for a few product categories that we need to create a report on. The report will cover the first few months of sales year 2007, as shown in Figure 8-1.

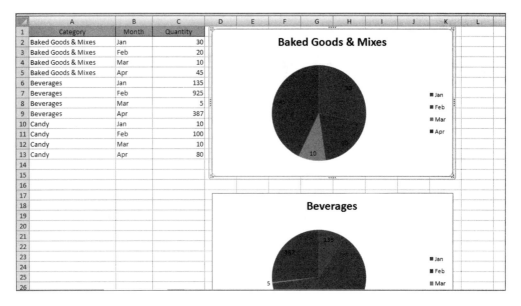

Figure 8-1. *Sales data and pie charts*

2. Open the VBE by selecting the Developer ribbon ➤ Code tab ➤ Visual Basic command, or by pressing Alt+F11.

3. Add a new standard module in the Project Explorer.

Before we can begin accessing and working with the Word DOM, we need to add a reference to Word in the References dialog box.

4. In the VBE, select Tools ➤ References to display the References dialog box (shown in Figure 8-2).

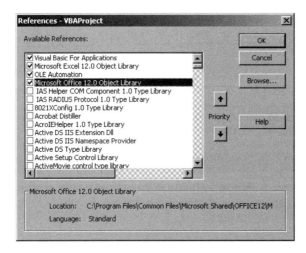

Figure 8-2. *References dialog box*

5. In the References dialog box, scroll down until you see the Microsoft Word 12.0 Object Library (shown in Figure 8-3).

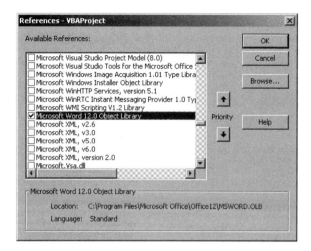

Figure 8-3. *Microsoft Word 12.0 Object Library selected*

6. Select the Microsoft Word 12.0 Object Library.

7. Click OK.

8. Add the following module-level variables:

```
Private m_oWordApp As Word.Application
Private m_oWordDoc As Word.Document
```

These variables will hold the instance of our Word application and the new Word document for the report.

9. Create a new subroutine named MakeWordDoc.

10. Add the following variable declarations:

```
Dim i As Integer
Dim sTitle As String
Dim sBody As String
```

These will contain a counter value used when we loop through our charts, and two string values to hold the title and introductory text for the report. Next, we'll assign the title of our report, "2007 Sales Report," to the sTitle variable. Since we'll also be creating a PowerPoint presentation from our VBA code, let's create some routines to provide that information to our application. This way, we can reuse it in both processes.

The Helper Functions

We are going to add three separate text entries for our report:

Title text: The title of the report

Title body text: A description or introduction to the report

Subject body text: Brief descriptions for each product chart

For this, we will create three helper functions.

1. In the VBE, add a new standard code module.

2. On the new code module, add the function shown in Listing 8-1 to return the report title:

Listing 8-1. *GetTitle Function*

```
Function GetTitle() As String
  GetTitle = "2007 Sales Report"
End Function
```

3. Below GetTitle, add a function to return the title body text, as shown in Listing 8-2.

Listing 8-2. *GetTitleBody Function*

```
Function GetTitleBody() As String
Dim sBody As String
  sBody = "Sales for the first four months of 2007 were generally stable.  "
  sBody = sBody & "Although Baked Goods & Mixes were somewhat flat "
  sBody = sBody & "Beverages and Candy showed improvement."

  GetTitleBody = sBody
End Function
```

4. On the same code module, add the function shown in Listing 8-3 to return the subject body text.

Listing 8-3. *GetSubjectBody Function*

```
Function GetSubjectBody(Index As Integer) As String
Dim sBody As String
    Select Case Index
    Case 1
      sBody = "Sales in this category were average " ➥
              & "for the first third of the year."
    Case 2
      sBody = "Sales in this category were slightly above average " ➥
              & "for the first third of the year.  February was " ➥
              & "very good for the season."
```

```
    Case 3
      sBody = "Sales in this category were above average " ➥
              & "for the first third of the year.  February and April " ➥
              & "showed spikes due to holidays."
    End Select

  GetSubjectBody = sBody
  End Function
```

5. Save the project.

In a production application, you are probably not likely to store these string values in your VBA code. For the purposes of our examples, I've included the text here, but a more realistic scenario would be if this information came from a database, an XML or text file, or even a worksheet in an Excel project.

The last subroutine we added, `GetSubjectBody`, takes a parameter named `Index`. This is used to match and display the correct text for the corresponding chart.

Let's move back to Standard Module1 and resume programming our Word report.

Creating an Instance of Word

Before we begin, let's outline the steps involved in creating a report with text and charts in Word from Excel VBA code:

1. Open the Word application.

2. Create a new Word document.

3. Add formatted headings and text.

4. Add charts with formatted headings and text.

5. Display Word and the new report.

Let's begin. Our first tasks are to open an instance of the Word application and load a new document into that instance.

1. In the `MakeWordDoc` subroutine, add the following statements:

```
Set m_oWordApp = CreateObject("Word.Application")
Set m_oWordDoc = m_oWordApp.Documents.Add
```

We are using the `CreateObject` function to create an instance of the Word application. `CreateObject` creates a new instance of Word even if one is already open. To use `CreateObject` to create an instance of a Microsoft Office product, you call the method and pass in an argument containing the class name of that application. The *class name* is a combination of the application name plus the object type. In this case (and in most cases), our object type is `Application`. All Microsoft Office products expose an `Application` object type. Word and Excel provide a few other object types that can be created with `CreateObject` as well, as shown in Table 8-1.

Table 8-1. *Microsoft Office Object Types*

Office Application	Object Type	Class
Access	Application	Access.Application
Excel	Application	Excel.Application
Excel	Worksheet	Excel.Worksheet
Excel	Chart	Excel.Chart
Outlook	Application	Outlook.Application
PowerPoint	Application	PowerPoint.Application
Word	Application	Word.Application
Word	Document	Word.Document

When using any of the additional object types provided by Word or Excel, a new instance of Word or Excel is created. To use `CreateObject` to open an instance of Outlook, the syntax would be the following:

```
CreateObject(Outlook.Application)
```

CREATEOBJECT VS. GETOBJECT

Another way to return an instance of an Office application is to use the `GetObject` function. `GetObject` differs from `CreateObject` in that it uses an existing instance of the application. There are a couple of instances where `GetObject` may make sense for your applications. One is when you want to use an existing instance of an application object that is already loaded. The other is when you want to start an instance of an application with a file loaded.

The syntax for using `GetObject` is `GetObject(pathname, class)`, where *pathname* is the path to a Microsoft Office document. The class parameter is not required in this case, as `GetObject` will find which application to launch. If no file name is given, the class parameter is required. The class parameter takes the same object class identifier as the `CreateObject` function.

2. Next, fill the variables with title and body text by adding the following lines of code:

```
sTitle = GetTitle
sBody = GetTitleBody
```

3. Then, use the Word `Application` object to insert the title and body text into the Word document, by adding the following code to the `MakeWordDoc` subroutine:

```
With m_oWordApp
    .Selection.Style = .ActiveDocument.Styles("Heading 1")
    .Selection.TypeText sTitle
    .Selection.TypeParagraph
    .Selection.TypeText sBody
End With
```

This code defines the document style for the first line of text and inserts the title text. Next, we add a new paragraph break and insert the report's descriptive body text.

Before we begin inserting our charts, let's add some cleanup code and take a quick look at our progress by running and displaying Word from the VBE.

4. Add the following code after the `With...End With` block:

```
m_oWordApp.Visible = True
MsgBox "word s/b  open now"
m_oWordApp.Quit
Set m_oWordApp = Nothing
```

Here we are displaying the Word application and our new document. The message box is here to stop the code from running so we can navigate over to the Word window (if it's not already the active window). Once we click the message box to close it, our cleanup code runs and shuts down the instance of Word and kills the Word `Application` object.

5. Save your work.

The code so far should look like Listing 8-4.

Listing 8-4. *MakeWordDoc Subroutine*

```
Sub MakeWordDoc()
Dim i As Integer
Dim sTitle As String
Dim sBody As String

  Set m_oWordApp = CreateObject("Word.Application")
  Set m_oWordDoc = m_oWordApp.Documents.Add

  sTitle = GetTitle
  sBody = GetTitleBody

  With m_oWordApp
    .Selection.Style = .ActiveDocument.Styles("Heading 1")
    .Selection.TypeText sTitle
    .Selection.TypeParagraph
    .Selection.TypeText sBody
  End With

  m_oWordApp.Visible = True
  MsgBox "word s/b open now"
  m_oWordApp.Quit
  Set m_oWordApp = Nothing
End Sub
```

Let's run the code we've generated so far and see what we get.

6. Put your cursor anywhere in the MakeWordDoc subroutine.

7. Click the Run button on the VBE toolbar or press F5.

■Note Depending on the speed of your computer, the code may run for a bit before Word appears. Remember, you are loading an actual instance of Word, so this will take about as long as Word normally takes to load on your machine.

Figure 8-4 shows the Word instance displaying the report heading in Heading 1 style and descriptive text in the default (Normal) style formatting.

■Note We did not tell our code to format the body text in Normal style, did we? The default behavior of Word's heading styles is to format text at the following paragraph marker to Normal style (saving us a line of code in the process!).

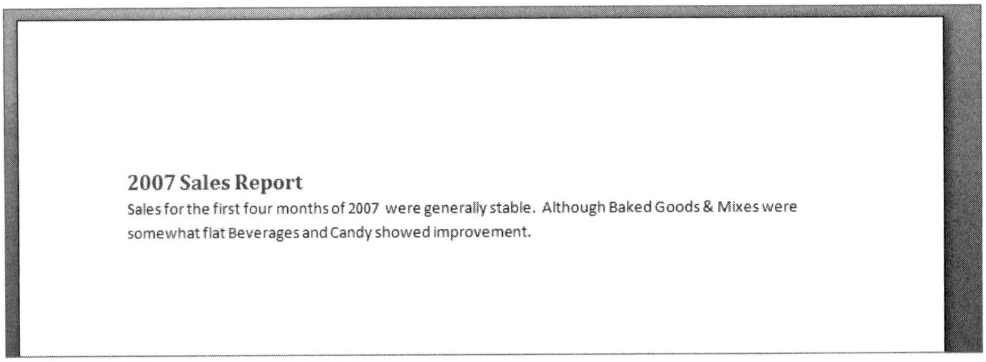

2007 Sales Report
Sales for the first four months of 2007 were generally stable. Although Baked Goods & Mixes were somewhat flat Beverages and Candy showed improvement.

Figure 8-4. *The report heading and text*

■Note The formatting of the Heading 1 and Normal styles may differ in your Word installation.

---

8. Navigate back to the main Excel window and click OK on the message box to let the code finish running, as shown in Figure 8-5.

Figure 8-5. *The message box stops the code so that we can check results.*

9. Click No when prompted to save the Word document (unless you really want it).

Adding Charts to the Report

We've seen now that our code works. Word opened and the heading section of the report displayed successfully. Now let's return to the VBE and add our charts and their descriptive text.

We have three charts to insert and three sets of descriptive text. In this section, we will add a loop that will do the following:

- Insert a blank line between each section

- Insert the descriptive text

- Insert the chart

1. In the MakeWordDoc subroutine, place the cursor at the beginning of the End With statement.

2. Press Enter.

3. Move the insertion point into the blank line you just created and add the following lines of code:

```
For i = 1 To 3
  .Selection.TypeParagraph
  InsertText i
  InsertChart i
Next i
```

I've created a couple of helper functions to insert the text and charts according to the index passed into the procedure. The InsertText subroutine finds the chart with the index value passed in and grabs its title. It then calls the GetSubjectBody function to get the text corresponding to the chart. Finally, it formats the text area and inserts the appropriate section heading and text.

4. On Standard Module1, add the code shown in Listing 8-5.

Listing 8-5. *InsertText Procedure*

```
Sub InsertText(Index As Integer)
Dim sTitle As String
Dim sBody As String

    Worksheets(1).ChartObjects(Index).Activate
    sTitle = ActiveChart.ChartTitle.Text
    sBody = GetSubjectBody(Index)

    With m_oWordApp
        .Selection.Style = .ActiveDocument.Styles("Heading 2")
        .Selection.TypeText sTitle
        .Selection.TypeParagraph
        .Selection.TypeText sBody
        .Selection.TypeParagraph
    End With
End Sub
```

The InsertChart subroutine finds the chart based upon the index value passed in, and then applies its Copy method to place a copy of the chart on the Windows clipboard. Then we move to the Word document and apply the Paste command at the insertion point.

5. On Standard Module1, add the code shown in Listing 8-6.

Listing 8-6. *InsertChart Procedure*

```
Sub InsertChart(Index As Integer)
    Worksheets(1).ChartObjects(Index).Copy
    m_oWordApp.Selection.Paste
End Sub
```

This completes the MakeWordDoc procedure. The finished code should look like Listing 8-7.

Listing 8-7. *Complete MakeWordDoc Subroutine*

```
Sub MakeWordDoc()
Dim i As Integer
Dim sTitle As String
Dim sBody As String

  Set m_oWordApp = CreateObject("Word.Application")
  Set m_oWordDoc = m_oWordApp.Documents.Add

  sTitle = GetTitle
  sBody = GetTitleBody
```

```
With m_oWordApp
  .Selection.Style = .ActiveDocument.Styles("Heading 1")
  .Selection.TypeText sTitle
  .Selection.TypeParagraph
  .Selection.TypeText sBody
  For i = 1 To 3
  .Selection.TypeParagraph
  InsertText i
  InsertChart i
  Next i
End With

m_oWordApp.Visible = True
MsgBox "word s/b  open now"
m_oWordApp.Quit
Set m_oWordApp = Nothing
End Sub
```

Now let's run the code and see the finished product.

6. Place the insertion point anywhere inside the MakeWordDoc subroutine.

7. Click the Run button on the VBE toolbar or press F5.

The completed report will appear, and should look similar to Figure 8-6.

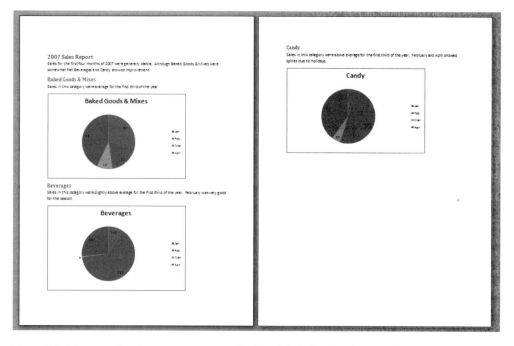

Figure 8-6. *The completed summary report displayed in Print Preview mode*

The Word DOM is very rich and contains many other useful objects for you to code against. Once you've added a reference to Word in the VBE, you can explore its many features in the Object Browser (which you can access by pressing F2). Figure 8-7 shows a view of the Word objects as displayed in the Object Browser.

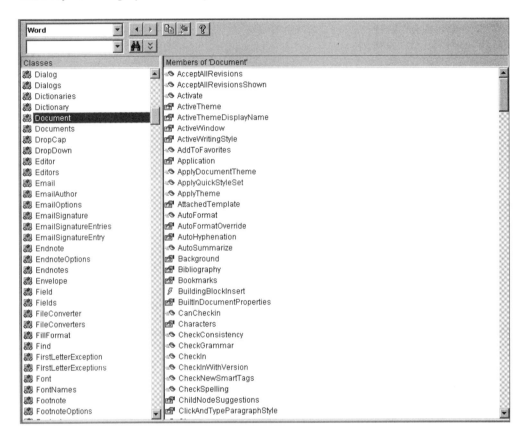

Figure 8-7. *Word objects displayed in the Object Browser*

   8. Return to the Excel window.

   9. Click OK on the message box and let the code run its cleanup.

Now that we've got our report completed in Microsoft Word, let's look at PowerPoint and create a presentation based on this data.

Creating a PowerPoint Presentation

Now that you've had a little experience in navigating Word's DOM, you should be comfortable enough to dive into the PowerPoint DOM. The process will be very similar, although the objects we will use will be very different.

In this example, we will build a series of slides, including a title page followed by one slide per chart in our Excel workbook project. The steps involved in this code will be as follows:

1. Open the PowerPoint application.

2. Create a new presentation document.

3. Create a Slide object.

4. Add a title slide.

5. Add chart slides.

6. Display the PowerPoint window with the new presentation loaded.

Coding the Presentation

Before we could access any of the Word DOM objects in the previous example, we had to add a reference to the Word Object Model to our code project. Before we can access any of the PowerPoint DOM objects, we must also add a reference to the PowerPoint Object Model.

1. Open the VBE by selecting the Developer ribbon ➤ Code tab ➤ Visual Basic command, or by pressing Alt+F11.

2. In the VBE, select Tools ➤ References to display the References dialog box (shown in Figure 8-8).

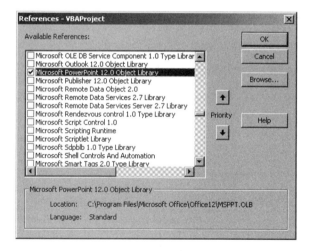

Figure 8-8. *Adding a reference to the PowerPoint 12.0 Object Model*

3. Select the Microsoft PowerPoint 12.0 Object Library.

4. Click OK to save the reference.

Now we can start coding against the PowerPoint DOM. For our PowerPoint example, we'll use a new empty code module.

5. In the VBE, add a new standard module in the Project Explorer. If you've only coded per the previous example, this should be Module3 (but don't worry if it's not).

6. Add the following module-level variables:

```
Private m_oPptApp As PowerPoint.Application
Private m_oPptShow As PowerPoint.Presentation
Private m_oPptSlide As PowerPoint.Slide
```

The object types of these variables are plainly named. We have a variable to hold a reference to the PowerPoint application, one for the Presentation object, and one to hold a Slide object.

7. Add a new subroutine to the code module and name it MakePowerPointPresentation.

8. Add the following lines of code:

```
Set m_oPptApp = CreateObject("PowerPoint.Application")
Set m_oPptShow = m_oPptApp.Presentations.Add
```

In this code, we are instantiating an instance of the PowerPoint application using the CreateObject function discussed in the previous example. Then we are adding a new presentation to that instance.

Now that we have a presentation to work with, our next tasks are to create a title slide and then add chart slides. In our Word example, we created helper functions to do this, and we will do something similar here.

PowerPoint Helper Functions

Our next chore is to create a title slide. The title slide will consist of a title line plus descriptive text, similar to the Word report we created in the last example.

1. Still working on the standard code module with your PowerPoint code, add a new subroutine and name it CreateTitleSlide.

2. Add the following line of code:

```
Set m_oPptSlide = m_oPptShow.Slides.Add(1, ppLayoutTitle)
```

The PowerPoint Presentation object contains a Slides collection that naturally contains all of the slides in a presentation file. The Slides collection's Add method adds a slide to the collection and returns a Slide object back. Here we are assigning that new slide to our m_oPptSlide variable.

The Add method takes two parameters. The first is the slide index. This tells PowerPoint where to put the slide. In our code, it's set to 1 since we're creating the first or title slide. The second parameter is the type of auto-layout to use. Figure 8-9 uses the Object Browser to show the many options available.

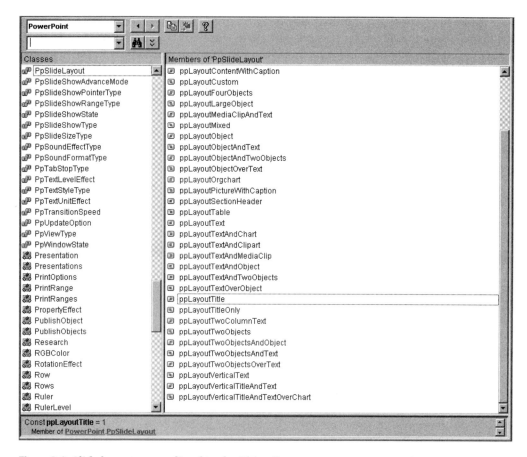

Figure 8-9. *Slide layout enums listed in the Object Browser*

The enum we've used represents a layout with a title placeholder and a text placeholder.

3. Add the following code to the CreateTitleSlide subroutine:

```
With m_oPptSlide.Shapes.Placeholders(1)
  With .TextFrame.TextRange
    .Text = GetTitle
    .Font.Bold = msoTrue
    .ChangeCase ppCaseUpper
  End With
End With

With m_oPptSlide.Shapes.Placeholders(2)
  With .TextFrame.TextRange
    .Text = GetTitleBody
    .Font.Bold = msoFalse
    .ChangeCase ppCaseUpper
  End With
End With
```

Within these two With...End With blocks, we are adding our title text and descriptive text to the Placeholder objects on the title slide. In the first With...End With block, we are setting the title and adding bold formatting to the text. In the second With...End With block, we are adding the title body (or descriptive) text with no bold formatting. The completed CreateTitleSlide subroutine should look like the code in Listing 8-8.

Listing 8-8. *Complete CreateTitleSlide Subroutine*

```
Sub CreateTitleSlide()
  Set m_oPptSlide = m_oPptShow.Slides.Add(1, ppLayoutTitle)

  With m_oPptSlide.Shapes.Placeholders(1)
    With .TextFrame.TextRange
      .Text = GetTitle
      .Font.Bold = msoTrue
      .ChangeCase ppCaseUpper
    End With
  End With

  With m_oPptSlide.Shapes.Placeholders(2)
    With .TextFrame.TextRange
      .Text = GetTitleBody
      .Font.Bold = msoFalse
      .ChangeCase ppCaseUpper
    End With
  End With
End Sub
```

Next, we'll create a procedure to add the slide charts.

1. Add a new subroutine to the code module we've been working in. Name it CreateChartSlides.

2. Add the following variable declarations to CreateChartSlides:

```
Dim i As Integer
Dim sTitle As String
Dim sngChartStart As Single
Dim spacer As Integer
```

The first variable, i, is the counter variable for the loop we'll use when enumerating through our charts. sTitle will store the title text for each chart slide. The sngChartStart variable will be used to help us determine where to place the chart on the slide and how to size it. The last variable, spacer, will be used to put a bit of space between the title placeholder and the chart.

3. Add a For...Next loop with two blank lines between the start and end of the loop, as follows:

```
For i = 1 To 3



Next i
```

The entire subroutine will take place within this For...Next block.

4. Add the following lines of code:

```
Worksheets(1).ChartObjects(i).Activate
sTitle = ActiveChart.ChartTitle.Text
```

The first line activates the chart with an index of i. The second line retrieves the title of the chart we just made active.

Next, we'll add a slide to place the chart on.

5. Add the following line of code:

```
Set m_oPptSlide = m_oPptShow.Slides.Add(i + 1, ppLayoutTitleOnly)
```

This line adds a new slide and gives it a layout that contains only a title placeholder.

6. Add the following code to the CreateChartSlides procedure:

```
With m_oPptSlide.Shapes.Placeholders(1)
  sngChartStart = .top + .height

  With .TextFrame.TextRange
    .Text = sTitle
  End With
End With
```

In this With...End With block, we are assigning a value to the sngChartStart variable, which is the total of the title placeholder's Top and Height property values. This will be used when we place the chart on the slide. Next, we add the chart title text to the title placeholder.

Next, we'll use the Excel Chart object's Copy method to place the chart in memory, and then we can paste it into the slide and place it in its proper location.

7. Add the following code to the CreateChartSlides procedure:

```
Worksheets(1).ChartObjects(i).Copy

spacer = 20
With m_oPptSlide.Shapes.Paste
  .top = sngChartStart + spacer
  .height = m_oPptSlide.Master.height - sngChartStart + spacer
  .left = m_oPptSlide.Master.width / 2 - .width / 2
End With
```

The completed `CreateChartSlides` subroutine should look like Listing 8-9.

Listing 8-9. *Complete CreateChartSlides Subroutine*

```
Sub CreateChartSlides()
Dim i As Integer
Dim sTitle As String
Dim sngChartStart As Single
Dim spacer As Integer

  For i = 1 To 3
    Worksheets(1).ChartObjects(i).Activate
    sTitle = ActiveChart.ChartTitle.Text
    Set m_oPptSlide = m_oPptShow.Slides.Add(i + 1, ppLayoutTitleOnly)

    With m_oPptSlide.Shapes.Placeholders(1)
      sngChartStart = .top + .height

      With .TextFrame.TextRange
        .Text = sTitle
      End With
    End With

    Worksheets(1).ChartObjects(i).Copy

    spacer = 20
    With m_oPptSlide.Shapes.Paste
      .top = sngChartStart + spacer
      .height = m_oPptSlide.Master.height - sngChartStart + spacer
      .left = m_oPptSlide.Master.width / 2 - .width / 2
    End With

  Next i
End Sub
```

Completing the MakePowerPointPresentation Procedure

Moving our attention back to the `MakePowerPointPresentation` subroutine, we will now insert our helper functions into the procedure and view our results. We will also add some cleanup code.

1. In the MakePowerPointPresentation subroutine, move the insertion point to a blank line after the two lines of code previously entered (shown in Listing 8-10 for reference).

Listing 8-10. *MakePowerPointPresentation Subroutine So Far*

```
Sub MakePowerPointPresentation()
   Set m_oPptApp = CreateObject("PowerPoint.Application")
   Set m_oPptShow = m_oPptApp.Presentations.Add


End Sub
```

2. Add the following two lines of code calling the helper functions:

```
CreateTitleSlide
CreateChartSlides
```

3. Add the following code to display the results of your work and to perform the necessary cleanup operations:

```
m_oPptApp.Visible = msoTrue
MsgBox "PowerPoint is open"
m_oPptApp.Quit
Set m_oPptSlide = Nothing
Set m_oPptShow = Nothing
Set m_oPptApp = Nothing
```

We are making our m_PptApp object visible and freezing the code with a message box, as we did in our Word example. The last few lines of this code close the PowerPoint application and destroy all of the PowerPoint objects.

The completed MakePowerPointPresentation subroutine should look like Listing 8-11.

Listing 8-11. *Complete MakePowerPointPresentation Subroutine*

```
Sub MakePowerPointPresentation()
  Set m_oPptApp = CreateObject("PowerPoint.Application")
  Set m_oPptShow = m_oPptApp.Presentations.Add

  CreateTitleSlide
  CreateChartSlides

  m_oPptApp.Visible = msoTrue
  MsgBox "PowerPoint is open"
  m_oPptApp.Quit
  Set m_oPptSlide = Nothing
  Set m_oPptShow = Nothing
  Set m_oPptApp = Nothing
End Sub
```

Running the Code

Now that we've completed the coding, let's run it and see our results.

1. Place the insertion point anywhere inside the `MakePowerPointPresentation` subroutine.

2. Click the Run button on the VBE toolbar or press F5.

3. If the Excel window appears with the message box displayed, make PowerPoint the active window.

The dynamically created PowerPoint presentation is displayed. It should look like Figures 8-10 through 8-13.

Figure 8-10. *Title slide*

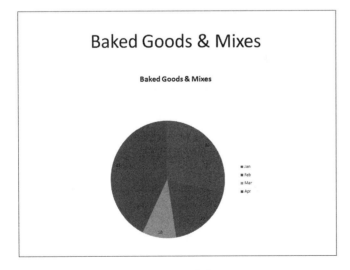

Figure 8-11. *Baked Goods & Mixes slide*

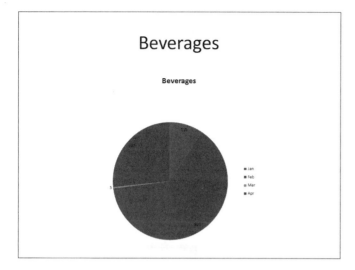

Figure 8-12. *Beverages slide*

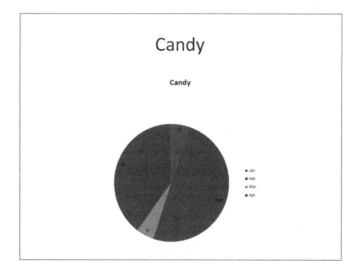

Figure 8-13. *Candy slide*

4. Return to the Excel window.

5. Click OK on the message box to finish running the code.

Very nice output, and not much more work than our Word document. If we want to include the text description on our chart slides, we can do that as well. For that, we need to do a few things differently, however.

In the previous example, we called on the Add method of the Slides collection using the following code:

```
Set m_oPptSlide = m_oPptShow.Slides.Add(i + 1, ppLayoutTitleOnly)
```

The layout type we used was ppLayoutTitleOnly, which gave us an empty slide with a Placeholder object to hold our title text. We used the remainder of the slide, which was empty, to place and size our chart. In our next example, we'll change the layout type to one that includes three placeholders: one for the title, one for the descriptive text, and one for the chart itself.

Adding Text to the Chart Slides

In this example, we'll use a different slide template for our text and chart. Figure 8-14 shows the empty template slide in PowerPoint.

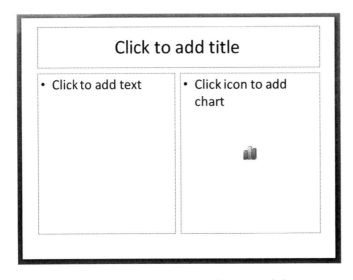

Figure 8-14. *PowerPoint slide template for text and chart*

Let's begin coding the CreateChartSlidesText procedure. In it we will add the title text in the title placeholder. We'll put our descriptive text in the text placeholder on the left side of the slide. Finally, we'll place our chart in the chart placeholder on the right side of the slide.

1. Open the VBE by selecting the Developer ribbon ➤ Code tab ➤ Visual Basic command, or press by Alt+F11.

2. On the standard module containing the PowerPoint code you've been working on, create a new subroutine and name it CreateChartSlidesText.

3. Add the following variable declarations:

```
Dim i As Integer
Dim sTitle As String
Dim oShape As PowerPoint.Shape
Dim top As Integer
Dim left As Integer
Dim height As Integer
Dim width As Integer
```

The first two variables, i and sTitle, serve the same function that they did in our original example. The first is a counter for our loop through our charts and text indexes, and the second will hold the title for each slide. The remaining variables will be used to hold the information for the third of the three Placeholder objects on our slide template. We'll need them in order to place the chart correctly on the slide.

4. Add the following empty For...Next block with one or two blank lines within the code block:

```
For i = 1 To 3

Next i
```

5. Within the For...Next block, add the following code:

```
Worksheets(1).ChartObjects(i).Activate
sTitle = ActiveChart.ChartTitle.Text
Set m_oPptSlide = m_oPptShow.Slides.Add(i + 1, ppLayoutTextAndChart)
```

This code is almost identical to our previous example—but notice the new layout type enum, ppLayoutTextAndChart. This gives us the slide template shown in Figure 8-14.

6. Next (still within the For...Next loop), add the following With...End With block to the CreateChartSlidesText subroutine:

```
With m_oPptSlide.Shapes.Placeholders(1)
  With .TextFrame.TextRange
    .Text = sTitle
  End With
End With
```

Again, this code is very similar to our previous example, minus the variable to hold the placeholder location (sngChartStart). In our current example, we already have a placeholder for our chart, but we have to use a different technique to get its location.

7. Immediately below the With...End With block, add the following code:

```
With m_oPptSlide.Shapes.Placeholders(2)
  With .TextFrame.TextRange
    .Text = GetSubjectBody(i)
  End With
End With
```

This code sets a reference to the second Placeholder object on our slide and inserts the descriptive text from the GetSubjectBody function.

8. Add the following line of code after the With...End With block we just added:

```
Worksheets(1).ChartObjects(i).Copy
```

This line of code copies the current Chart object onto the Windows clipboard for later pasting into our PowerPoint slide template.

So we've got our text elements in place and our chart sitting in memory waiting to be dropped into our slide template. However, we can't just paste our chart into the third place-holder area on our template as we could with the text-based Placeholder objects. To place the chart, we have to get the coordinates of the third placeholder (top, left, height, and width). Then we remove the Placeholder object and paste in the chart, placing it accordingly.

9. Add the following lines of code after the Copy command you just added:

```
Set oShape = m_oPptSlide.Shapes(3)
With oShape
  top = .Top
  left = .Left
  width = .Width
  height = .Height
  .Delete
End With
```

Here, we are setting oShape to hold the third shape, which is the chart placeholder. Then we are storing its dimensions and location in our top, left, width, and height variables. Once we have that information, we are deleting the Shape object using its Delete method.

10. Immediately after this code, add the following code:

```
With m_oPptSlide.Shapes.Paste
  .Top = top
  .Left = left
  .Width = width
End With
```

This code, which places and sizes the chart, is similar in function to our previous example. We are placing it in the exact location of the placeholder we just removed.

■**Note** You might notice that although we're retrieving and holding a reference to the height of the place-holder shape, we're not using it when we place the chart. It's included here for reference. If you need to resize the height in your projects, this is how and where you'd do it.

That's it for coding our For...Next loop.

11. Place the insertion point at the end of the loop and press Enter.

12. Add the following line of cleanup code:

```
Set oShape = Nothing
```

Once we're done with it, we destroy the oShape object. That's the last line of code in this procedure. The finished CreateChartSlidesText subroutine should look like Listing 8-12.

Listing 8-12. *Complete CreateChartSlidesText Subroutine*

```
Sub CreateChartSlidesText()
Dim i As Integer
Dim sTitle As String
Dim oShape As PowerPoint.Shape
Dim top As Integer
Dim left As Integer
Dim height As Integer
Dim width As Integer

  For i = 1 To 3
    Worksheets(1).ChartObjects(i).Activate
    sTitle = ActiveChart.ChartTitle.Text
    Set m_oPptSlide = m_oPptShow.Slides.Add(i + 1, ppLayoutTextAndChart)

    With m_oPptSlide.Shapes.Placeholders(1)
      With .TextFrame.TextRange
        .Text = sTitle
      End With
    End With

    With m_oPptSlide.Shapes.Placeholders(2)
      With .TextFrame.TextRange
        .Text = GetSubjectBody(i)
      End With
    End With

    Worksheets(1).ChartObjects(i).Copy

    Set oShape = m_oPptSlide.Shapes(3)
    With oShape
      top = .Top
      left = .Left
      width = .Width
      height = .Height
      .Delete
    End With
    With m_oPptSlide.Shapes.Paste
      .Top = top
      .Left = left
      .Width = width
    End With
  Next i
  Set oShape = Nothing
End Sub
```

All that's left to do now is modify our calling procedure, `MakePowerPointPresentation`, and then run it.

13. Navigate to the `MakePowerPointPresentation` subroutine.

14. Replace this line of code:

`CreateChartSlides`

with this line:

`CreateChartSlidesText`

15. Place the insertion point anywhere inside the `MakePowerPointPresentation` procedure.

16. Click the Run button on the VBE toolbar or press F5.

17. Once the message box appears, make PowerPoint the active window if it's not already.

Figures 8-15 through 8-17 show the chart slides with the descriptive text.

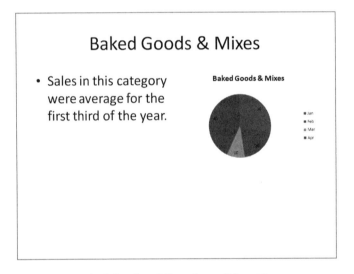

Figure 8-15. *Baked Goods & Mixes chart slide with text*

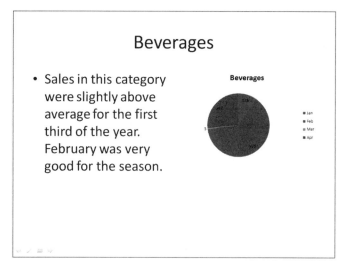

Figure 8-16. *Beverages chart slide with text*

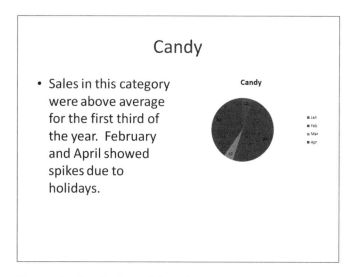

Figure 8-17. *Candy chart slide with text*

18. Return to the Excel window.

19. Click OK on the message box to finish running the code.

Summary

In this chapter, we took a look at automating other Microsoft Office products using Excel 2007 VBA. Office automation is a powerful concept that allows us to interact with Office applications for purposes of sharing information, creating documents, and creating workflow processes.

We are not limited to automating Microsoft Office products, however. Many applications support VBA, including some non-Microsoft products. For instance, versions 9 and later of WordPerfect support VBA, and Novell has added VBA support to the open source office suite OpenOffice.org (`www.openoffice.org`), which runs on the Windows and Linux platforms.

Throughout this book, we've explored various ways we can code in VBA in Excel 2007, and we've seen some pretty neat solutions. However, we are not limited to using code created from within the Excel VBE. We can create ActiveX components using Visual Basic (5 or 6) that we can access from our Excel projects. We can also create assemblies using the .NET Framework and Visual Studio Tools for Office, provided by Microsoft.

In Chapter 9, we will take a look at both of these tools and see how we can add functionality to our Excel 2007 projects using them.

CHAPTER 9

■■■

ActiveX and .NET

ActiveX? .NET? In a book about programming in Excel 2007? Of course! Yes, ActiveX controls and components are still kicking around. And .NET technologies are the wave of the future for those Microsoft-centric developers among us (which is why you're reading this book, I'd assume).

ActiveX, for the uninitiated, is Microsoft's technology for component software. ActiveX comes in two flavors: components and controls. The controls we added to our Excel UserForm in Chapter 4 were ActiveX controls. If you have any experience with VB 6 or earlier, you've used ActiveX controls on your forms, and perhaps you've downloaded free controls written by other developers or purchased control libraries written by third parties. The same is true of Microsoft Access controls. ActiveX components, on the other hand, do not necessarily provide a UI, but they do expose a set of functionality you can use in your programs. Sometimes you hear these described as "COM components," a term that is somewhat correct. ActiveX is based on the Microsoft COM (Component Object Model) technology, and the two terms are often used interchangeably.

The Microsoft development world is moving away from COM and ActiveX for many reasons, but there are so many classic VB applications out there that it is still a worthwhile exercise to see what they have to offer.

The .NET tie-in comes to us via Visual Studio Tools for Office Second Edition (VSTO SE), provided by Microsoft. By adding VSTO SE to your Visual Studio installation, you receive a rich set of tools that allow you to program Microsoft Office applications from the Visual Studio programming environment. Imagine opening a new Excel project and seeing Excel within the Visual Studio 2005 development environment. There is some really neat stuff here with so many possibilities.

In this chapter, we'll look at ways to incorporate ActiveX components in our Excel projects. Then we'll take a dive into VSTO SE and explore some of the advantages that this maturing platform can give us as Office developers.

Using ActiveX Components in Your Excel 2007 Projects

We are at a technology crossroads as year 2007 draws to an end. Microsoft's .NET technologies have reached their stride and are becoming more widespread. Classic Visual Basic (VB 6) applications will be supported throughout the Windows Vista life cycle (five years). This means

Microsoft will guarantee that applications and components (DLLs) created in VB 6 will continue to run in Windows Vista as they did in Windows XP. Not so for the VB 6 IDE (integrated development environment), for which extended support will be retired in April of 2008).

What does this mean for you? If you are currently using any ActiveX components, your applications should work just as they do now. The problem with VB 6 support going away as I see it is that VBA, being a subset of VB, has similar syntax. It's easy enough to create procedures and compile your code in classic VB if you're a VBA programmer.

If you're moving your Microsoft development tools to Windows Vista, you will not have this option available to you. Given that there are still plenty of ActiveX components available (both free and for pay), and since you can still create your own if you are not moving to Vista right away, we'll take a short look at incorporating them into your Excel projects.

Are There Any Benefits?

Absolutely. Consider that the code you create in VBA is very similar to VB code. How can one be more beneficial than the other? There are two major reasons:

Better performance: Code wrapped in an ActiveX DLL is compiled code. This runs much faster than interpreted VBA code.

Greater security: Your VBA code is not very secure in the VBE. Anyone who knows how to press Alt+F11 can see and modify your code. Code in a compiled VB component cannot be seen by users or any other interested party.

Custom Functionality with ActiveX

Way back in Chapter 2, we looked at various methods of bringing data into your Excel projects. These ranged from using Excel's import methods to getting DAO and ADO recordsets and placing their data on your worksheets.

In our ActiveX example, we'll take one of these data-driven samples and see how they'd happen in a compiled component or DLL. Then we'll look at how we can use that compiled component to add custom functionality to our projects.

I'm including the VB 6 code, but don't worry if you're not a VB programmer. The DLLs are also included with the source files for this book, so you can access the functionality. You just won't have access to the code.

■**Note** The supporting files and source code for this book are available at `www.apress.com`, in the Download section of this book's home page.

Using an ActiveX Component in Excel 2007

Our ActiveX example allows us to put data on the worksheet of our choice in our current workbook and pass in a SQL statement to retrieve whatever data we need. This example will mimic the functionality of our ADO example from Chapter 2 in the file `DataAccessSample03.xlsm`. Listing 9-1 shows the original VBA code we wrote in Chapter 2.

Listing 9-1. *ADOTest Macro from Chapter 2*

```
Sub ADOTest()
Dim cnn As New ADODB.Connection
Dim rs As ADODB.Recordset
Dim xlSheet As Worksheet
Dim sConnString As String
Dim arr_sPath(1) As String
Dim sSQL As String
Dim iFieldCount As Integer
Dim i As Integer

    arr_sPath(0) = "C:\projects\Excel2007Book\Files\northwind 2007.accdb"
    arr_sPath(1) = "C:\projects\Excel2007Book\Files\northwind.mdb"

    Set xlSheet = Sheets("Sheet1")
    xlSheet.Activate
    Range("A1").Activate
    Selection.CurrentRegion.Select
    Selection.ClearContents
    Range("A1").Select

    ' Open connection to the database
'    cnn.Open "Provider=Microsoft.Jet.OLEDB.4.0;" & ➥
        "Data Source=" & arr_sPath(0) & ";"
''When using the Access 2007 Northwind database
''comment the previous code and uncomment the following code.
    cnn.Open "Provider=Microsoft.ACE.OLEDB.12.0;" & ➥
        "Data Source=" & arr_sPath(0) & ";"

    Set rs = New ADODB.Recordset
    ' Open recordset based on Orders table
    rs.Open "Select * From Orders", cnn

    iFieldCount = rs.Fields.Count
    For i = 1 To iFieldCount
        xlSheet.Cells(1, i).Value = rs.Fields(i - 1).Name
    Next i

    ' Copy the recordset to the worksheet, starting in cell A2
    xlSheet.Cells(2, 1).CopyFromRecordset rs

    xlSheet.Select
    'Range("A1").Select
    Selection.CurrentRegion.Select
    Selection.Columns.AutoFit
    'Range("A1").Select
```

```
      rs.Close
      cnn.Close
      Set xlSheet = Nothing
      Set rs = Nothing
      Set cnn = Nothing
End Sub
```

This code dropped the result of a SQL SELECT statement onto Sheet1 in our sample file. Our ActiveX component allows us to choose which worksheet we put our data on and select which data we want, giving us a quick tool for querying the Northwind database.

The VB 6 code here is also split into a data class and a second class named cExcelNwind. The data class, cData, is doing some work this time. Its GetData method will return a recordset to the cExcelNwind class. The cExcelNwind class will do the work of placing the data on the worksheet that is passed into the ActiveX component. Listings 9-2 and 9-3 show the VB 6 code.

Listing 9-2. *cData Class from the ActiveX Component*

```
Option Explicit

Const m_sDBPathName As String = "C:\Book\Files\Northwind 2007.accdb"
Private m_oCnn As ADODB.Connection
Private m_oRS As ADODB.Recordset
'

Public Function GetData(Which As String) As ADODB.Recordset
    m_oCnn.Open "Provider=Microsoft.ACE.OLEDB.12.0;" & ➥
        "Data Source=" & m_sDBPathName & ";"

    Set m_oRS = New ADODB.Recordset

    m_oRS.Open Which, m_oCnn

    Set GetData = m_oRS
End Function

Private Sub Class_Initialize()
    Set m_oCnn = New ADODB.Connection
    Set m_oRS = New ADODB.Recordset
End Sub

Private Sub Class_Terminate()
    Set m_oCnn = Nothing
    Set m_oRS = Nothing
End Sub
```

Listing 9-3. *cExcelNwind Class from the ActiveX Component*

```
Option Explicit

Public Sub PlaceData(TheWorksheet As Excel.Worksheet, WhichData As String)
Dim oData As cData
Dim xl As Excel.Application
Dim rs As ADODB.Recordset
Dim iFieldCount As Integer
Dim i As Integer

    Set xl = TheWorksheet.Application 'hook into the current Excel session
    TheWorksheet.Activate
    TheWorksheet.Range("A1").Activate
    xl.Selection.CurrentRegion.Select
    xl.Selection.ClearContents
    TheWorksheet.Range("A1").Select

    Set oData = New cData
    Set rs = oData.GetData(WhichData)

    iFieldCount = rs.Fields.Count
    For i = 1 To iFieldCount
        TheWorksheet.Cells(1, i).Value = rs.Fields(i - 1).Name
    Next i

    TheWorksheet.Cells(2, 1).CopyFromRecordset rs

    TheWorksheet.Select
    xl.Selection.CurrentRegion.Select
    xl.Selection.Columns.AutoFit

    rs.Close
    Set TheWorksheet = Nothing
    Set rs = Nothing
    Set xl = Nothing
End Sub
```

■**Note** Once again, the VB 6 code provided here is for reference only, showing the similarities to code we've already experienced. We will not dig into the specifics of compiling DLLs or ActiveX EXEs here.

As you'll see in this next bit of client code, accessing the data from an external component really helps keep the code on the client application simple. The compiled version of this code is available at www.apress.com in the Download section of this book's home page. It is called Nwind2Excel.dll. You must register the DLL before you can access its functionality.

Registering Nwind2Excel.dll in Windows XP or 2000

1. Copy the file to a folder on your local machine.

2. Click Start ➤ Run.

3. Type **regsvr32.exe**, followed by a space, and then the full path to Nwind2Excel.dll. Listing 9-4 shows an example of this command.

   Listing 9-4. *Example of Run Command to Register a DLL*

   ```
   regsvr32.exe C:\MyComponents\Nwind2Excel.dll
   ```

4. Click OK to register the DLL.

5. Click OK when the success message appears.

Caution In the VB code, be sure to change the path to the Northwind 2007 database to wherever it can be found on your local machine. If you are using the compiled DLL, it needs to find the Northwind database in C:\ExampleDBs. You must create that folder and put the Northwind 2007 database there.

Registering Nwind2Excel.dll in Windows Vista

1. Open a command prompt window by selecting Start ➤ All Programs ➤ Accessories ➤ Command Prompt.

Note This command prompt must be run using the Run as Administrator right-click menu option.

---

2. Type **regsvr32.exe**, followed by a space, and then the full path to Nwind2Excel.dll. Listing 9-4 (shown previously) shows an example of this command.

3. Press Enter to run the command.

4. Click OK when the success message appears.

Figure 9-1 shows the success message you should see.

Figure 9-1. *regsvr32.exe shows a success message upon registering a DLL in Windows Vista.*

Now we can use the DLL in our project.

1. Open a new workbook in Excel.

2. Open the VBE by choosing the Developer ribbon ➤ Visual Basic or by pressing Alt+F11.

3. Add a standard code module in the Project Explorer.

4. Add a reference to the new DLL by selecting Tools ➤ References.

5. In the References dialog box, scroll down until you see an item named !Northwind2Excel Object, as shown in Figure 9-2.

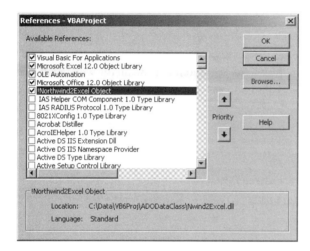

Figure 9-2. *Adding a reference to !Northwind2Excel Object*

■**Tip** When you create custom objects, they tend to get lost in the list in the References dialog box. Adding the bang (!) character as a prefix helps keep your custom objects near the top of the list and makes them easier to find.

---

6. Select it from the list and click OK to close the dialog and store the reference.

Now we are ready for a small bit of client code.

The Client Code

The really neat thing about using custom DLLs to provide functionality is that it lets us use such a tiny bit of code in our applications.

On the standard module you just created, add the following code:

```
Option Explicit

Sub GetNorthwindData()
Dim oNwindData As cExcelNwind

  Set oNwindData = New cExcelNwind

  oNwindData.PlaceData ThisWorkbook.Sheets("Sheet1"), "Select * From Orders"
  oNwindData.PlaceData ThisWorkbook.Sheets("Sheet2"), "Select * From Employees"

  Set oNwindData = Nothing
End Sub
```

That's about it. The two lines of code between the Set statements do all the work, with each line placing the result of its SQL statement on the worksheet referenced. Let's run the code.

1. Return to Excel.

2. Save the file.

3. Open the Macros dialog box by selecting the Developer ribbon ➤ Macros command.

4. Choose GetNorthwindData from the List of macros.

5. Click the Run button.

Caution As noted earlier, if you are using the compiled DLL that comes with the source code for this book, you must create the path C:\ExampleDBs and place the Northwind 2007 database there.

The result is shown in Figure 9-3. Sheet1 contains the order information and Sheet2 contains the employee information.

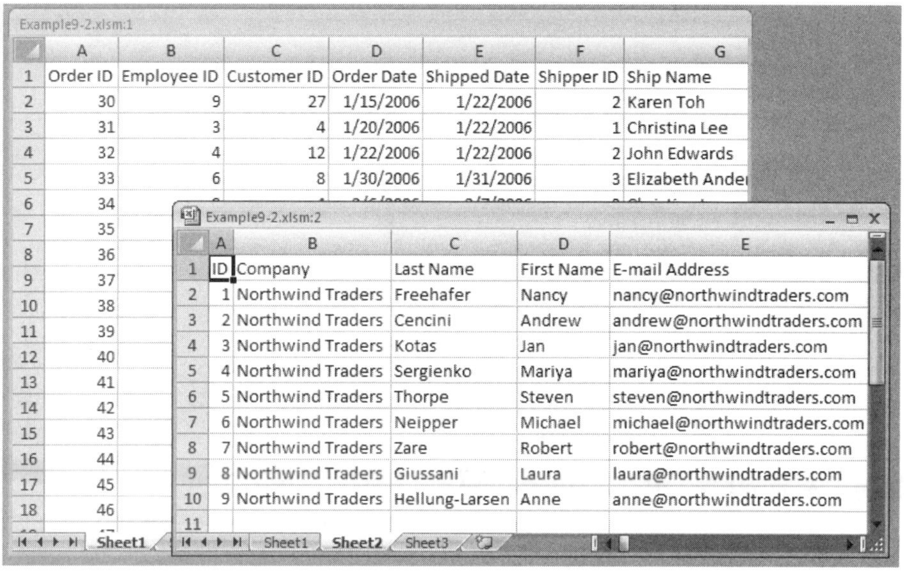

Figure 9-3. *Result of GetNorthwindData macro*

6. Save the workbook if you like.

■**Note** Here's one of the comparative advantages of the .NET platform vs. ActiveX. In the .NET world, we do not have to deal with registration of components like we do with ActiveX components. We can simply copy our component to any machine that has the correct version of the .NET Framework installed, and it will run.

One benefit that we see from this example is minimal code in our project. Let's take a look now at how .NET technologies can actually take the code out of our Excel projects.

Excel in the .NET World

We can't code directly in the Excel 2007 VBE to use .NET components, but we can download tools from Microsoft that will let us create Excel projects from within Visual Studio 2005. VSTO and VSTO SE each come with a suite of tools that allow us to access various functions within an Excel project.

VSTO, which interfaces with Office 2003 applications, allows direct access to an Excel workbook and gives us programmatic control within the managed code environment. VSTO project templates include the ability to create the following:

- Excel workbook projects

- Excel template projects

- Word template projects

- Word document projects

- Outlook add-in projects

Figure 9-4 shows the Visual Studio 2005 New Project dialog box for Microsoft Office 2003 projects from the original version of VSTO.

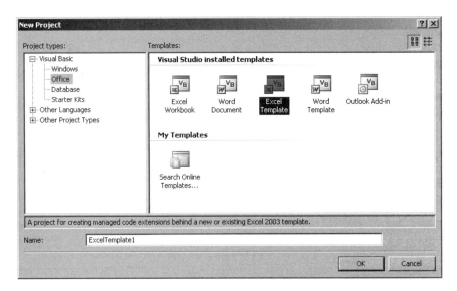

Figure 9-4. *VSTO Microsoft Office projects*

VSTO SE adds some new project types to the toolbox, as shown in Figure 9-5.

Figure 9-5. *New project types included in VSTO SE*

VSTO SE provides us with two new project categories, Excel 2003 Add-ins and Excel 2007 Add-ins. It adds an InfoPath template project to the Office menu, as shown in Figure 9-6 (which shows the Windows Vista interface).

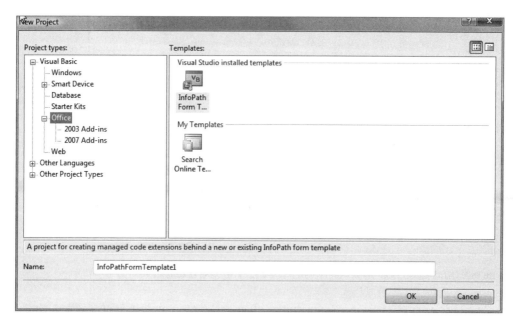

Figure 9-6. *InfoPath Form Template project added in VSTO SE*

■**Note** If you already have VSTO installed, you can safely add VSTO SE. The existing Office 2003 project types will still be available. The new project types of VSTO SE will be available in addition to the original project types.

Figure 9-7 shows the VSTO SE Office 2003 Add-in projects available in the New Project dialog box.

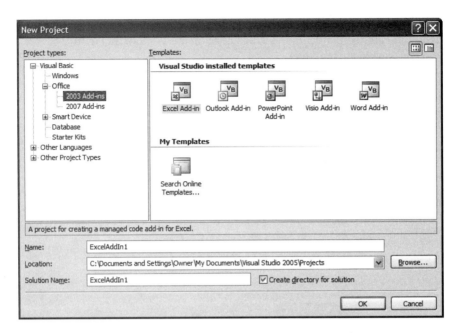

Figure 9-7. *Office 2003 Add-in projects added in VSTO SE in Windows XP*

Another new project category containing Office 2007 Add-in projects is also added. The new selections are shown in Figure 9-8.

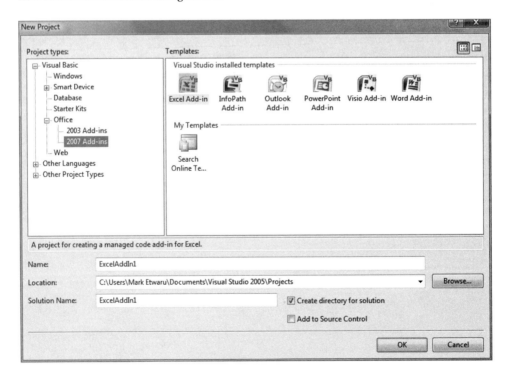

Figure 9-8. *Office 2007 Add-in projects added in VSTO SE in Windows Vista*

VSTO is no longer available, but if you have a copy, you can still write code for Excel 2003 that will run in Excel 2007 Compatibility mode. VSTO SE provides add-in programming only.

■**Note** VSTO SE is available as a free download from Microsoft at www.microsoft.com/downloads/ details.aspx?familyid=5E86CAB3-6FD6-4955-B979-E1676DB6B3CB&displaylang=en (if this link fails to work in the future, you can search the Web for "VSTO SE").

Managed Code in an Excel Project

We are going to look at two examples of running managed code in Excel. In our ActiveX examples, we revisited some of the functionality we'd already built directly in Excel using VBA. The first example .NET project will duplicate some of the functionality from our previous VBA projects, but you'll see how the .NET versions require absolutely no code on the Excel client workbook. Our second example will show how to create a custom task pane in an Excel 2007 Add-in project in conjunction with the .NET version of an Excel UserForm.

■**Caution** If you do not have Visual Studio 2005, you can still run the sample workbooks as long as you have placed the Northwind 2007.accdb file in the same path that the sample code refers to. The only other prerequisite is that the .NET Framework 2.0 must be installed on your PC.

Retrieving Data Using .NET

In this example, we'll reach out to the Northwind 2007 database and populate a worksheet with data from the Employees table. The end result will look a lot like one of our early data access samples in Chapter 2, where we imported data from the Northwind database and then resized the columns using the AutoFit command. We will create a data access component and then use it from within our add-in.

1. Open Visual Studio 2005, and the start page will appear.

2. In the Recent Projects area (shown in Figure 9-9) in the Create section, click the Project link to open the New Project dialog box (shown previously in Figure 9-8).

Figure 9-9. *Recent Projects section of Visual Studio 2005 start page*

3. In the Name text box, name the project NWindDataAddIn.

4. Leave the "Create directory for solution" check box checked.

5. Click OK.

The new project is created, as shown in Figure 9-10.

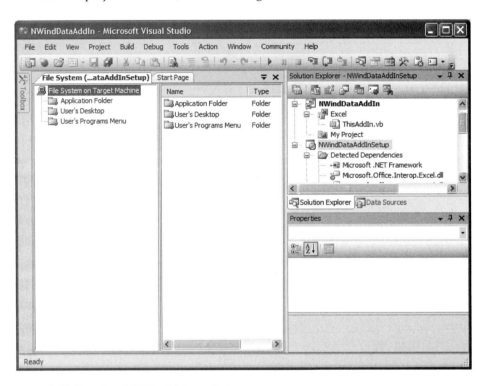

Figure 9-10. *New Excel 2007 add-in project*

We'll look at the default contents of the add-in project in a moment, but first let's create our data access component. We will add another project to our add-in project. Once the coding is finished, we'll have to add a reference to our data access project before we can use it.

The Data Access Component

We could add a new class directly in our add-in project, but it makes sense to put that in its own project where it will become a separate component. This gives you the option to easily use your data access layer in other projects.

1. Select the NWindDataAddIn project in the Solution Explorer.

2. Select File ➤ Add ➤ New Project (Figure 9-11).

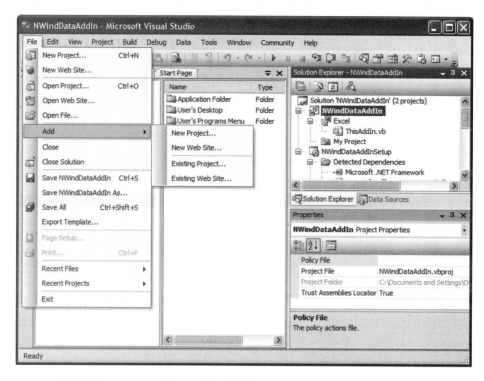

Figure 9-11. *Adding a new project to the solution*

3. In the Add New Project dialog box, select Windows from the "Project types" list.

4. Select Class Library from the Templates section.

5. Name the new project NWindDataAccess, as shown in Figure 9-12.

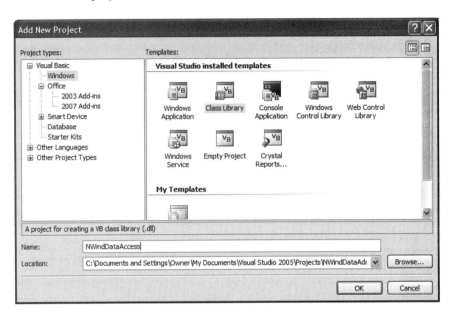

Figure 9-12. *Creating a new class library project*

6. Click OK.

A new project is added to the Solution Explorer and an empty class module is created, as shown in Figure 9-13.

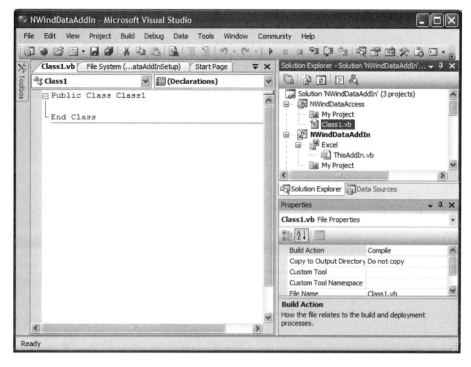

Figure 9-13. *New class library project added*

The default name for the new class is Class1. Let's change that.

1. Select the Class1.vb file from the NWindDataAccess project in the Solution Explorer.

2. In the Properties pane (below the Solution Explorer, as shown in Figure 9-14), change the File Name property to NWindData.vb.

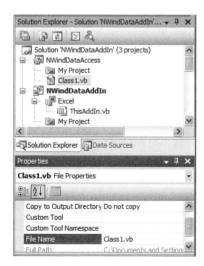

Figure 9-14. *Changing the class name*

Once that's done, all references to Class1 will be changed to reflect the new class, as shown in Figure 9-15.

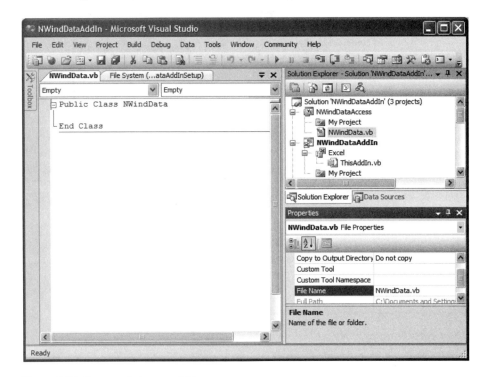

Figure 9-15. *Renamed class and file name*

Now we'll add some code to our class. This will be a very simple class that does nothing more than query the Northwind 2007 database for a list of employees.

1. On your local PC, create a folder called C:\ExampleDBs (if you did not already do so for the ActiveX example).

2. Copy the Northwind 2007.accdb file into the new folder.

Note These two steps are more of a necessity for those who do not have Visual Studio 2005 (so the code will run from the sample files you downloaded from www.apress.com). If you are using Visual Studio 2005, you can modify the code to refer to the Northwind 2007 database from any location on your PC.

---

3. Put your cursor in the class module code window and press Ctrl+Home to position the insertion point at the very beginning of the code.

4. Press Enter.

5. Add the following statement to reference the OLEDB library:

```
Imports System.Data.OleDb
```

6. Move the insertion point to the blank line inside the class code.

7. Add the following module-level declarations:

```
Const TABLE_NAME As String = "Table1"
Private m_sNwindName As String
```

The constant TABLE_NAME will hold the table name we'll use when we fill a DataSet from the Northwind Employees table. The sNwindName variable will hold the path to the database. Next, let's add a public property to the data access class to store and retrieve the location of the database.

8. Add the following property to the NWindData class module:

```
Public Property NwindPathFileName() As String
    Get
        Return m_sNwindName
    End Get
    Set(ByVal value As String)
        If System.IO.File.Exists(value) Then
            m_sNwindName = value
        Else
            Throw New System.IO.FileNotFoundException
        End If
    End Set
End Property
```

The Property Get is very straightforward in that it's just returning the value from the private variable. The Property Set has a bit of validation code. We're checking to see if the file exists before we assign the new value to the private variable. If it does not exist, the class will throw a System.IO.FileNotFoundException error to the client code.

■**Note** Managed code does not raise errors as classic VBA and VB did. In the .NET world, exceptions are thrown by our code and caught in exception handling blocks.

Now we'll add a method that accepts a SQL statement to get the data and returns the data in the form of a .NET DataSet object.

9. Add a new function named GetData to the NWindData class, as follows:

```
Public Function GetData(ByVal Which As String) As DataSet
```

10. Add the following variable declarations:

```
Dim dsReturn As New DataSet()
Dim cnn As OleDbConnection
Dim sConnString As String
```

11. Create the connection to the data by adding the following code:

```
sConnString = "Provider=Microsoft.ACE.OLEDB.12.0;" ➥
             & "Data Source=" & m_sNwindName & ";"
cnn = New OleDb.OleDbConnection(sConnString)
```

12. Create a DataAdapter to hold the data and fill the DataSet by adding the following code:

```
Dim da As New OleDbDataAdapter(Which, cnn)
```

Next, we are going to fill the DataSet from the DataAdapter. We will add exception handling to this process. As VBA programmers, we're used to using the age-old On Error Go To syntax in our error handlers. In our managed code, we use Try...Catch blocks to catch any exceptions our code throws.

13. Add the following code to fill the DataSet and watch for and handle exceptions:

```
Try
    da.Fill(dsReturn, TABLE_NAME)
Catch ex As Exception
    MsgBox(ex.Message)
End Try
```

This Try...Catch block includes the optional Finally clause. Any code inserted here will always run regardless of errors. It's a good place for cleanup code. The last thing to do is return our filled DataSet.

14. Add the following code after the Try...Catch block:

```
Return dsReturn
```

The complete GetData function looks like Listing 9-5.

Listing 9-5. *Complete GetData Function*

```
Public Function GetData(ByVal Which As String) As DataSet
    Dim dsReturn As New DataSet()
    Dim cnn As OleDbConnection
    Dim sConnString As String

    sConnString = "Provider=Microsoft.ACE.OLEDB.12.0;" ➥
                 & "Data Source=" & m_sNwindName & ";"
    cnn = New OleDb.OleDbConnection(sConnString)

    Dim da As New OleDbDataAdapter(Which, cnn)
```

```
    Try
        da.Fill(dsReturn, TABLE_NAME)
    Catch ex As Exception
        MsgBox(ex.Message)
    Finally
        MsgBox(dsReturn.Tables("Table1").Rows.Count & " Records")
    End Try

    Return dsReturn
End Function
```

That completes our work on the data access component. Let's bring our attention back to the add-in project that Visual Studio 2005 created for us.

The Add-In Project

When we created our add-in project, Visual Studio 2005 created the NWindDataAddIn project, and it created a deployment project named NWindDataAddInSetup. Within the NWindDataAddIn project, we have one file, named `ThisAddIn.vb`. This is where we'll put the code that will run on our client Excel applications.

Before we begin, we must add a reference to our data component.

1. In the Solution Explorer, select the NWindDataAddIn project.

2. Right-click the project and choose Add Reference to display the Add Reference dialog box.

3. On the Projects tab, select NWindDataAccess, as shown in Figure 9-16.

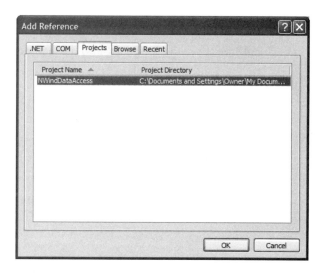

Figure 9-16. *The Add Reference dialog box*

4. Click OK.

5. In the Solution Explorer, double-click the `ThisAddIn.vb` file to open the code window.

Add-in projects include one line of code in the `startup` method referencing the Excel application, as shown in Figure 9-17.

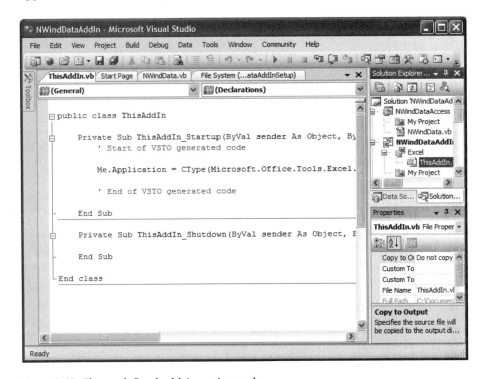

Figure 9-17. *The predefined add-in project code*

6. Place the insertion point in the blank line above the `ThisAddIn_Startup` method.

7. Add the following module-level variable declarations:

```
Private m_oNWind As NWindDataAccess.NWindData
Private m_oSheet As Excel.Worksheet
Private m_oDS As DataSet
```

Here, we create an object to hold a reference to our data component and create variables to hold references to an Excel worksheet and our `DataSet`.

8. In the `ThisAddIn_Startup` method, put the insertion point in the blank line under the last comment.

9. Add the following code:

```
m_oNWind = New NWindDataAccess.NWindData
m_oSheet = Me.Application.Worksheets("Sheet1")
GetData()
```

This code instantiates an instance of the data component, fills `m_oSheet` with a reference to Sheet1 in our Excel workbook, and calls a function named `GetData`. Visual Studio 2005 may bark at you because this function does not exist, yet but that's only temporary.

10. Put the insertion point inside the `ThisAddIn_Shutdown` method.

11. Add the following line of cleanup code:

```
m_oNWind = Nothing
```

Now let's create the `GetData` method.

Getting the Data   Since we added a reference to our data access project, we can refer to its properties and methods from our add-in. The `GetData` method will call out to our data access layer and fill our module-level `DataSet` variable. Then it will push the data out to the Excel sheet.

1. In the ThisAddIn class module, add a new subroutine named `GetData`.

2. In the `GetData` procedure, add the following variable declarations:

```
Dim sDB As String = "C:\ExampleDBs\Northwind 2007.accdb"
Dim iCols As Integer
Dim i As Integer
Dim row As Integer
```

We're passing in the location of the database to the `sDB` `String` variable, and then we have the remaining `Integer` variables to hold our place as we walk through the `DataSet` and display our data.

3. On the first blank line below the variable declarations, type the following line of code:

```
Try
```

4. Press Enter, and Visual Studio 2005 will add a complete `Try...Catch` block for you.

5. Place the insertion point in the first blank line below the `Try` line of code.

6. Add the following code to set the file name in the data access component and call its `GetData` method:

```
With m_oNWind
    .NwindPathFileName = sDB
    m_oDS = .GetData("select * from employees")
End With
```

7. Add the following code to walk through the `DataSet` and insert the column headings in the worksheet:

```
For i = 0 To iCols - 1
    m_oSheet.Cells(1, i + 1).Value = ➡
                        m_oDS.Tables("Table1").Columns(i).Caption
Next
```

8. Place the insertion point in the blank line following the previous code, and press Enter.

9. Add the following code to walk through the DataSet and insert the employee data on the worksheet:

```
row = 2
For Each RowIterator As DataRow In m_oDS.Tables("Table1").Rows
    For i = 0 To iCols - 1
        m_oSheet.Cells(row, i + 1).Value = ↵
                RowIterator(m_oDS.Tables("Table1").Columns(i).Caption)
    Next
    row = row + 1
Next
```

Next, we'll add the code to format the Excel worksheet by applying the AutoFit command to size each column to show its longest data entry.

10. Place the insertion point in the blank line following the previous code, and press Enter.

11. Add the following code:

```
Dim r As Excel.Range
m_oSheet.Select()
r = m_oSheet.Range("A1")
r.Select()
Application.Selection.CurrentRegion.Select()
Application.Selection.Columns.AutoFit()
r.Select()
```

The last thing for us to do is a bit of exception handling.

12. Place the insertion point at the beginning of the line containing the Catch statement, and press Enter.

13. Move the insertion point up into the blank line you just inserted.

14. Add the following code to trap for the FileNotFoundException:

```
Catch ex As System.IO.FileNotFoundException
    MsgBox("File: " & sDB & " not found")
```

That's all the code for the GetData method. The completed subroutine looks like Listing 9-6.

Listing 9-6. *Complete GetData Subroutine*

```
Private Sub GetData()
    Dim sDB As String = "C:\ExampleDBs\Northwind 2007.accdb"
    Dim iCols As Integer
    Dim i As Integer
    Dim row As Integer

    Try
        With m_oNWind
            .NwindPathFileName = sDB
            m_oDS = .GetData("select * from employees")
        End With

        iCols = m_oDS.Tables("Table1").Columns.Count
        For i = 0 To iCols - 1
            m_oSheet.Cells(1, i + 1).Value = _
                            m_oDS.Tables("Table1").Columns(i).Caption
        Next

        row = 2
        For Each RowIterator As DataRow In m_oDS.Tables("Table1").Rows
            For i = 0 To iCols - 1
                m_oSheet.Cells(row, i + 1).Value = _
                        RowIterator(m_oDS.Tables("Table1").Columns(i).Caption)
            Next
            row = row + 1
        Next

        Dim r As Excel.Range
        m_oSheet.Select()
        r = m_oSheet.Range("A1")
        r.Select()
        Application.Selection.CurrentRegion.Select()
        Application.Selection.Columns.AutoFit()
        r.Select()
    Catch ex As System.IO.FileNotFoundException
        MsgBox("File: " & sDB & " not found")
    Catch ex As Exception

    End Try
End Sub
```

15. Save the project, and then run it by selecting Debug ➤ Start Debugging, or by pressing the F5 key.

Excel 2007 will appear with the Northwind Employees table loaded into Sheet1, as shown in Figure 9-18.

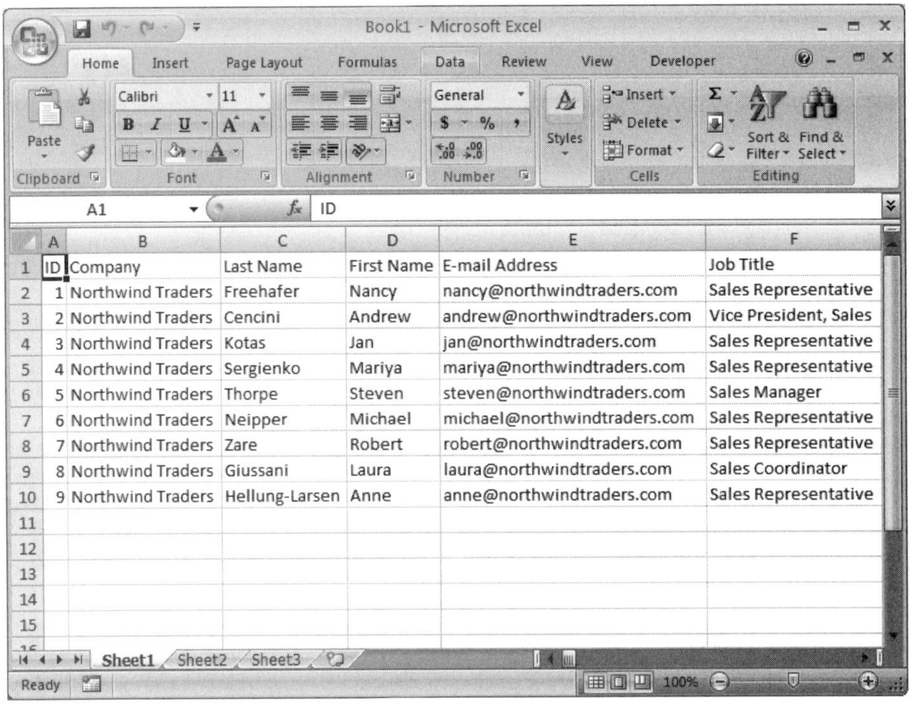

Figure 9-18. *Northwind data added to the worksheet from the add-in project*

I mentioned earlier that this is accomplished with no code at all in the workbook. Let's take a look at the VBE in the Excel workbook we just opened through our code.

Open the Excel VBE by selecting the Developer ribbon ➤ Code tab ➤ Visual Basic command, or by pressing Alt+F11. Look through all of the built-in code modules and you will not find one bit of code.

Note All Excel workbooks ship with built-in code modules representing the code behind the workbook (ThisWorkbook) and its worksheets (Sheet1, Sheet2, etc.). You can find this code in the VBA IDE Project Explorer by double-clicking the item in the Project Explorer's Microsoft Excel Objects folder.

How does the workbook know where to find the data, then?

1. Return to Excel and click the Office button, and then select Excel Options.

2. Select Add-Ins from the left-hand navigation to display the Add-ins list, as shown in Figure 9-19.

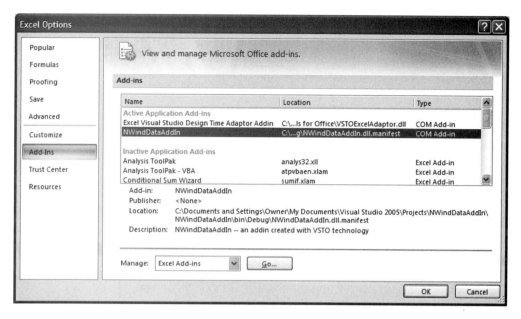

Figure 9-19. *The Add-ins list in the Excel Options dialog box*

This section gives you a snapshot of available and active add-in applications. Excel will leave these add-ins loaded even after you close Visual Studio. Before you close the workbook, and while the Excel Options dialog is still open, unload the add-in as follows.

3. From the Manage drop-down list, choose COM Add-Ins, and then click the Go button.

4. Deselect the NWindDataAddIn project, as shown in Figure 9-20.

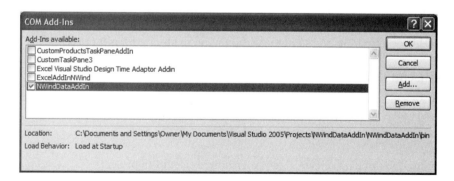

Figure 9-20. *Unloading an add-in*

5. Click OK to unload the add-in.

6. Close the workbook without saving.

7. Close Visual Studio 2005.

Creating a Custom Task Pane and Data Input Form Using .NET

In this example, we'll look at a .NET project that creates a custom task pane and a simulated Excel UserForm. A *task pane* is a window that anchors itself to the right of an Office application and contains commands to perform various functions. A common Office task pane is the Getting Started task pane, shown in Figure 9-21.

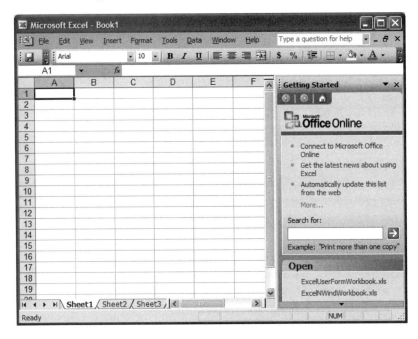

Figure 9-21. *Getting Started task pane in Excel 2003*

Our example task pane will contain commands used by a human resources department to enter new hire information and send that information to other groups for processing.

Creating the HR Task Pane Add-In

To begin, we'll need to add a couple of new items to our add-in project: a user control that will contain the task pane and a Windows form to act as our Excel 2007 UserForm.

1. Open Visual Studio 2005.

2. From the start page, create a new Microsoft Excel Add-in project.

3. Name it UserFormAddIn.

4. Add a new user control to the project by selecting Project ➤ Add User Control.

5. In the Add New Item dialog box, name the user control HRTaskPane.vb.

6. Add a new Windows form to the project by selecting Project ➤ Add Windows Form.

7. In the Add New Item dialog box, name the Windows form NewEmpForm.vb.

The Custom Task Pane   Our custom task pane will contain two commands. The first will open our Windows form to collect new employee information. The second will send that information to other departments who might need it.

1. Open the User Control Designer by double-clicking HRTaskPane.vb in the Solution Explorer.

2. Click the Toolbox (on the left side of the Visual Studio window) to unhide it (if it's not already displayed).

3. Click the pin (Auto Hide) button to leave the Toolbox displayed.

4. Add two Button controls from the Common Controls section (Figure 9-22) to the user control by dragging them onto the Designer.

5. In the Properties pane, change the Text properties of the two buttons to New Employee and E-mail Info, respectively, as shown in Figure 9-22.

6. In the Properties pane, name the New Employee button btnLaunch.

7. In the Properties pane, name the E-mail Info button btnEmail.

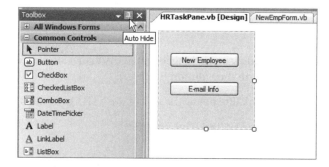

Figure 9-22. *Completed HR task pane with Auto Hide command displayed*

8. Double-click the New Employee button to open its code stub.

9. Add the following code to btnLaunch_Click:

```
Dim oForm As New NewEmpForm
oForm.ShowDialog()
```

This code creates a new instance of our NewEmpForm and opens it in dialog mode (so it remains attached to the Excel window).

10. Click back on the HRTaskPane.vb [Design] tab, and then double-click the E-mail Info button.

11. Add the following code to btnEmail_Click:

```
Dim rng As Excel.Range
rng = Globals.ThisAddIn.Application.Range("A6")
'code to handle e-mail here
MsgBox("Sending new hire information for" & rng.Text & " to Systems Group")
```

This is basically a dummy function to simply show that we can process the data from the task pane and place it anywhere else we'd like.

12. Close the HRTaskPane design and code windows. If prompted to save changes, choose Yes.

Showing the Custom Task Pane   Now that we've got our custom task pane set up, we need add code to show it when our add-in starts up. The ThisAddIn.vb code file that Visual Studio 2005 created for us came complete with two code stubs for handling add-in startup and shutdown.

■Note The startup method contains one line of code generated by VSTO. This tells the add-in what application it's attaching itself to.

---

1. Display the ThisAddIn.vb code window by clicking its tab in the Visual Studio display area (if it's not there, double-click it in the Solution Explorer).

2. Place the insertion point in the blank line below the end of the VSTO-generated code.

3. Add the following code to display the HRTaskPane control:

```
Dim MyTaskPane As New HRTaskPane
Dim MyCustomTaskPane As Microsoft.Office.Tools.CustomTaskPane = ➥
                Me.CustomTaskPanes.Add(MyTaskPane, "HR Tasks")
MyCustomTaskPane.Visible = True
```

This code adds our HRTaskPane control to the add-in's CustomTaskPanes collection. In the call to the CustomTaskPanes.Add method, the second argument is the text that will display in the title bar of the task pane when it is displayed. Finally, we make the task pane visible.

Creating an Excel UserForm Using a Windows Form   So far, we've created a task pane with two commands and added code to our add-in project to display the custom task pane. The last things for us to do are add controls to our Windows form to collect data and add commands to put the data on the active worksheet.

1. Open NewEmpForm.vb in Design view by double-clicking it in the Solution Explorer.

2. Add six labels, six text boxes, and two Button controls from the Common Controls Toolbox, and lay them out as shown in Figure 9-23.

Figure 9-23. *Completed employee data entry UserForm*

3. Name the text boxes and buttons per Table 9-1.

Table 9-1. *New Employee Form Control Properties*

Item	Property	Value
Form	Text	New Employee Form
TextBox1	Name	txtFName
TextBox2	Name	txtMidInit
TextBox3	Name	txtLName
TextBox4	Name	txtDOH
TextBox5	Name	txtTitle
TextBox6	Name	txtReportsTo
Label1	Text	First Name
Label2	Text	Mid Init
Label3	Text	Last Name
Label4	Text	Date of Hire
Label5	Text	Job Title
Label6	Text	Reports To
Button1	Name	btnSave
Button1	Text	Save
Button2	Text	btnCancel
Button2	Text	Cancel

Now that we have our controls set, let's add code to create the display form in Excel 2007 and place the data from our Windows form onto the worksheet.

4. Display the Save button code stub by double-clicking the Save button.

Our Save button will do three things:

- Set up the worksheet by adding headings and adjusting column widths

- Put the data from the data entry form on the worksheet

- Close the data entry form

5. Add the following code to the btnSave_Click event:

```
FormatForm()
PlaceData()
Close()
```

As you can see, each command maps to one of the three functions that the Save command will perform. The Close method is a built-in method of the Windows form object. Let's add the code for the FormatForm and PlaceData methods.

6. On the NewEmpForm.vb code module, add a new subroutine and name it FormatForm.

7. Add the following code to the FormatForm subroutine:

```
DoHeadings()
Dim rng As Excel.Range
With Globals.ThisAddIn.Application
     rng = .Range("A5")
     rng.Value = "First Name"
     rng.Font.Bold = True
     rng.ColumnWidth = 15
     rng = .Range("B5")
     rng.Value = "Mid Init"
     rng.Font.Bold = True
     rng.ColumnWidth = 15
     rng = .Range("C5")
     rng.Value = "Last Name"
     rng.Font.Bold = True
     rng.ColumnWidth = 15
     rng = .Range("A8")
     rng.Value = "Date of Hire"
     rng.Font.Bold = True
     rng = .Range("B8")
     rng.Value = "Job Title"
     rng.Font.Bold = True
     rng = .Range("C8")
     rng.Value = "Reports To"
     rng.Font.Bold = True
   End With
   rng = Nothing
```

The DoHeadings method will put the title and subtitle on the worksheet. The repeated reference to the rng variable sets the active cell, formats it, and places any text labels in the cell.

Note We have a reference to the Visual Basic Globals module in our With block. We saw the same reference earlier in our btnEmail_Click event on our custom task pane object. In order to access objects in an Excel workbook (or any Office application object), we must go through the Globals module. This module supports the runtime library members that contain information about the runtime currently being used.

8. Add another subprocedure and name it DoHeadings.

9. Add the following code:

```
Dim rng As Excel.Range
With Globals.ThisAddIn.Application
    rng = .Range("A1")
    rng.Value = "HR Data Entry System"
    rng.Font.Bold = True
    rng.Font.Size = 16
    rng = .Range("A2")
    rng.Value = "New Employee Information"
    rng.Font.Italic = True
    rng.Font.Size = 14
End With
rng = Nothing
```

There's nothing new here. This code works exactly like the FormatForm subroutine. Next, let's add the code to put the data on the worksheet.

10. Add a new subroutine, and name it PlaceData.

11. Add the following code:

```
Dim rng As Excel.Range
With Globals.ThisAddIn.Application
    rng = .Range("A6")
    rng.Value = Me.txtFName.Text
    rng = .Range("B6")
    rng.Value = Me.txtMidInit.Text
    rng = .Range("C6")
    rng.Value = Me.txtLName.Text
    rng = .Range("A9")
    rng.Value = Me.txtDOH.Text
    rng = .Range("B9")
    rng.Value = Me.txtTitle.Text
    rng = .Range("C9")
    rng.Value = Me.txtReportsTo.Text
End With
```

Again, we're not doing anything new here—we're just breaking the functionality up into smaller pieces.

The last thing to do is to code the Cancel button.

12. Select btnCancel from the Class Name drop-down list on the code designer.

13. Select its click event from the Method Name list.

14. In the `btnCancel_Click` event code stub, add the following line of code:

```
Close()
```

That is all the code we need to write. Now let's run the application and see how it works.

Running the Add-In   Now that the user control, the Excel Add-in, and the Windows form have all been coded, let's run the project and take a look at what we've done.

1. Run the project by selecting Debug ➤ Start Debugging or pressing the F5 key.

Excel 2007 opens with a blank workbook displayed and our custom task pane anchored to the right of the workbook, as shown in Figure 9-24.

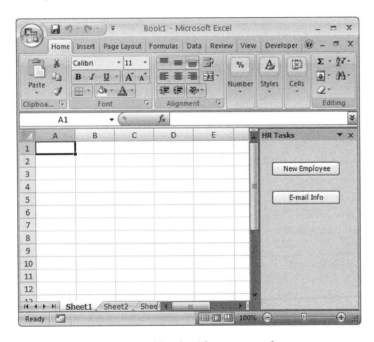

Figure 9-24. *Excel 2007 workbook with custom task pane*

2. Click the New Employee button on the HR task pane to display the data entry form.

3. Enter data on the New Employee form. Sample data is shown in Figure 9-25.

Figure 9-25. *New Employee form with sample data*

4. Click the Save button to place the data on the worksheet and format the sheet, as shown in Figure 9-26.

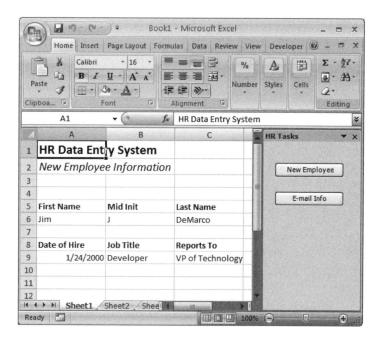

Figure 9-26. *Data and formatting applied to active worksheet*

5. Close the workbook without saving.

6. In Visual Studio 2005, save the project file.

■**Caution** As with the previous example, the add-in will remain loaded for all Excel workbooks until you manually remove it.

Summary

We've created some very interesting code using both classic VB (6.0) and VSTO SE from within Visual Studio 2005. Although Microsoft is supporting VB 6 applications for the five-year product life cycle of Windows Vista, it is retiring support for the classic VB development environment. The good news is that .NET technologies, while not directly supported in Microsoft Office applications, are available to us via the VSTO SE package. Where previous versions of VSTO gave us direct access to Office products from within the Visual Studio development environment, the SE version does not. All access to Office applications is now done via add-in applications created in VSTO SE.

In this chapter, we looked at a method of bringing data into an Excel workbook using an ActiveX component created in VB 6.0. The code is almost identical to the code we wrote in Chapter 2 when we looked at data access in Excel 2007. With very few lines of code in the Excel VBE, we were able to accomplish what filled up multiple code modules in the original examples, by wrapping that code in a COM object.

We then built a couple of components using .NET technologies. These components made code nonexistent in our Excel workbooks. By running the code from an add-in, all we have to do is load the add-in, and the code runs. We built a simple data access tool that loads Northwind Employee data when a workbook is opened, and we designed a custom task pane that calls a data entry form to collect data and place it on the active worksheet.

Index

You Need the Companion eBook

Your purchase of this book entitles you to buy the companion PDF-version eBook for only $10. Take the weightless companion with you anywhere.

We believe this Apress title will prove so indispensable that you'll want to carry it with you everywhere, which is why we are offering the companion eBook (in PDF format) for $10 to customers who purchase this book now. Convenient and fully searchable, the PDF version of any content-rich, page-heavy Apress book makes a valuable addition to your programming library. You can easily find and copy code—or perform examples by quickly toggling between instructions and the application. Even simultaneously tackling a donut, diet soda, and complex code becomes simplified with hands-free eBooks!

Once you purchase your book, getting the $10 companion eBook is simple:

❶ Visit **www.apress.com/promo/tendollars/**.

❷ Complete a basic registration form to receive a randomly generated question about this title.

❸ Answer the question correctly in 60 seconds, and you will receive a promotional code to redeem for the $10.00 eBook.

THE EXPERT'S VOICE™

2855 TELEGRAPH AVENUE | SUITE 600 | BERKELEY, CA 94705

Offer valid through 9/08.